Family, Faith & Fragile X

The Raw Story of a Mother With Three Special Needs
Children

Kirsten Fowler

Chizel Books Publishing

For more information, email contact@kirstenfowler.com

ISBN Ebook: 979-8-9858118-1-0

ISBN Paperback: 979-8-9858118-0-3

Cover design by: Rachael Gibson

Printed in the United States of America

Contents

Dedication   VII

Forward   VIII

Introduction   X

1. In the Beginning   1

2. Falling in Love   9

3. Making Tough Decisions   15

4. Diagnoses   33

5. Early Intervention, IEPs, and ABA   46

6. Respite and Care-Giving   60

7. Hiring a "Nanny"   75

8. Me Time and Marriage   84

9. Fragile X Carriers   98

10. Siblings, Family, and Caregivers   115

11. Specialized Vacations and Activities   134

12. Extracurricular Activities   145

13. Media Time, Noise, and Unseen Expenses   152

14. Other Self-Harm and Aggression   163

15. Trying to Help   171

16. Doctors, Medication, and Oils   181

17. The Dentist   189

18. Church and Religion   199

19. Diapers and Potty Training   209

20. Hygiene and Grooming   221

21. Sleep...or Lack Thereof   236

22. Parenting Tips   245

23. A Day in the Life of Fragile X   254

24. Final Thoughts   274

To my loving husband, Jeremy, who never gives up on me, and my four children, Millie, Isaac, Eliza, and Evelyn, who have taught me the most important lessons I never wanted to learn.

Forward

Fragile X research and clinical work has been the main feature of my academic life and I have seen thousands of families that are raising children with Fragile X syndrome. However, Kirsten Fowler, tells it like it is in a "raw", unfiltered fashion with descriptive prose. She is able to describe the chaos of trying to meet the needs of 3 children with Fragile X syndrome when overwhelmed by the screaming, aggressive hair pulling and scratching of all who are involved in a poop fiasco that requires dedicated cleaning. It is truly chaotic at times and heart-wrenching, but this family has the strength to get through the chaos and find enjoyment as a family as they bring fun into the house since they cannot travel elsewhere. Their Mormon religion (The Church of Jesus Christ of Latter-day Saints) gives them strength as does their community and extended family. This is a big family with mother's siblings who are also struggling with children who have Fragile X syndrome. Kirsten receives advice from doctors who are ignorant and tell her that girls cannot have Fragile X syndrome. This book goes a long way in educating families and even professionals about what families need. The advice is solid and useful for what many are going through as they struggle to raise children with Fragile X syndrome.

What Kirsten is dealing with is the over-reactivity of these children to environmental stimuli and their inability to habituate to these experiences. So the behavior can be out of control and often aggressive because of their anxiety coupled with enhanced sympathetic responses. Her son Isaac has severe problems in this area, compared to others with Fragile X syndrome, but many mothers have experienced aggression which dramatically increases their own stress. This book goes a long way in describing the stress so the reader feels it and this is what professionals need to know. Kirsten has also experienced the many health problems such as fibromyalgia, neuropathy, and autoimmune disease, specifically Hashimoto thyroiditis and Lupus that are associated with the premutation. Fragile X-associated neuropsychiatric disorders (FXAND) include the anxiety and depression that she has experienced, all related or exacerbated by stress. These problems also relate to the Carrier's exquisite sensitivity to sensory stimuli although this is a milder version of what those with Fragile X Syndrome experience.

Kirsten describes it all in harried scenarios which may be scary for the newly diagnosed families but the guidance that she gives is priceless. Her ability to deal with the behavior problems and keep her marriage together is remarkable. We are emboldened by her strength and I have spent my career learning from courageous women who are Carriers and Kirsten is no exception.

Randi Hagerman MD
University of California Davis MIND Institute

Introduction

My husband, Jeremy, turned to me one night after a rough battle with the kids and said, "You should write your story." I looked up from scheduling out the coming week, gave a tired half laugh, and said, "I don't have time." Then we sat there in silence for a moment, thinking. My four kids were actually asleep all at the same time, which is a rare and precious occurance. I had a million things I should have been doing, wanted to be doing, needed to be doing...but I got out my laptop and began.

At the age of sixteen, I learned I am a Carrier of Fragile X Syndrome. I wanted to read all the books I could find about it, especially personal stories and insights. Unfortunately, there were too few. Even now, twelve years later, books addressing what it is like to be a FXS Carrier and mother of Fragile X children are not as prevalent as one might think, considering millions of individuals who are affected.

So now I feel it is my turn to share my story. I don't have all the answers, but I'm writing this book for those who want to see someone walking the same road, finding joy in an arduous journey, and sharing experiences for others to learn from.

I am a mother of four children—three with FXS. Over the years I have read books, studied articles, and given speeches about FXS. I graduated with a Bachelor's degree in Family Life with an emphasis in child development from Brigham Young University, where I expanded my studies into children with disabilities, siblings of children with disabilities, and healthy marriages. I combined my previous love of journalism and my new love of family life to write articles for *yourdivorcequestions.org*, writing a three-part series about couples with special needs children who stick together despite many challenges.

After struggling with my own health issues once I began having children, I dug deep into any research I could find about Carriers and related health issues. You start to become an expert in the things that most impact you.

This is the first book to address what it is like to be a Carrier of Fragile X Syndrome with all its challenges, while addressing the overwhelming task of raising special needs children at the same time. You will find:

- Tools to help your marriage
- Special needs parenting tips
- Insights into what it is like to be a Carrier of FXS
- Access to links for my favorite products
- Insights into IEPS, therapists, and ABA
- Real life experiences of day-to-day life
- Tips to help in finding respite and supported living

What is stopping you from stepping into my shoes to find common ground and helpful information to navigate Fragile X? Don't continue to be left in the dark or feel alone. No matter what mountains you are currently climbing, begin a new journey to find joy in this crazy life of family, faith, and Fragile X.

*Note: Names outside of my family circle will be changed for privacy reasons.

Note from the Author

Writing this story was difficult. Not because I don't like writing. I love writing. It was probably a good therapeutic thing for me. But reliving things and the PTSD that comes with it is awful. Much of the time I just couldn't dig too deep, so some things might seem superficial. It was hard to write this also because things change so much each day and as much as I want to give hope to people, I would sometimes cry and feel like a fraud when the days came that I just felt so hopeless. So much more could have gone into this book. I could write chronicles, but I won't. I hope I have included just enough to help someone, even just one person. Good luck on your journey, readers. Much love, Kirsten

1

In the Beginning

Kirsten with her siblings and parents

"Knowledge is power."
–Francis Bacon

I grew up in a wonderful family with two loving parents and five children. I am the youngest of my siblings, and as such will always be the "baby." We are all members of the Church of Jesus Christ of Latter-day Saints, and this has shaped us as individuals and as a family unit. Going to church every

Sunday and attending different church activities during the week has always been the norm, and I gained a strong personal testimony of my Savior and His gospel on the earth at a very early age. I am so grateful my parents raised me in the Church, because it is a huge part of how I manage through daily struggles and trials.

I grew up poor on a small dairy farm in rural Benjamin, Utah. As kids, we explored acres of land, jumped ditches, made forts with straw bales, avoided (or tried to avoid) pools of cow sludge, and caught various little critters. Mostly, we spent a lot of time at home with family. We were not the vacationing type, but life in our house was always fun: we made homemade taffy and caramel, canned apricots, and juiced tomatoes. Whenever possible, we talked Dad into playing catapult, which involved him lying on his back and launching us upward and forward with his feet. We sailed through the living room, trying not to hit the rock wall fireplace. Old worn floral couch cushions made great landing pads.

Being the youngest of the family has its ups and downs. My siblings always say I'm the "spoiled" one, but I am also the one that spent the most time alone at home and missed out on a lot of the farm life and family time. My children never got to meet my grandparents, or were too young to remember them.When I was about eight years old, my grandpa passed away and the dairy farm was sold. My cousins moved away not long afterward. Moving away became normal for me. My oldest sister, Rachael, married Marc after some time in college and then moved out. Jessie, the next oldest, followed suit and married her husband, Joel. My oldest brother, Daniel, went on a two-year mission to Brazil, and when he got home he married Tynelle. Aaron and I were best friends, even though he was more than five years older than I. I was definitely the caboose. It was hard when he left on his mission to Texas, and I was alone at home with my parents. He got married and moved to his own home, too, shortly after he came back from Texas.

At the age of ten I became an aunt. Rachael brought Brighton into the world as my parents' first grandchild. Several years later, her daughter Avery came. Jessie had three children during that time: two boys and a girl. They were all quite close in age. My brother, Daniel, had a little boy about the age of Jessie's second-born. I recall a distinct memory from about this time. Every other Sunday since my siblings began to marry, we all got together for dinner and birthdays. This time we were gathered at Rachael's home.

"Okay, everyone, it's almost time to eat cake!" Rachael hollered to gather our family around the patio table. It was a late summer evening and the two horses in their stalls behind her house whinnied loudly in approval. The miniature goats and chickens came to celebrate, too, but Rachael quickly shooed them away. Their new house in Santaquin was becoming quite the little farm with a horse corral, chicken coop, and beautiful country air.

Avery, the birthday girl, was sitting in the middle of the patio table with the cake in front of her, waiting to blow out the candles. She was "nervicited," as we say, a combination of nerves and excitement. All the family gathered around her, chatting and smiling.

"Look at this family," my mom said, looking around glassy-eyed at us all gathered together. "We are so lucky. It's not everyone that has a family like ours."

"I know, my friends are always saying, 'Is your family for real?'" replied Rachael, chuckling as she uncovered the cake and reached for a small packet of matches.

"There's definitely a difference with your family," said Joel. "You are all so close and no matter what happens, you stay close."

My dad replied, looking at mom with love in his eyes, "It isn't because of us two crazy kooks!" he said, laughing. And then a little more seriously, he added, "We just got lucky with the best kids."

"It must have been the orange carpet," my mom said, making another joke. We all laughed knowingly because we had ugly 70s era carpet that resembled orange and yellow tie-dye cottage cheese that got thrown up in chunks. It was all throughout our house until about the year 2000. We also had low-pile carpet complete with holes worn from wear in the kitchen and dining area.

As we were caught up in our childhood for a moment, Rachael lit a match and touched it to the wick of the first candle. Then she put out the match and lit the remaining two candles with the first. Wax began to bead at the top and drip down the multicolored candles.

"Do you want us to sing 'Happy Birthday?'" Rachael asked.

"NOOOO!" Avery screamed out. We all looked at one another.

"It's okay. What if we just whisper?" Rachael asked calmly, trying to de-escalate the situation.

"Ahhhh! NOOOOO! Stop it! Stop it!" Avery continued to scream.

I wasn't sure what to think. I felt embarrassed, awkward, and a bit sorry for Rachael. Every parent loves spoiling their child for their birthday and singing "Happy Birthday" with the family, but that is *not* what Avery wanted. At the same time, Brighton came running to the scene, flapping his hands and running around, his twig legs carefully slid into his favorite skinny jeans. Without any warning, he blew and spit on the candles to huff them out, then ran off again, smiling and giggling. Avery cried harder.

"Brighton!" Rachael said, disappointed and embarrassed, "It's Avery's birthday. She gets to blow out the candles."

While Rachael tried to comfort Avery, I heard someone yell out in pain, "Ouch! What in the world?" It was Rachael's niece who was there to celebrate. Brighton had bit her arm, leaving red teeth marks.

"Brighton! We do NOT bite," Rachael said, exasperated. Brighton giggled and ran away again.

"Marc! Grab him! He's headed for the road again!" Rachael called to Marc, who immediately went running after Brighton.

Meanwhile, Rachael began lighting the candles again for Avery to blow out—this time with no attempt at a birthday song. We all smiled and tried to help, but I wasn't sure how. I was just a young teen wondering why my niece and nephew struggled so much. I often wondered this as I watched them stim, flap their hands, bite, poop on the floor, watch the same movie over and over, or run around the house with no signs of stopping. Sometimes I wondered, "Why does Rachael let them watch so much TV? How does she do anything in public? Are they going to do anything about this?" I had no clue. Even though I was a generally kind and understanding person, I just didn't get it. Of course, now I realize how inconsiderate and judgmental I was.

I recall another Sunday evening years later, but this time at my parent's house, where I grew up and my parents still live. Again, Rachael was in the spotlight.

"We got the results back from Brighton's blood test," she said, while we all sat around the small country kitchen in Benjamin, Utah. "He has Fragile X Syndrome."

None of us had ever heard of it before. We likely had the same reaction as most would and thought, *Fragile...what?* Rachael was the pioneer of FXS in my family. She led the way and was the bearer of hard news. I knew this was difficult for her. Even though it wasn't her fault that Fragile X was a part of our lives, she felt it was because she was the first to tell us about it.

She continued, "Fragile X is actually a genetic disability. We have discovered that Dad is a Carrier. The way genes work, this means Kirsten, Jessie, and I are also Carriers, but Aaron and Daniel aren't affected." Dad looked solemn. He had heard the news before the big announcement, knew before I did, and now there was a look of guilt and sorrow on his face, as if he felt responsible for bringing this into our family. But this was all new to me—I was only sixteen at the time and did not yet comprehend what it all meant.

It was different, on the other hand, for my sisters. At that time, Rachael had two children and Jessie had three. I later found out that Jessie and Joel decided to stop having children because of the now-known chance that she could pass on Fragile X. She felt lucky to have three children who showed no signs of delay. For me, a teenager with my whole life ahead of me, suddenly so much was uncertain and unknown. Later that night, my dad and I talked about what might change in my life because of this news.

"I know you're still young, but you need to understand that because you are a Carrier, you need to think about some things," my dad told me. "When you think about having children, you should think about the 50/50 chance of having one with Fragile X like Brighton." In the background my mom was fidgeting, walking back and forth between the living room and kitchen, listening in on the conversation. She couldn't hold it in any longer.

"Do we really have to talk about this now?" she worried. Dad gave her an exasperated look.

"It's okay, Mom," I replied, "I want to talk about it." It was true—I did. I was interested, at least on an academic level, and talking about it did not bother me. I always cherished the chance to have a heart-to-heart with my dad, even if the subject was difficult. Besides, at that point I didn't yet feel the weight of my reality. I didn't cry or fret very much about what my future held. Maybe I was in shock or denial but I didn't fully understand the gravity of the situation.

"Maybe there will be a cure by the time I have kids," I said hopefully. "Surely in five to ten years there will be some big breakthroughs." My dad looked thoughtful and agreed, but we both knew there was no guarantee. "Plus, there's adoption and in vitro. I'm not sure if that's what I want, but there are options, right?" I looked to him for validation and comfort.

"Yeah, sure. We'll just have to see when we get there," he replied. We chatted for a while longer, then I gave him a hug.

"It'll be okay," I said. As I pulled away, I looked him in the eye and gave him a reassuring smile. I hoped he could tell I didn't hold him responsible for this and I felt things really would be okay. I knew it was in God's hands. We then called it a night, but before I went to bed, I said a prayer as I continued to wonder about my future.

"Dear Heavenly Father, I just found out Brighton has Fragile X Syndrome and I'm a Carrier. But I guess you already knew that. Will I be able to find someone that wants to have kids with me? Will my kids in the future have it, too? I am kind of scared, but I am also grateful for the comfort and peace I felt while talking with my dad tonight. Please help my dad. He thinks it's his fault, but we don't blame him. It was all meant to be. Help me to know what to do now," I prayed and closed in the name of Jesus Christ. I fell asleep with peace, knowing that no matter what was in my future, Heavenly Father and Jesus Christ would be with me.

Talking with my dad helped me to feel stronger and more capable. I am glad I was told as soon as the family understood the genetic fallout instead of right before I was about to get married or have children. It was my right to know, and I would have felt betrayed if such significant information had been hidden from me. I really appreciated that my dad could talk to me in a real and honest way while also being caring and understanding. It was hard and maybe even scary to talk about, but because I learned about it sooner rather than later, I had time to accept and embrace it, which made things easier as I made decisions later on and grew in my understanding of health issues.

As we have grown as a family, this genetic disability has brought us together. It was never about blaming Rachael because she was the first one to find out, or blaming my dad because he passed it to us, or even blaming some great-great-great uncle who possibly started it all years before. Instead, we tried to come together to get through hard times with greater understanding.

I would be lying, however, if I said everything in the family has always been peachy. As Carriers, we tend to be moody and anxious and suffer from depression. It can lead to heavy conversations, unfair comparisons, and misunderstandings. But what is family without disagreements and heartache? And without the growth that comes with making up afterwards?

Overall, knowledge has opened doors, created understanding, and brought empowerment. At sixteen *I* was given new knowledge: I am a Carrier of

Fragile X Syndrome. I was lucky to have many years to prepare myself to face the challenge of telling my future spouse our children might have special needs. I did not dwell on it all the time, though. In fact, most of the time I didn't even think about it, and I certainly did not feel limited by it day to day.

What I did worry about, though, was how my future spouse would react. My biggest fear was I would be rejected by the man I would someday love because of the possible future we and our children could have. I prayed, even at sixteen, that the person I loved would love me back, despite knowing I am a Carrier of FXS with all of its repercussions. It is one thing to accept it yourself and have years to think it over, and another to tell the man you want to marry about the situation and hope he doesn't change his mind about you.

2

Falling In Love

Kirsten and Jeremy right before he served his mission in Africa

"Truth without love is brutality, and love without truth is hypocrisy."
–Warren W. Wiersbe

I didn't start dating until I was sixteen years old because I chose to follow the recommendation of the leaders of my church, the Church of Jesus Christ of Latter-day Saints. I still had my fair share of crushes and heartbreaks—all the stuff that comes with the territory of being a teenage girl. I was nineteen when I had my first official boyfriend, a boy who knew my sister, Rachael, through church, and who was aware of her two special needs children. After just a few months of dating, he broke up with me. I was devastated.

"I think it's because he figured out that Fragile X is genetic and didn't want to have anything to do with it," speculated Rachael.

"I don't know…maybe he just didn't like me enough. But who knows, maybe he thinks I am tainted," I replied, feeling dejected.

"Well, he had to have known," Rachael loyally insisted. She was trying to help me feel better and convince me I am beautiful and amazing, and he was an idiot for walking away. She continued, "I really think that's the reason behind it all."

"Actually, I'm pretty sure he is seeing someone else right now. I think he's been hanging out with her for a while behind my back and he was feeling guilty," I said sadly. I found out later he married that girl, so I guess I was the stepping stone.

At the time, I was heartbroken and felt the first taste of depression. With hindsight, however, I am grateful he decided to go a different way. A person should be loved and accepted unconditionally for who he or she is, even while they are in the process of becoming who they will be. As we remain in that process, we must realize everyone around us is in the process of "becoming," too, and we should continue to love through the growing pains—both our own and theirs.

Fortunately for me, there was another guy in the wings. I had had my eye on him for years. While some things just are not meant to be, other things seem destined. It all started years before, when a small group of my friends and cousins decided we would go to a religious youth camp for fourteen- to seventeen-year-olds called Especially For Youth (EFY). The camp was in Logan, Utah, and we felt so cool going on a road trip without our parents. Like all the other girls, I hoped to meet some cute guys there. Little did I know that first day at EFY I would meet the cutest guy in the world. One day while I walked through the hallway, I came upon Jeremy, who was sitting alone on some stairs, looking at his phone. I felt kind of bad for him sitting alone, so I got brave enough to talk to him. He was very easy to talk to and I was attracted from the start. I saw him throughout the week at service projects, activities, and in classes. He was kind and had a handsome face and a maturity I was drawn to; that may have stood out to me mostly because he was one of the few out of hundreds attending who were over fifteen years old. He and I were among the oldest teens there. In fact, we were almost the same age as the counselors leading us.

It wasn't just his age, though. He had an "older" look—in a very good way. He treated me with respect by walking me to classes. In our group discussions about the gospel, I was surprised at how well he knew the scriptures. It wasn't one specific thing or another, but there was something about Jeremy overall that made him stand out to me in a big way. Throughout the week I kept my eye on this new crush. When EFY came to a close, I had no intention of leaving without some way to contact him.

There were a handful of people I wanted to keep in contact with, and Jeremy was at the top of my list. Of course there were girls swarming him. Eventually, I got my turn and got his address. Writing letters back and forth ended up being an important part of our relationship: we exchanged poems, songs, things about ourselves that we never told others, and all our favorite things. We even shared a cassette tape back and forth on which we recorded ourselves playing music, singing, and just talking. Jeremy and I knew more about each other than almost anyone else did, even our closest family and friends. We wrote constantly for a year before he left on a two-year mission for the Church to South Africa. The day he left I went to his house, along with many other friends and family. At this point in time, I only saw us as friends, but when I hugged him goodbye I had a special feeling and an impression that I should date him when he got home.

Fast forward two years. He came home and I was a student at Utah State University, which conveniently happened to be close to his home. We immediately began dating and there were a lot of cute moments in our courtship, including our first kiss high up in a tree, dinner dates, and dances that brought us even closer and more in love. It was not long until we both just kind of knew marriage was in our future. We even talked about how many kids we wanted.

"How many kids do you want?" I asked him first. I realize this is a weird question, but we were getting to the proposal stage, and in Utah culture, that is a pretty standard issue to address.

"I think maybe seven or eight," he said matter-of-factly. That, too, is normal around here, but I knew, given my situation, that was really pushing it.

My eyes got big and I smiled, but inside my heart sank. "I think maybe three or four," I said, feeling generous in that number. I felt as a Carrier of a genetic disability, I could not give Jeremy the children he desired. I knew I had to tell him about my Carrier status before he proposed.

One Wednesday evening I felt I could not hold it in any longer. I called him to tell him I needed to talk about something important. I can't imagine what he was thinking this "something" was, but I know it was not Fragile X. Even though by this time he had met my niece and nephew who have FXS, he did not know what it was—or that it is genetic. All the way down the canyon from Logan to where Jeremy lived in Brigham City, I prayed for strength, love, peace, and understanding. A few minutes before I got to his parents' house, I turned on the radio to distract myself and heard a song by Keith Urban called *Only You Can Love Me This Way*. I remember hearing the words of that song and feeling in my heart Jeremy would continue loving me—unlike others who may have shunned me. But still, I wasn't completely sure, and doubt and fear still lingered in my mind. Before I knew it, we were sitting on his couch alone and I just came out with it.

"I have something important to tell you," I paused for a moment, not looking at him. "And I understand if, after I tell you, you don't want to pursue a relationship with me anymore." He looked at me, concerned, but lovingly put his arm around me. The tears welled up and silently fell down my cheeks. I had feared this moment since I was sixteen, and I could hardly believe I was now facing that fear.

"You remember my sister Rachael's kids? They have Fragile X, which I think I have told you before," I said plainly, pausing for a moment to sniff and calm my breathing. "Well, Fragile X Syndrome is actually a genetic disability, which means there are Carriers, or those that pass on the affected gene. My dad is a Carrier, Rachael and Jessie are Carriers, and..." I paused for a second and then rushed through to the end. "...and I am a Carrier." I let out a breath. I did it. I said it. Breathe.

"Okay," Jeremy said calmly. "What does this mean, exactly?"

"Well, it means if we get married and have children, we have a 50/50 chance of having a child with Fragile X Syndrome," I said these words, closed my eyes, and began to shake and cry. "I'm so sorry. If you don't want to date me anymore, I understand," I said, trying to be brave. I felt defective and wanted to give him everything. The last thing I wanted was to lose him, but I knew I had to give him a choice. I had to give him the knowledge willingly entrusted to me all those years ago.

"Kirsten," he said gently. "Kirsten, look at me." I had purposely avoided his gaze, staring at the ground or the wall as I spoke. I took a slow breath and timidly looked up into his brown eyes.

"This doesn't change anything. I still love you," His eyes were wet, his expression sincere and full of love. He still wanted to marry me? He still wanted to marry me! He loved *me*, and we were going to figure this out together. We sat and hugged on the couch with me crying on his shoulder for a long while. I knew Keith Urban's song would be our wedding song as I thought of how Jeremy could have easily "turned a different corner" or "gone another place," but he didn't. When it all became too much, he was right there beside me, just like the song said. And I just remember thinking no other man could love me the way Jeremy loves me. I felt like the luckiest girl in the world.

That night I felt pure, unconditional love from Jeremy—just like the love I feel from my Heavenly Father. I remembered the day I hugged him goodbye for two years and felt something special between us. It was as if God had brought us two unlikely people together for a journey that would be the greatest adventure we never could have imagined.

Later I came to realize I should never be afraid to tell my truth, nor should I feel I am any less because of it. For Jeremy, the news of my Carrier status and unknown outcomes with unborn children didn't change his love for me in any way. I know to Heavenly Father I am loveable despite my flaws and issues—or maybe because of them.

It was from that point forward that Jeremy and I went together into an unknown future, paving the way with unconditional love for one another and with the Savior as our guide.

3

Making Tough Decisions

Kirsten and Jeremy at the hospital after the birth of their first child

"A person's a person, no matter how small."
—Dr. Seuss, Horton Hears a Who!

J eremy and I made the decision to get married, but we still had to decide
about having children. For our first child, Jeremy and I thought little about
our options, because just starting out, we felt going ahead with a natural
conception was going to be okay. Some have asked me if we really knew what

we were getting into. Although I feel I had a better idea than most, I don't think anyone can really understand what it is like having a special needs child until they are living it. Having said that, we made our decisions and stuck with them. After all, we would love that child no matter what, right?

After just eight months of marriage, I got pregnant with our first daughter, Millie. With the potential of having a child with Fragile X, we made sure to talk with our physician, Dr. Duggard, about these possibilities. Unfortunately, he was not well informed on the subject; no doctors really were at that time, at least in the area where I was living. When the possibility of amniocentesis was brought up, he brushed it off, because "Girls can't have Fragile X Syndrome, so there is no reason to test for it."

"Well, actually I know several girls in my family with the full mutation," I countered, confused that I was explaining to a doctor what I thought was simple genetics.

"No, the X-chromosome is affected, so only boys have the full mutation. Girls can be Carriers, but they can't have the full mutation," Dr. Duggard replied, fully confident. I just looked at my husband across the room, and we gave each other a look that said, *seriously?*

But I didn't argue with him any more on the subject, because we had already decided against prenatal testing. I was worried about the risk of losing the baby and I had made up my mind that I would love this child as she is, whether she had FXS or not. My overarching belief was and still is if a child with a disability is worthy of life once he or she is living on the earth, they are just as worthy of life before they are born.

And so came the day when Millie was born. I had pre-eclampsia, so I was taken into the labor room earlier than expected. They broke my water and I had a quick, comfy epidural delivery—just the way I like it. It was a very quick labor, and she was the most beautiful baby I had ever laid eyes on. We had her tested at the hospital for FXS soon after she was born. We endured the waiting period without much worry before the results came back. Rachael was not concerned. I was not concerned. She was a happy, healthy baby and, besides, I had never had a baby before and was hopeful in general about the prospects. There just wasn't a lot of stress waiting for the results.

Results came back in about four weeks. We found out she does not have the full mutation. In fact, she is not even a Carrier! Honestly, Millie's negative test came as no surprise because she was doing so well and showed no signs of delay. I felt blessed because she would not have to walk the difficult road I had traveled, although of course she will have her own challenges. Unfortunately, however, Dr. Duggard's false belief that girls cannot have FXS was sort of confirmed by our negative test results. I hope he has learned the truth in the meantime so he can be a help to other families in similar situations.

Because Millie was way ahead in her development, after a short ten months we decided to go ahead and have another child. Our second-born, Isaac, and Millie are just nineteen months apart! By the time Isaac was born, Millie was communicating well and already sleeping through the night in a toddler bed in a room of her own. I tried to potty train her, hoping to only have one child in diapers, but she was not ready for that, and it didn't happen until much later. Naive me—little did I know I would be changing diapers for many years to come.

We felt good about the decision to have another child, but I was worried about how fast the labor would be since Millie had come so quickly.

"Dr. Duggard, you know how fast my labor was with my first pregnancy. She was here within an hour! Is there any way I can be induced early? I really don't want to have this baby in the car. How about October nineteenth?" I begged. Dr. Duggard just chuckled.

"Well, you've got a point there, but I don't feel comfortable starting you too early, and this baby is measuring small. I wonder if maybe you miscalculated your period. The earliest I feel comfortable would be November second." Back then I didn't question the doctor's orders. I thought he knew best.

Finally, it was November first and I went to bed happy, expecting tomorrow to be the big day. It came as a great surprise when I was awakened at two a.m. by a strange feeling. I thought perhaps my water broke (this wasn't how my first birthing experience had started out. This was going to be a whole different rodeo).

"Jer?" I called from the bathroom. "Jer? Honey?"

A groggy, half-asleep Jeremy called back from the bed, "What?"

"I...I think my water broke," I said. I wasn't 100 percent sure since I'd never experienced this before, but a quick Google search confirmed it, as silly as that sounds.

"Oh! Are...are you sure?" He asked, fully awake once he realized what was going down.

"Yeah, we gotta go. Call Mom, quick," I said, panicking just a little. She lived about twenty-five minutes away and Millie was sleeping at the time. My mom rushed out of bed and raced to our home. We grabbed our hospital bags, got into the car, and pulled away just as she turned into the driveway.

Thankfully, we made it to the hospital before Isaac decided to make his grand appearance.

"I need an epidural *now*," I breathed after another contraction. The nurse smiled sweetly at me.

"I'm sorry, but we have to wait for the doctor to get here before we do that. You likely have several hours to go anyway, Sweetie," said one nurse.

Oh really? I thought. "Actually I go really fast. I've talked to my doctor about it. I want an epidural before it's too late," I said.

"Well, let's check you and see where you are," said the nurse calmly. She checked me and then said, "Okay. I'm going to grab another nurse to have a look." I was confused, but soon another nurse came in. Sure enough, Isaac was right at the door, but something wasn't right and the doctor still wasn't there. As the second nurse was checking me, she said, "I don't feel the head."

"What do you mean?" I asked, confused and in pain. I thought, *Seriously? He's gotta be right there!*

"In order to give you an epidural, I need to be sure the head is down. I don't feel a head, so we need to wait for the doctor." Neither Jeremy nor I was sure what was going on. All I knew was I didn't have my epidural and the baby was coming. Dr. Duggard finally arrived and checked me yet again. As the authority, he looked at me and said, "I'm sorry, but the baby's head isn't down. He's feet-first." My eyes grew wide and his next words scared me. "We will have to do an emergency C-section."

What? My brain screamed. *How could he be feet-first? He's been head-first this whole nine months! The doctor has been checking me the old fashioned way and hurting my belly feeling around. I know he's head-down!* But then I remembered something. I kept feeling a large round thing up in my ribs. The thought had occurred to me that this might be his head. I even told Jeremy. I brought it up with my doctor once, but he dismissed me and I just thought, *Well, okay!* I have since learned to always go with my gut feelings.

It was at this point in the hospital while I was in pain and contractions were coming quick and hard that I realized my doctor had put me in this awful position. He had not used ultrasounds to check me and the baby regularly. He was a family doctor at a family clinic and he used outdated practices. He used his hands to feel around my uterus and used that as his guide to determine how large the baby was and what position he was in. As panic set in, I had the thought that maybe we would have to sue this doctor, especially if things went wrong! But other things caught my attention—I was still in so much physical pain that it was hard to focus on what was happening outside of my body. As Dr. Duggard left to prepare for the C-section, a nurse came in.

"Can I have the epidural now?" I asked, desperate.

"Now that you are getting a C-section, you will need a spinal, not an epidural," she said, somewhat apologetically. This would mean I would have to wait longer for pain relief and I wasn't too happy about that. Eventually an anesthesiologist or nurse anesthetist came in to do paperwork so I could get my spinal.

"Okay, hi, my name is Andrew. I'll be giving you your spinal today, but first I need you to answer some questions," he said. At this point my pain was unbearable, so I didn't acknowledge him. He plowed ahead, "What is your full name and birth date?"

But I was now in the zone. When I'm in the pain zone, I do not talk to anyone. Jeremy could see I was in pain and not capable of talking. He looked at the guy like, *Are you serious? You are expecting my wife to answer all these questions right now?* But the man kept pressing on, so Jeremy stepped in to answer the questions while still trying to hold my hand and comfort me.

"AAHHHHHHGHH!!" Before I knew it, screams came out of my mouth. I felt like one of those ladies on soap operas. I never thought I'd scream while giving birth, but there I was, screaming full voice! Before I knew it, there were a dozen people in the room and the man taking notes got pushed over into the corner with nothing to do. The doctor was there at the foot of my bed quickly putting on some gloves and still in his regular clothes with a smock halfway on.

"There's the feet!" Dr. Duggard suddenly called out at the foot of my bed.

I thought, *Feet!? Wait, what? He can't come out feet-first! Is this even possible?* Apparently it is. Isaac was coming, ready or not. Within a matter of seconds, he was delivered. By some miracle, there was no cord wrapped around his neck and no broken bones. They laid him on my belly, but I didn't even know what was going on. He started to slide off, so Jeremy reached out with his bare hand to hold him steady.

Less than one hour elapsed between my water breaking and holding my baby in my arms. There was no way a C-section could have happened. I don't know where that little anesthesiologist ended up in all the chaos, but Jeremy and I still laugh about him in his hair net and scrubs, getting pushed to the corner with nothing to do.

That was the first and only time I gave birth naturally, without medication, and it certainly was not by choice. The nurses tried and tried in vain (no pun intended) to put the IV in, but when I am in labor my veins go flat, so when I say "natural," I mean completely natural. I was not even hooked on an IV. I am grateful nothing serious happened to me or the baby during delivery since there was no IV in place and virtually no monitoring of contractions or heart rates.

Once the cord was cut, the nurses checked Isaac and weighed him. I saw him for a quick moment before a nurse took him, saying, "We need to take him to the NICU. Because of the traumatic birth we want to make sure everything is functioning properly." I heard no updates about him and I did not see my baby for hours. I finally got word that they would bring him to me soon. After all, he did need to eat *some*time.

Even though they did not find anything physically wrong with Isaac, Jeremy and I had the feeling he had Fragile X Syndrome. I cannot pinpoint exactly what gave us that feeling; there was just something *different.* He looked different from our first child and he had larger ears, which is one physical characteristic of FX.

That first day, we had a flood of family members come to see our new son. They came soon after he was born, but the nurses kept him for hours. Everyone wondered what was taking so long and where the baby was. My guess is they were running every possible test to be sure he was okay after a breech delivery, but we called and asked for him several times, and the minutes just kept ticking by with no baby. Finally, after more than four hours, they brought him to me, but he needed to be fed immediately, so the family had to keep waiting—I wanted to breastfeed in private for our first time. Isaac was not good at latching, another possible sign of disability, and I did not feel like he was eating much.

During the rest of my stay at the hospital, I was mostly alone. I was moved to three different rooms because the hospital was full. I was in a lot of pain from the traumatic birthing experience and my back ached more than ever before, which I assumed was due to the surprise breech delivery. I was not happy to repeatedly be moving from room to room. At one point, I was placed in the pediatric wing on one of the upper floors, away from the nurse's station and therefore from my baby, too. I felt forgotten and neglected. I wondered if anyone even remembered I was up there.

This was so different from my first experience. I let the nurses take Isaac at night so I could sleep—something I never thought I would do, but I was overwhelmed and in pain. Everything seemed difficult and dark during that time, whereas looking back on my first birthing experience, everything seemed calm, happy, and light. Millie had stayed with me the entire time I was at the hospital.

Isaac was very fussy overall, and even the nurses could not soothe him. He would not take a pacifier, even though he calmed down when I held it in his mouth. I think the nurses even tried giving him sugar water while he was in their care, which I did not approve of. Eventually, they brought him to me, and I felt guilty he had been crying. Actually, he never really cried; it would start out as little grunts and turn into a type of wail when he really got mad.

Finally, Jeremy and Millie brought us home. During the next four weeks I tried to think positive thoughts and chose to see all the things that proved Isaac had no disability. My friends visited and there were "kind" comments about how different he looked. At church, little kids called him Elf, because he had big ears that were almost pointy. I found his ears endearing and once in a while called him "my little elf," but when others insinuated it, it was hard not to be offended and go home to cry a little. It was my first taste of future interactions with others and my son.

Years before Isaac was born, I heard a song entitled, *I'll Walk With You* by Carol Pearson and Reid N. Nibley. The lyrics became more and more real to me. It pained me to think of Isaac's future and I knew this song would stay with me:

If you don't walk as most people do, some people walk away from you, but I won't! I won't!

If you don't talk as most people do, some people talk and laugh at you, but I won't I won't!

I'll walk with you. I'll talk with you. That's how I'll show my love for you.

Jesus walked away from none. He gave his love to everyone. So I will! I will!

Of course I could not know for certain what the future would bring; however, I tried to stay optimistic while we anxiously awaited Isaac's test results for FX. At that time, Rachael was into photography and offered to take some newborn pictures of Isaac before he got too much bigger. During the photo sessions, he held his head up. He was only about two or three weeks old. A typical baby is not physically able to do that. I thought, *Wow, he must not have disabilities because he's holding his head up like a champ! And so early!* When I got the pictures back, they were so cute. He looked like a little man.

A week or two later when we received his diagnosis, I finally understood why Isaac kept his head up so well on picture day: muscle stiffness and rigidity is another sign of FX. In fact, many affected children learn to walk with their knees locked and legs stiff.

This little man of ours came about by a choice—our choice to conceive Isaac naturally changed everything. And with change comes growth.

The first few weeks after Isaac was born were a time of intense learning for Jeremy and me. I learned new lessons about forgiveness and moving on from terrible experiences without holding a grudge, thanks to Dr. Duggard. I found I did not want to blame him for what happened that day in the hospital, although there probably would have been legal grounds for me to do so. I distinctly remember that while I was in labor, I had the presence of mind to say a little prayer, and I told God I forgave the doctor and I would not hold a grudge against him, and I prayed I would be free of hate. I am glad I did not hold any of that in, because I had enough on my plate. My prayer was answered, and I moved on right then and there, even in my pain. I was still frustrated with the whole situation, and I didn't go back to that doctor again except for a few check-ups with Isaac right after his birth.

I learned that not all hospitals are created equal based on my postpartum care. I learned things about my body and what I need during childbirth. For example, I vowed to go to a highly recommended OB/GYN in the future—not a family doctor—who would take ultrasounds at every checkup, especially during the last half of pregnancy. I would demand an epidural the second I arrived at the hospital and not just ask for one.

Most of all, I grew closer to my husband as together we accepted the possible hardships in our future. The choice to have a second child was between me, Jeremy, and God—no one else. We felt our faith in God would pull us through no matter the outcome; admittedly, however, our faith did waiver when the choice we made did not turn out the way we wanted.

With all of the trauma of Isaac's birth and the depression I experienced during and afterward from a tough diagnosis, I felt logically and emotionally that we were done having babies. I wanted more children, but I did not believe it was possible, nor did I feel it was ethical. One Sunday afternoon I was in the mother's room at church attempting to nurse Isaac. Another woman with a new baby was there as well. I got settled in as she packed up her diaper bag to leave. We started some small talk as women do, and then she said something that put a dagger in my heart.

"I can't believe this is my last one!" she said. This was probably her fourth or fifth child. "I have to prepare myself for all those 'last' moments! I guess it will be nice not to carry this fifty-pound diaper bag around anymore," she laughed. I laughed, too.

"Yeah, I bet!" I said. "That's probably so weird to think about!"

"It really is, but I think we are ready for the next stage of life," she replied. We said goodbye and I was left by myself with my baby. As he nursed, the conversation hit me. *This is my last child, too*, I thought. *But I'm not ready. How can I accept this? How can I already be done? Lasts? I just started Firsts!* I started to cry and my throat hurt from keeping in the brokenhearted sobs. I stayed in the mother's room until church was over and quickly made my way out of the building with a smile plastered on my face.

While Isaac was still just a little toddler, I sold or donated every last baby item from the crib to the little booties. It was a heart-wrenching day, but I felt I was turning a new leaf and helping myself move on to new dreams. Still, I felt too young to be "done." I was only twenty-four. Many women are not even married at that age; yet, there I was with two children and at the end of that road. During this time, I had a friend recently married and struggling with infertility. I got a taste of what she felt, but it was different. For one thing, I had two children, so I should be happy and content. The other part is I *could* have children easily, but I was closing that door—not because I wanted to, but because I felt nature and society were forcing me.

The hardest part of trying to move forward was watching three of my closest neighborhood friends become pregnant when I normally would have started trying for a third child. I wanted to carry my baby right alongside them, but I felt that would never happen again for me. It seemed so unfair.

One day Jeremy walked into our bedroom and found me sitting and looking blankly at the wall. I was still in my Sunday clothes. I felt okay mentally and physically that morning and felt good going to church. I went into a meeting of the Relief Society, our women's auxiliary. Normally those meetings are inspiring and uplifting, but today touched a sore spot.

"What's the matter, hon?" Jeremy asked.

"I dunno," I said lamely, finally replying to Jeremy's inquiry after a moment of silence. We both knew that was not true.

"Mommy," Millie, with her cute little voice, came into the bedroom to find me. "I want barg barg." I smiled at her with pride at how much she was talking now and how she always called granola bars "barg bargs." She called vanilla "ganilla," which was also the name of her favorite doll for a time.

"Okay, let's get you a granola bar," I said. I walked past Jeremy, still questioning me with worried eyes, but I avoided his gaze and made my way to our kitchen. As I pulled a box of granola bars out of the cupboard, I kept thinking about what my friend had said in Relief Society that day.

"Here you go, sweetie," I said to Millie as I handed her a "barg barg." She ran off, happy to go play in her room, content for now with her snack. Jeremy followed us in the kitchen and as Millie left to play, he came up and hugged me close, planting a gentle kiss on the top of my head. Tears formed behind my closed eyes as I tried to be strong. I took a deep breath.

"It's nothing," I said, my throat closing off at the end from trying to hold back tears. "It's just stupid."

"It's not stupid, it's okay. What's bothering you?"

"Well," I began slowly, "Shelly announced today that she is expecting another baby. I can't help but feel that should be *me*," I said, my voice cracking as I squeezed my eyes shut to the flow of tears now coming full force. "This would be about the time we would be having another one. Isaac is two years old and I wanted our kids to be close."

"Yeah," Jeremy agreed, thoughtful. "I know, honey. I'm sorry," he said, still holding me close.

"It's not fair. I don't understand. We're still young. I am perfectly capable of having kids, and yet...I *can't*," I sobbed. Black mascara ran down and landed on his slightly wrinkled white shirt, so I pulled away. He took a deep breath and put his hand under my chin to pull my gaze up to his, my eyes a watery, black mess. I felt sheepish, but I held his compassionate gaze.

"I want more kids, too, but it's going to be okay. We will figure this out together. Heavenly Father is aware of us. We just need to trust in Him that things will work out," he said with tears in his eyes. Then he kissed my forehead and pulled me into his chest, not caring about his shirt.

In the next few months, two other women I was close to announced their pregnancies and I smiled and congratulated them while holding in my jealousy. I will never forget sitting among those three pregnant friends of mine at church during Sunday School when someone said, "Look at this! It must be the expecting mother row! Careful, Kirsten, you may be joining them soon! It could be contagious!" I smiled and we all had a laugh, but I wasn't really laughing. The comment hurt because I wanted to be pregnant but felt I couldn't be ever again. The individual didn't mean any harm whatsoever and I truly was happy for those expectant women, but my mind kept chewing on the comment and I eventually had to hurry out of the room. I spent the rest of the meeting time outside the church building bawling my eyes out and praying to God for help, comfort, and understanding.

That is when I started to learn more about in vitro fertilization. There were more children that needed to come to my family, but I just could not see how unless we used science to rule out the genetic factor of Fragile X. I caught myself thinking, *If you don't feel that a baby with special needs should be aborted in the womb, why is it okay to 'abort' all the embryos that have Fragile X before they are implanted?*

This was just one aspect that made me feel this option was not right for us. Then again, I would look at the other side and think, *I would be giving that child a better life. I could still have children and take care of them all properly. I wouldn't have greater burdens on my family and community. The conception would have barely taken place and, like an early miscarriage, it would not become a life.* As a Christian, my view of children and adults, no matter their issues, is that all individuals are worthy of life and are loved by God. I went around and around in my mind as I considered this option, and there was so much I was not sure about. It became very confusing.

"IVF costs so much more than we could ever afford," Jeremy said one night as we discussed the issue. "I mean, I am willing to do whatever it takes to bring a child to our family, but I don't even know if I want to do IVF. It just doesn't seem like it is what we should do."

I agreed. "But I don't know if we should have another child. I don't know if I have enough faith to have one naturally. What if this child also has a disability? What will people think? How can we handle it?" I said, wondering what we would do.

"And what about you?" Jeremy asked softly. "You would have to go through all kinds of hormones, injections, pain, and stress to make it all work."

"I know," I said. Then I paused. "Well, I don't fully know, but I'm willing to do whatever it takes."

"But we can have children naturally. If Heavenly Father's will is for us to have a child with FXS, even if we did IVF, it could still happen. We have heard so many stories where it does happen."

"I know," I replied sadly. "I know. I just don't know if I have enough faith that this child won't have FXS."

"Maybe we can pray that we can have another child that has no disability," Jeremy said thoughtfully.

"I don't know if it's right to ask. How is it better to use IVF than to tell Heavenly Father what we want and how to do it?" I asked. No matter what we explored, I questioned myself and our decisions.

Another aspect of our hesitancy in this decision to have another little one in the home was Isaac. At the time he was about four and showing more signs of aggression as he became bigger and stronger. I was wary of being pregnant, making sure I didn't get hit or kicked in the belly or later having a tiny, innocent newborn and the potential dangers that could come about. Not only that, but Isaac required a lot of time and attention as a toddler. He was still in diapers, still waking up in the middle of the night, and the honor of parent was mentally and physically exhausting.

However, over the next few months Jeremy and I prayed, discussed, pondered, and weighed our options. Eventually we decided to have another child. We prepped Isaac by using baby dolls to teach him how to be soft. We also used social stories to help him know what to expect when the baby came and did our best to help prepare him for a new baby in our home. Along with our decision to have baby number three, we also made the decision to have it naturally. So I canceled the appointments I had made with the IVF doctor and we moved forward in faith. But in moving forward, we purposely changed our point of view. Instead of asking Heavenly Father to take away FXS, we prayed that His be done. I also prayed daily for the strength to accept His will and for His help to carry out His plan for me—whatever it may be.

About a year later our third baby, dear Eliza, was born. I asked for an epidural as soon as I got to the hospital, because I didn't want any more natural births. Unfortunately, there was only one anesthesiologist there in the middle of the night and he was already involved with another patient. By the time he got to my room, I was about ready to push. They asked if I still wanted the epidural and I said yes, because that was part of the plan and I was traumatized from Isaac's birth. Looking back, I think I would've preferred to just go natural, because I was so numb afterward. I think they put a nice heavy dose to make sure it would work before I pushed. As soon as she appeared, I could see she was our chubbiest baby yet! She didn't have any obvious indication of Fragile X and looked a lot like Millie. In fact, she was my best eater and didn't have any complications, like jaundice, to deal with. I was grateful she was an easy baby.

Thankfully, the preparation we did with Isaac seemed helpful, because he often came over to touch her head softly and say, "Baby." It was cute, but I just wondered if there would be a day he might seriously injure her without even realizing it. Thankfully, that day never came, although we had some rough moments that left physical and emotional scars. Even still, a little over a year after Eliza was born, Jeremy and I found ourselves pondering about having another child. We felt an overwhelming peace and decided to proceed. Soon after, Evelyn was born.

As soon as Evelyn was placed in my arms, I knew she was affected. She seemed to look more like Isaac had, but without the big ears. She was taken from me soon after we had skin-to-skin contact and placed in a NICU to address some breathing issues. Once again, I spent much of my time alone in my hospital room. She was my fourth child, so Jeremy stayed home taking care of the other children. Child number four is a little more "old hat," and does not get the kind of press the first child does.

Physically I felt really great after this delivery, though, which was a blessing. I did everything I could to feel normal—I put on makeup and wore regular clothes so I did not get depressed. I went up to the NICU often to hold Evelyn, to feed her, and to enjoy her presence. I also took the time to rest a lot. When the day came for me to leave the hospital, however, I did not get to take her with me.

"She will have to stay in the NICU until her oxygen levels are consistently higher and she is showing sustained improvement," said one of the doctors. I was heartbroken. Jeremy came to pick me up and we said goodbye to our little girl. I never imagined what it would be like to leave the hospital without my baby. Tears ran down my cheeks as we drove away.

"I can't imagine having a baby stillborn or losing your baby just after having it," I said thoughtfully to Jeremy. "I am so grateful I can come back and see her, knowing that soon she will be home with us, even though it is hard to leave her here now." After I got home I became very good at pumping breast milk and managed to arrange times where I could visit Evelyn, bring milk, hold her, and check in with her while neighbors, friends, and family watched my other kids.

The day we finally brought her home was so wonderful. We were all a family again. Unfortunately I felt like I had triplets. Isaac, Eliza, and Evelyn were all still dependent on me and I was constantly on the go. I had to lock myself in my room just to nurse Evelyn without Isaac trying to sit on us or Eliza begging for chocolate milk. When the baby napped I attended to the needs of the other children, but we kept the door to our room locked so no one would go in and cause a disturbance or bring in more germs.

One day I forgot to lock the door after putting Evelyn down. I was doing dishes when I heard a faint cry coming from my bedroom. As I got closer I heard Isaac's mischievous giggles. The door was wide open and when I came into the room I saw that Isaac had gotten into the pack-n-play where Evelyn slept. He was nestled close to her, smiling and giggling while she wailed. I'm sure he hurt her as he tumbled into the bed and over her body to snuggle. It was terrifying and adorably cute at the same time. For both reasons, I took a picture to always remember this moment.

Many people look at me and my family with our struggles and honestly wonder why I kept having children, considering my circumstances. Having children naturally as a Carrier is a very debated issue, both in the Fragile X community as well as from those watching from the outside. Some feel Carriers should not have children naturally unless an affected fetus is aborted. Others feel it doesn't matter whether the child has Fragile X or not, the baby should live. Others are of the opinion to only do IVF. The truth is there are a lot of options, a lot of differing opinions, and sometimes it can feel that others are shouting at you that you did the wrong thing and are a horrible person. For me, I feel I am looked down upon and judged by many others for having four children naturally. Many have said it's my fault that my kids have disabilities, so I have no one to blame but myself. Others say I condemned my children and myself to a less-than-desirable life and I should be ashamed. I just have to remember that I did what I felt was right at the time and I love each of my children. Everyone is entitled to their own opinion. I respect the decisions of others, even those I don't agree with, because I know it is a difficult decision to make. Sometimes people don't have much of a choice.

Maybe that's why I love this quote by Elder Neil L. Andersen of the Church of Jesus Christ of Latter-day Saints: "The decision of how many children to have and when to have them is between a husband and wife and the Lord. We should not judge one another on this matter."

This is the grace I would like to receive from others and the grace I want to hold for others, because there is no way I can ever know exactly what is going on in another person's life or even understand fully what another person's experiences mean. I am learning to trust in God and in my own decisions, and working to have faith that things will all work out for good.

None of our decisions to have a child were made easily or quickly—each was made with a lot of thought, discussion, prayer, and consideration of all options. I admit I have sometimes thought back with a trace of regret or self-doubt, because the life Jeremy and I have made is not an easy one; each time we received a diagnosis of FX for one of the children has been very difficult and even disappointing. Each diagnosis was hard to take, although one was admittedly harder than the others.

4

Diagnoses

Isaac's footprint Christmas ornament

"Welcome to Holland...there's been a change in the flight plan...and there you must stay."
–Emily Perl Kingsley

Isaac

It was getting closer to Christmas time and a few friends in my neighborhood decided to get together to make a craft. The three of us each ha a cute little baby of our own, so we wanted to immortalize those tiny baby feet by making imprinted clay Christmas ornaments. While the ornaments baked in the oven, we laughed and talked around the table as we handled fussy children. Suddenly, I heard my phone buzz and looked down at the caller ID. It was the doctor. This was likely the call I had waited four week for.

"Excuse me, ladies, I have to take this call," I said to my friends. Then I stepped out of the kitchen. Even though I didn't want to answer in front of my friends, I couldn't let that call go. I wanted to know and let the torturing guessing games end. I answered with a tentative "Hello?" and heard the doctor's voice respond, "Hello, Ms. Fowler."

Oh no, I thought, *it's not just his secretary. This must be bad news.* You don't usually get a phone call directly from the doctor if it's good news. Nurses can deliver happy news, simple news, or even leave you a voicemail. I have since learned this concept many times over.

"We have the lab results back from Isaac's test," the doctor quickly got to the point. "I'm sorry to have to tell you this, but Isaac has the full mutation. He has Fragile X Syndrome." Before he even finished his sentence, I knew. I immediately started sobbing in shock and complete despair. I could feel the worried eyes of my friends on my back. I struggled to stay calm.

"Okay," I told Dr. Duggard, then sniffed and said, "Thank you for letting me know." The last part was choked off by a sob that escaped my throat.

"I'm sorry. Please, if there is anything I can do or if you have any questions, please call," Dr. Duggard reassured me in a calm, saddened voice.

"Okay...um...I...I gotta go. Thank you, bye," I hurried and ended the phone call through stumbling, tearful words. I wiped my tears and tried to put on the "I'm fine" face when I turned to look at my friends, but it didn't work.

"Are you okay?" they both asked with concern.

"Yeah, I...sorry. Um...I think I need to go. Thanks for inviting me...um...Sorry I'm a mess," I said, trying to smile and hold back tears. They didn't know what to say, but that was okay because I didn't want to talk.

Some may wonder why I did not confide in supportive friends at such a difficult time—I wonder myself and there are multiple reasons. One is I was fairly new in the area and these were newer friends. Also, I was in shock and denial, so I just couldn't. Looking back now I realize that deep down I may have been embarrassed to admit aloud that my child was different from their "perfect" children. Feelings of embarrassment, sadness, resentment, and guilt bubbled up inside me. I knew playdates would be different and likely few and far between from here on out, given my newly-acknowledged circumstance.

At that mom

ent, the previously happy playdate was over, and I left as soon as I could. I don't even remember waiting for the ornaments we had made to finish baking, but I have them, so I must have waited. For years when it came time to decorate the Christmas tree I took that little imprinted foot out of the box of decorations, and my heart sank and ached as I remembered that horrible day now immortalized in baked clay by a footprint with five cute little toes.

That day my life changed forever. It broke me in every way. It dawned on me that he had been delivered feet-first with no broken bones—he had low muscle tone and was double-jointed. I remembered how he could hold his neck up, stiffening his muscles to compensate. I could not believe I would ever feel happiness again. How could I? My future seemed clouded in darkness. Suddenly, my dreams of my little boy growing up, having friends over to play, going on dates, marrying and moving on into his independent life was now replaced with reality: a disabled child dependent on me for the rest of my life—I would never be an empty-nester, never be a grandma to his children. How could I go on day to day as if things were *normal?*

Every time I resolved to be happy and move on with life, Fragile X came into my mind and with it came fear, despair, resentment, and most of all, the feeling of being trapped. Even the thought of Fragile X squeezed every happy thought and peaceful image out of my mind and replaced it with anguish. My free spirit was now caged under a heavy lock and key, covered by a shroud of pain. There was no doubt I still loved my baby boy, but I hated Fragile X; I hated what it meant for his future and mine.

Of course, part of me felt the situation was entirely my fault. Jeremy could have easily blamed me. Others have pointedly said, "You have no one to blame but yourself." Sometimes I still feel that way, but I am coming to believe that my Heavenly Father had a hand in it as well. Unfortunately, in those early days, I found it difficult to feel His love. I could not shake the darkness following me as I walked around the house, fulfilling my duties like a zombie.

When I shared the news with Jeremy on that first night after receiving the diagnosis, he focused more on the positive. I was surprised at how differently we reacted to that first bout of knowledge. He said to me, "Isaac is still my little buddy. That hasn't changed." I was reminded of the unconditional love and acceptance he expressed when I told him I am a Carrier. To him, life was *not* over. Life was still moving forward, even though I was feeling like I was at a dead end—even feeling dead myself.

Don't get me wrong—I was thrilled and amazed that Jeremy felt this way. I am so grateful he was strong through those first months so our family could push through even though I was shattered. But it was hard.

I was going crazy. I wondered if what I was feeling was normal, because it sure didn't feel like it. Thankfully, one day I stumbled across an article that brought understanding and knowledge, which, in turn, gave me greater peace. It lightly touched upon Elisabeth Kubler-Ross' stages of grief, which include denial, anger, bargaining, depression, and acceptance. So apparently what I was going through *was* normal! I wasn't crazy! I also learned these stages are different for everybody and the stages do not always proceed in any specific order. Jeremy and I were living side by side, but going through stages at different paces. I believe for many years he was in denial while I was in depression. I think my denial stage was those four weeks between birth and diagnosis. After that, there was no denying for me, but Jeremy's denial actually gave me hope things would be okay, even though Fragile X was here to stay.

Later, when Isaac was about seven years old, he was also diagnosed with autism. It wasn't hard to get this diagnosis, because there really was no question of whether he had it, just a matter of paperwork and testing. The biggest reason we went forward with getting a dual diagnosis was to get him the support, ABA therapy, and other opportunities we needed. Unfortunately a FX diagnosis doesn't always mean much in today's world, but an autism diagnosis does. I hope one day Fragile X will be as widely recognized as autism.

Eliza

I had no reason to believe Eliza had FXS. From the first time I saw her beautiful face, she was happy and ate well. When she was just two weeks old, I took her to a newborn checkup with Dr. Baird.

"Well, it looks like you've got yourself a healthy baby girl," he said with a smile.

"Yeah," I laughed, "I think so, too. She is eating so well and is such a good baby."

"I'm glad to hear it. You know, I bet we could look at her results for Fragile X online," said Dr. Baird, wheeling his chair away from Eliza and back over to the computer.

"Wow. Already?" I said, a bit nervous. I wasn't prepared to hear this news. Not yet. Isaac's results took four weeks. I thought I still had time.

"Yep," he said, typing in information and clicking around the screen. "Aw yes, it's right here. Let me print it out and let's take a look."

"Okay," I said nervously. As the printer came to life and printed out our future, I sat with Eliza smiling on my lap, innocent and cute. I said a little prayer in my heart: *Heavenly Father, please help me be okay.* The printer stopped and Dr. Baird rolled over to grab the fresh document.

"All right, let's see what we've got," he said, glancing over the results. I looked at him anxiously. He met my eyes. "She has Fragile X Syndrome," he said, trying not to look at me with pity.

"Oh. wow. Okay." I said, stuttering.

"I'm sorry, Kirsten. I really didn't think she had it, so I thought the sooner we tore off the bandaid the better."

"It's okay," I said as tears spilled down my cheeks. The corners of my mouth involuntarily pulled downward, unable to stop the sadness from showing. I tried to be brave. "I'm glad we know. Now I can start getting her on lists for help, programs, and therapy," I said, trying to smile. The room felt quiet and awkward. He handed me the test results.

"I really wish you the best. Girls often are high functioning and we can still be optimistic," he said reassuringly. I nodded and didn't dare speak in case my voice betrayed me.

I left that appointment, got in the car, and cried in the parking lot. I called my husband, even though he was at work, because I didn't want to wait. He couldn't talk much because he was in a truck with several other guys, but he just said, "Okay, thanks for telling me. It's going to be all right. We will talk more when I get home, okay? Are you going to be okay?"

"Yeah, I just wasn't ready. I was caught off guard and now I have to tell all my family. I just feel so stupid. Like, 'Hey, we had another kid and she also has Fragile X! Aren't we smart?'"

"You know that's not how it is and your family will be loving and supportive."

"I know, but I just feel...embarrassed to tell them," I said, ashamed.

"Honey, I need to go, but please tell your family. It will be okay," he said, reassuring.

"I know. Okay, I love you. We can talk more when you get home tonight," I said, wiping snot and tears on my sleeves. I didn't even care.

"Love you, hon. You got this," he said.

"Love you, bye," I said and hung up. Eliza made cute noises behind me, all nestled in her car seat. I reached back and grabbed her little fingers. "Hey, we got this. I love you so much. It's going to be okay."

Later that day, I called each of my family members one by one to tell them the news. They were sad along with me, but hopeful Eliza would continue to be high functioning. They were nothing but kind, loving, and supportive. I am forever grateful that my family is this way. I don't know what I would do if they looked down on my family, ridiculed us, or shunned us. Rejection like that makes a hard thing so much harder, and my heart goes out to those who don't have the family love and support they desire and need.

Evelyn

It was my twenty-ninth birthday and I was having quite a pleasant day. The sun was shining through my front room window and I was sitting on the couch, soaking up the rays, and taking a moment to myself while baby Evelyn slept and the older three children watched a show downstairs. It was the only respite I got at the time. I had a thought that maybe, just because it was my birthday, I would receive *that* call from my doctor. Sure enough, I felt my phone vibrate in my pocket, took it out, looked at the screen, and saw that it was the doctor's office. For a moment I didn't want to answer. It was my birthday, after all, and I didn't want sad news ruining it. But I couldn't wait. I picked up the phone.

"Hi, this is Dr. Baird." I took a deep breath.

"Hello," I said simply.

"I have the test results right here for Evelyn. Do you have a minute?"

"Yes, I do," I tried not to hold my breath.

"It looks like she is Fragile X as well," he said.

"Okay, thank you for letting me know. I was hoping to hear something else, but that's okay. She's been doing really well and we sure love her," I said, trying to be calm, trying to be okay.

"I'm sorry to deliver such news, but if anyone can do it, you can," he said.

"Thank you," I said.

"Let me know if you have any questions or anything," he said.

"Okay, I will. Thank you, Dr. Baird. Buh-bye."

"Bye."

I stopped what I was doing. It was time to call my family. Again. It was time to tell them. Again. I already felt like they were unsure about the whole pregnancy in the first place and they always worried about me, but it is hard to go through this three times and still feel confident in your decisions. I called my parents first, then trickled down through my siblings, and then Jeremy told his side of the family on his own timetable.

I will never forget that birthday. It doesn't hold the sting some might think, but a tenderness. That day my sister Jessie came by to visit and brought a precious painting of a girl praying with an angel standing behind her, comforting her.

"I felt like I should get you something, so I went to the bookstore and looked around," Jessie told me. "When I saw this, I just knew that was it." We both started to cry. That day I felt like Jessie and many others on both sides of Earth and Heaven were there to help me through this.

I truly felt angels around me that day and so many other days, helping me and lifting me up. Of course, my mom—an angel on Earth—stopped by like she often does and brought my kids snacks, treats, and some food for that night. She also gave me a figurine of a mother and baby with a poem she wrote:

You are my special needs baby who I will truly loveTo nurture and take care of you with help from up aboveI know that God has chosen me to be your Earthly motherI must have asked him, "Oh, my Father, can there be no other?"He held me and he said, "I know you can do this for me.""You do not understand but as for now it needs to be."I will send these special little angels down to youYou are valiant and I trust that you will love them like I do.

Over time I am learning there is a reason each of my children are here with me just the way they are. I love that my mom wrote this poem capturing my thoughts and feelings so well. She was inspired. There have been so many good, spiritual, and happy moments—still, in the end, three of my four children are diagnosed with FXS, despite my great faith; however, I have discovered it is my faith in *Christ* that matters most and not just a hope in something I desire to happen in my life. No matter what happens, I know He lives. I trust in Him and will follow Him. Still, life is hard every day.

I recently came upon a song by Hillary Scott called *Thy Will* which sums up many of my feelings concerning this matter. These lyrics really hit home:

I'm so confused.
I know I heard you loud and clear,
So I followed through.
Somehow I ended up here.
I don't wanna think
I may never understand
that my broken heart is a part of Your plan.
When I try to pray
All I've got is hurt and these four words:
Thy will be done....
I know You're good
But this don't feel good right now...
Sometimes I gotta stop,
Remember that You're God
And I am not, so
Thy will be done.

No one's life turns out exactly the way they thought it would. Mine certainly didn't. We just make the best choices we can with the knowledge we have at the time, then accept the consequences and move forward in faith. Having a child with a disability means taking on a new mission to take care of them, advocate for them, and love them unconditionally. The initial shock of a diagnosis can feel like a punch to the gut, but Jeremy and I know God is in charge and had a plan for us all along.

I have never lost a child to physical death; I know many parents who have. In fact, my brother and sister-in-law have lost three baby boys. It is devastating and heartbreaking, and it seems so unfair. I have similar feelings, though, concerning my three children diagnosed with FXS. I suppose it would be fair to say I have experienced a type of emotional death with each of them. As I mentioned before, in many ways, accepting that diagnosis includes mourning the death of hopes and dreams—such as prom, grandkids, family reunions, friendships, dating, marriages, having the kids' friends over for parties, special vacations as a family, traveling, couple experiences later in life and being empty nesters, missions for our church, sports teams, social acceptance—the list goes on and on. All of that and more seems to get snatched away, like having a rug pulled from under your feet when you hear the words, "Your child has Fragile X Syndrome."

I have so many feelings, a jumble of feelings really, wrapped up in the diagnoses and day-to-day life after each of them. It took me many years to recognize and acknowledge that one of the feelings I experience is resentment. It hurts me to admit to these feelings in black and white, but I am sure I am not the only one that has felt or is feeling resentment in similar situations.

As I have explored it, I have found my resentment came from feeling unsatisfied in my life, disappointed in the outcomes, and harboring bitterness toward God. And, of course, the deep feelings of anger and guilt came from blaming myself because I am the Carrier of this genetic nightmare. Over time I realized the best antidotes to resentment are gratitude and acceptance. I am actively working to change my mindset to focus on the things my children and I CAN do. I look at all the things I DO have. This is much easier said than done, and sometimes feels almost impossible during a bout of depression, anxiety, guilt, and a mix of so many other emotions Carriers and mothers of special needs children deal with. Letting myself feel these emotions when they come and understanding where they are coming from and why helps me to overcome some of the root issues. Going to therapy on a regular basis and coming to an emotional understanding led me to realize I was holding resentment in the first place. Once I recognized and acknowledged the resentment, I could work on rectifying it, and my life has been much better since then. It was not a one-day or a one-and-done circumstance but a process. There are other difficult emotions, both new and recurring, that need to be felt, accepted, and addressed.

One stage of grief from Kubler-Ross' research is acceptance. Once I continued with my life after Isaac's diagnosis, I thought that was acceptance. Logically, I knew I had to move forward. I knew which steps to take to keep on living in my new life, taking care of my children, and being a wife and mother. What I did not realize, though, is I had not accepted the diagnosis emotionally. I did not let myself feel the hard feelings or be okay with those feelings. It has taken years of therapy and it takes a continual effort to accept this reality and learn to cope.

A big reason for this ongoing process of acceptance is ongoing grief. Every time a child chooses not to play with my child. Every time Isaac poops on the floor and smears it. Every time he pulls out someone's hair. Every time my child reaches a specific chronological age but fails to reach anticipated milestones. When an adult gives me a disgusted look in the grocery store for not parenting "right." When we can't participate in an event with friends or family because it just will not work for our kids. Every day is a bombardment of choices we make to let ourselves feel, accept, move forward, and find joy.

I love each one of my children so much just the way they are. They are capable of love and progression. I cannot imagine my life without any single one of them. They have shown me love, laughter, compassion, understanding, patience, priorities, and SO much more. They have changed other people's lives for the better as well. I know they are mine for a reason and they are here for a reason. Is it hard? Yes. But the best things in life require beauty from the ashes, or a refiner's fire. You grow most in the hardest moments and become more beautiful for it. Growth looks a little different for everyone. I just keep trying every day, because I want that joy available to us all, no matter our circumstances.

Finding joy is likely tied into another stage Ross's colleague, David Kessler, discovered years later called "finding meaning," which happens to be the name of his recent book. Going through a traumatic, grieving experience can lead you to many places, but many people find greater peace when they look for and find meaning in the pain they have experienced. Some people start foundations in the name of a deceased loved one. Others continue a deceased individual's dream. People who have children with disabilities might start a 5k to raise money or begin their own business making products for special needs children. It is beautiful to see with new eyes how others are finding meaning in their grief. It is truly empowering.

As for me, I am trying to find meaning in Fragile X by writing this book detailing my experiences in hopes it will help someone else and all that I have been through will not be in vain. After all, I am starting to realize that my "normal" is NOT normal for most people. That first realization came when a slew of people began coming to my home telling me and my child what we needed to do and what we should stop doing. I raised Millie like many other children are raised where the parents are the main caregivers, disciplinaries, influencers, and decision-makers; however, when Isaac came along, he got an army to escort him every step of the way and suddenly I wasn't the only one. At the time I saw this as a nuisance and much of the time I felt threatened as a mother and anxious to have people coming into my home all the time. It was a humbling and difficult experience but it was something we all needed and from which we learned. Early intervention was a roller coaster of emotions for me.

5

Early Intervention, IEPs, & ABA

Millie and Isaac during a visit with our Early Intervention Service Coordinator

"Starting something new or making a big change requires effort, persistence, and motivation."
–Doe Zantamata

Early Intervention

One of the first things I did after each diagnosis was sign up my child for government and community assistance. Thanks to Rachael, I knew it can take years to get off the waiting list for benefits in the United States, so

I wanted to get on that as soon as possible. I advocated to set them off on the right foot. I signed up for speech therapy, occupational therapy, physical therapy, parent support, and various social opportunities. Life got really busy, but it helped me not think about the weight of my reality and made me feel like I was doing *something* for my kids. Doing something was better than feeling like a failure. If I just focused on my kids and did my best, they would all be okay—I would be okay. As essential as these things are, there is more to life than therapy sessions and in the beginning, especially with Isaac, I overdid it.

"Jerika is coming tomorrow at eleven a.m. for a Speech and then we have a back-to-back session with Marc, the OT," I said to Jeremy, looking at my calendar. "His physical therapist isn't coming until next Wednesday, but we have to work on his kneeling technique before then."

Jeremy just looked at me. At that time he was busy with work and school and unable to have as much involvement in early intervention as I had. He had his own bucket of worries. I continued, talking to myself more than to him, "Oh, and then Julie will be coming Friday for a family check-up of some kind. I think next week there is a family meet-and-greet where we can connect with other families."

To be honest, it was all a bit much, especially for a Carrier almost guaranteed to struggle with anxiety. Multiple therapies and interventions for Isaac started before he was even six months old. Having half a dozen strangers coming in and out of my home, telling me what to do, was not easy for me. Often I felt judged for my messy home. I felt inadequate for not doing enough for Isaac and fulfilling his every need. One aspect I didn't consider was Isaac getting all the attention. Sometimes Millie needed to be distracted or pushed away so Isaac could do what was being asked in the at-home therapy sessions. I wish now that I would have ignored the therapists and used Millie as a tool to help. It would have been better for Isaac and Millie to play together and learn. I think she would have felt needed and a part of the therapy and there would have been a better relationship between the two as siblings, which would have been better for everyone. Unfortunately, I was so stressed and agitated that when therapists came over, I couldn't think clearly or perform at full capacity.

As I came to learn more about being a Carrier of Fragile X, I found it is common for us to have anxiety. Personally, I had social anxiety, despite the desire and need to be social. When speech therapists, occupational therapists, early intervention specialists, and physical therapists started to come into my home, I was quite simply overwhelmed. Each provider came multiple times a month. I experienced major anxiety before every visit. Sometimes I canceled at the last minute because I just could not do it that day. My house was a mess much of the time, and I could not bear having people come to my home in that condition; maybe I didn't put on makeup, which made me worry, too. Sometimes my anxiety got the best of me and I would duck out of appointments.

"I have to cancel Julie tomorrow," I once told Jeremy in defeat. "Our house is a mess. I just can't. There is laundry strewn across the couch and I haven't vacuumed in days. Isaac's goldfish crackers are crushed all over the floor. It's embarrassing," I said. I felt like I had to have everything together, even though that is certainly not what Julie expected of me.

Julie was a college student and newly married, in her early twenties, and not much younger than me. She was our Early Intervention Service Coordinator and looked out for the overall family welfare and made sure the kids were getting what they needed. Having another woman come to my home who seemingly had it all together and about the same age was hard at first. Slowly—very slowly—I learned to let people in despite my fear and embarrassment. I recognized she was there because she cared and honestly wanted to help, not because she wanted to judge me. She came for Isaac, but she was really there for the whole family. She even included Millie so she would feel part of it all. Millie went to preschool because Julie helped her get into an early intervention program. That was a huge turning point for Millie, and she started to come out of her shell and shine.

Julie was not just there for my kids, she was there for me. Later I found what she most enjoyed about her job was being a help to the parents. Julie helped me not feel guilty for what I was or wasn't doing for Isaac. She encouraged me and talked with me. She saw me in the lowest of low times because I let her in. Being vulnerable, humble, and teachable as a parent is key to having successful early intervention. No matter what therapists do or say, if you as a parent or caregiver do not do your best to implement their techniques, there will not be much progress. Predictably, this fact made me feel even more overwhelmed.

"Marc is coming over today and I still haven't worked on that kneeling technique with Isaac," I told Jeremy before he left for work. "I feel like a naughty school girl going to face my teacher."

"Honey, it's okay. You are doing your best. We have a lot going on," Jeremy reassured.

"I know, but I feel like I'm a failure. I feel like I'm letting Isaac fail," I said, defeated.

"You're not a failure. Look, having the therapist come over twice a month alone is more help than many kids out there get. We are still doing good things. You can't beat yourself up about this," Jeremy said softly. But it was hard not to.

Here I was trying to help my son, but it was causing me so much stress. People don't realize how hard it can be, especially for introverts and anxiety-ridden individuals, to accept therapists in their home all the time. Although early intervention and all the therapies were a good thing for Isaac, I had some learning and adjusting to do. I ended up reducing visits so people weren't in and out of my house so frequently. I set goals to work with Isaac one-on-one on a more regular basis and even recruited some young women in my neighborhood to come help with his physical therapy. It was a challenge and I often felt guilty if I did not work on goals each day for a specific amount of time. I feared if I did not invest that time, the child would not progress and

I would be to blame. It certainly did not help that there were a few bad eggs in the therapy department. It took me a while to learn that I could ask to switch therapists.

"Don't bite on that!" one speech therapist snarled. "I just sanitized that. Now I'll have to do it all over again." Isaac was putting a plastic train in his mouth, which is expected of little children (especially one with special needs), but apparently the old crone didn't know that. I'm not sure how—or why—she was in the speech therapy business to begin with. She was not good with children at all, even neurotypical ones. She never included Millie during play sessions and often got after her, making her cry. It was a mess often making Millie feel even more left out and ostracized.

"You know," this therapist said to me once, "he's just manipulating you." She sounded disgusted. "He's manipulative and he won't progress much." I was dumbfounded. I could not believe she was so negative and saying things when she should have known better. Needless to say, we soon switched to a new speech therapist. Thankfully, by the time Eliza and Evelyn were ready for speech therapy, we came across the best therapists. The two girls shared the same occupational therapist and speech therapist, both of whom were fantastic. I stayed friends with their speech therapist, Barbara, even after my girls graduated out of early intervention. I even received an invitation to her wedding!

The truth is, there are good and poor practitioners in every field. Some will be a good fit for your family and some will not, but do not stop fighting to find the right person to help your child. Toss out the bad ones! Work with the therapists and together you will find the right approach to really help your child progress. In fact, when we started doing Zoom sessions during the COVID-19 quarantine, Evelyn did better because her anxiety levels were lower—she no longer had to interact with the therapist face-to-face or feel a pressure to perform. Instead, I did what the therapist asked, showed them her progress, and they saw more of her ability than ever before.

Of course, this approach does not work for everyone. In-person visits are often a more ideal way. Zoom therapy sessions were completely and utterly useless for Isaac—I cannot emphasize that enough! The point is to do what works for you and your child, but do not be afraid to let therapists into your home if that is what works best. The good therapists we found never criticized my messy house or even implied I was a terrible parent—they were there to support me, my family, and my children.

Sometimes it takes a type of bravery, sacrifice, and compromise to make things work. I had to remind myself consistently that this is for my children so they can become their best selves. Early intervention is just the beginning. An army of people have helped and are helping me raise my children and assisting them in becoming their best, most successful, happy selves throughout their entire life. This took some getting used to. It took me understanding my own limits and boundaries as well. As Albert Einstein once said, "There is only one road to human greatness: through the school of hard knocks." Ain't that the truth!

IEPs

After early intervention, Special Needs Preschool came next for each of my three Fragile Xers (or Fraggles, as some lovingly say) once they were three years old. My kids have been all over the area each going to different schools as we try to fit their individual needs. It opened my eyes to the various pros and cons of my neighboring schools, but it can be tricky to balance buses, projects, programs, and holiday parties for each of them. Not to mention I worry I'll never get all my children gathered if there were ever a natural disaster. Overall, the IEP process at each of these schools has been mostly the same. Eliza's Individual Education Plan (IEP) meetings have been simple thus far, entailing mostly just speech therapy. She has done so well that it has been suggested we do away with the IEP and just keep up with speech therapy, but

I highly recommend never getting rid of an IEP, because it allows the child to get the help they need all along the way.

Evelyn is just getting started in school, but her first IEP went relatively smoothly and we are working on several developmental goals. Before she started preschool, I took her in for a two-hour preschool evaluation. Now, this isn't my first rodeo; I know the preschool teacher and the Physical Therapist like old friends. This will be my third child in her special needs class. And the PT was with Isaac when he was in early intervention and at different schools the past eight years of his life. I can't help but say, "It's me again" when I go to these types of things.

Overall, I'm proud of my little Evelyn. She is doing very well cognitively and will need continued speech therapy going into preschool this summer. By some miracle and the "binky fairy," we got rid of her pacifier, but her blanket is still here to stay. Isaac and Eliza each still have a favorite blanket, so I'm not sure that will end any time soon. Overall, I was proud of how well she performed at the evaluation, despite her high anxiety. I hate the final part of any evaluation, though, when the evaluator has to tell you results. They have to tell you how it is and can't sugar-coat it. If it is your first evaluation and you have high hopes, you are likely to cry right there or when you get home. But I am learning to be proud of my children, no matter how they compare to typical kids. That doesn't mean I never cry about their reality, but I am immensely proud of how far each of my children have come. Their worth is not based on test scores. Still, I understand the reasons why they have to be tested this way.

Isaac was my first child with an IEP and it was, to say the least, a difficult process. One IEP in particular will live in our minds forever.

"We need a name for this," said Ms. Barker, Isaac's main teacher. She was addressing the whole IEP team consisting of me, Jeremy, Rachael, a Fragile X researcher, our DSPD support coordinator, the teacher, the principal, the speech therapist, and a few others. We smiled but nodded in agreement. "Let's call it the blue period." The Blue Period. It had a nice ring to it and it stuck.

That was the day the IEP lasted over two hours straight. Jeremy and I had brought chips, cookies, and snacks to share. I printed list of what I wanted to address and so did Ms. Barker. It felt like we were going to war, but really we were on the same team—both frustrated with each other because of dealing with Isaac. One conversation I'll never forget was when Ms. Barker explained, "Isaac smeared his feces on several of his classmates." My first reaction was horror, though not totally surprised, and my thoughts were, *how did that happen? Wasn't anyone watching him? I thought he had a one-on-one technician?* But we all know how fast and sneaky Isaac can be and his poop can appear out of nowhere like a Houdini routine! Sadly, I am not exaggerating. We will talk about this again later, but the IEP was so much more than poop stories. Several ideas were put out there, a tentative solution agreed upon, and then we'd address another issue. Then it was my turn.

"You keep sending Isaac home because he throws up at school. I know it is school policy that he be sent home and stay home for forty-eight hours, but it is getting kind of ridiculous. He just stays at home watching his iPad and having a regular day, because he is not sick," I tried to explain to everyone. "I have a letter from his doctor stating he has anxiety and a possible rumination problem and he should be able to stay at school unless he has a fever or is actually sick." The school policy was brought up again and shocked faces said, *How dare you?* Eventually we came up with a compromise to make a plan for Isaac with the best outcome.

It can be tricky to find compromise when there are rules to follow in schools—as there of course must be—but being open and kind with one another and keeping the child's best interest at heart is key to finding workable and reasonable solutions.

We generally covered just about everything during these two-hour meetings, but here are a few sneak peeks:

- When Isaac bolted out the door, staff had to try to get him back into the classroom safely and without force, if possible. This was a tough topic, because teachers are not supposed to be rough or use physical force on their students (i.e. drag them), but an escaping student cannot be allowed to run outside of the school and into the street where they could be hit by a car or become lost. It's a fine line to walk.

- Sometimes Isaac would self-harm by continually banging his head on brick or concrete. It was an awful sight. He would often look at you, walk over to the brick wall of the school, then pound his head and start crying, or he would sit down on the concrete and throw himself back to hit his head. He also might use his fists to punch the sides of his head over and over, sometimes causing bruises. If you gave him attention, looked worried, or said, "No," he would just do it more and harder, but if you ignored him he might really hurt himself. I always worried he would cause a concussion or further brain damage. He would not wear a helmet and we feared if he did, if he was ever not wearing it, he would hit the ground harder, thinking he still had extra protection. You had to show no reaction to the awful scene and remain neutral while also trying to prevent injury or predict the outburst to help him. You have to have some wicked ninja skills as a special needs parent or teacher!

- It is best to use Isaac's stroller for transportation, transition, security, and safety. Yes, Isaac *can* walk. It is a blessing for sure, but also very dangerous. During transitions between classrooms and activities he would melt down, which meant self-harming, scratching others, or running away. Isaac now uses the stroller to get on and off the bus, too. When he pulled the hair of an innocent girl while being coerced to his seat on the bus, we knew things needed to change. He still puts up a fight over getting into his stroller, though. Sometimes it takes two adults to pick him up and put him in his seat, then one buckles him in while the other tries to hold the chair still, all while both adults get kicked and scratched.

- Sensory needs are different for every child. You cannot give Isaac a fidget spinner and chewy tube and be done. He does not enjoy typical sensory items like those. He likes water play, which is very involved, and he loves dog piles/squishies, needs which are difficult to fulfill at school. The school purchased a ball pit pool with him in mind, and that helped a great deal. They installed a mini tramp where he could access it at any time, as well as a swing in one of the side rooms for him to use during speech lessons.

- Potty training was an ongoing process. Much of the time Isaac would not use the toilet at school and the teacher or technicians had to wrestle his kicking, poopy legs to get him cleaned up. This often led to multiple showers at school each day, especially when he had blowouts. I think I can count on one hand the number of times he came home in the clothes in which I sent him to school.

- Hurting teachers and classmates was a big issue. He gave one technician a concussion by jerking his head back while sitting on her lap and he ruined another technician's hearing aid. Sometimes he scratched or pulled another student's hair. When he spread poop on one classmate, we were all at the end of our ropes in dealing with his behavior.

You can see why the meeting lasted so long. After that first Blue Period IEP, his IEPs lasted about two hours. It was the new normal. Then COVID-19 hit and IEPs changed. I took all my children out of school and did homeschool. One big reason for this is Isaac has no hygiene skills and if there was any germ at school, he would not only get it but spread it to everyone in our family, guaranteed. As you can imagine, homeschooling four children, three of whom have special needs, was not an easy task.

All therapy and IEPs were online. The good thing was they were all short and sweet. The hard thing is Isaac did not respond at all to online therapy sessions and the IEPs were really just intended to get from point A to point B. Overall, I enjoyed homeschooling because I had more control over my children's lives and education than ever before. I learned more about each child and their abilities as well as their struggles. Everything became more apparent. Don't get me wrong, it was difficult and I found it to be extremely stressful. I started out gung-ho and was doing great, but after Christmas break, I was pretty much toast and we did the bare minimum to get by. I will never do homeschool with all of my children at the same time again...unless we have another world crisis. But even then, I will change my approach for sure and not be as rigid. I think it was good for me and my kids to have that year to learn together.

Even though it took everything I had, I do not regret the decision to homeschool. Now I feel better able to help my children and their teachers succeed. I also came to a surprising realization, especially concerning Isaac: others need to have the chance to work with him. Even though he can be very difficult to handle, he is a sweetheart and teaches us all to be more loving and patient. I am learning to open my home and heart to more people. I am discovering that raising my kids is not a one-woman job. It really does take the whole community to raise children, especially those with special needs. Even those scratched, kicked, and bitten by Isaac have a special place in their hearts for him. He changes people's lives.

ABA Therapy

There is, however, one program I have not been able to fully open my house or heart to: Applied Behavioral Analysis (ABA) therapy. I know this type of therapy is a lifesaver for some and has changed their children's lives for the better. I encourage each family to try it out and see if it works for their child. Maybe your child will be one drastically improved by this practice. Maybe one day I will get the courage to try ABA for Isaac again, but it will not be any time soon. I suppose it might work differently for my two FXS girls, but overall, it was definitely something I do not want to experience again unless absolutely necessary.

"Hi, I'm Nancy. I am your ABA coordinator. We will be coming into your home from four to eight p.m. each day to help Isaac." At first this sounded nice. Isaac would come home from school and there would be someone here to help and entertain him. How bad could it be?

"Unfortunately, there is a high turnover in this job and right now we will have to switch off who comes into your home to help with Isaac," Nancy said. I remember having a flashing red warning light in my head. Having someone different come each day did not sound pleasant to anyone, particularly Isaac. I find it funny—in an annoying and frustrating way—that so many times in the special needs world there is constant change when what these kids really need is consistency. Different caregivers, new teachers, switching schools, and changing rooms, all seem part of the special needs world, while my oldest daughter, who does not have a disability, often has more consistency and structure, especially in the school system. Unfortunately, there isn't often much choice. So it was with ABA. I was at the mercy of whoever could come that day.

There were several workers Isaac decided he just did not like. Pretty soon he did not like any of them, though, because they made him do things he did not want to do. There is a reason he has adopted the nickname, "The Boss." He likes to do things his own way on his own terms and on his own time. He does not like to be forced. Even bribes and reward charts can be a downward slope with him. For example, ABA decided in order for him to go on the potty, they would turn off the TV or whatever he was watching. If this worked and he didn't end up hurting himself and others in the process, he learned something new: if I go into the bathroom, then I get media time. Well, guess what? You cannot expect to go to the potty every five seconds and watch TV all day. That is not how it works, but it's what he discovered. The ABA technicians became his personal TV remote and pretty soon they used the TV reward to get him to do simple things he already knew how to do, like pointing to the apple picture when asked. It all seemed so pointless and caused other issues with TV time. He started tricking the ABA people with what he could and could not do. I tried to step in and change things, help them understand, but it was not working. Isaac just did not fit this program and it was frustrating to everyone.

The worst was when we decided to really go all in on a new potty training idea. He wore underwear and we took him every so often to the potty. Well, guess what? I was the one cleaning up the accidents. I pleaded for them to help me, especially after one particular incident when Isaac peed at the top of the stairs. I tried to clean up and Evelyn, just a baby, cried in the other room. Eliza came and slipped and fell in the urine. All of my kids were crying and the ABA person just stood there and watched. The truth was I could not do this alone—I needed their help. We had to get special permission so they could help clean up pee. It was all waste.

The last day we had anyone for ABA at the house, the kids were crazy, and I was sick of having someone sit and stare at me eating or dealing with children. I started to cry and turned to the girl and said, "I'm sorry, but can we be done for the day?" That's when I called Nancy and said we were done. It wasn't worth the awkward dinners with a hovering stranger, the unsuccessful potty training fiascos, the increased anxiety on my part that pushed onto the kids, or the huge increase in Isaac's self-harming behavior. Whatever they were or were not doing was NOT working and I was not going to wait for it to *maybe* get better. I feel like ABA may work better for a higher-functioning individual, but there are a lot of other options in that case and much more hope for success anyway.

Even at this point, the days of people coming in and out of our home to help were not finished. Even though we did not *want* the help, the fact was we *needed* the help. It was just a challenge trying to find the right people, the right programs, and the right fit.

6

Respite & Care-Giving

Melina and Isaac

"Nothing in the world is worth having or worth doing unless it means effort, pain, difficulty..."
–Theodore Roosevelt

G etting help for special needs children is not easy—and that's an understatement. Whether you hire and pay someone yourself, plead for government help through loads of paperwork and frustrating fiscal agents, or find an angel to help you, it sometimes seems like an impossible task—and all of this while you are trying to raise a child or children with special needs of varying degrees. Isaac was on the waiting list for about four years. That's nothing. I was definitely blessed. I think I got lucky...kind of.

One morning I came to Isaac's room to get him ready for the day when I got hit with a putrid smell a few feet away. I looked under his door and saw fingerpainted poop smears peeking out from under his door and heard giggling. *No*, I thought. *No, no, no, no. Not again.* I tried to take a deep breath to calm myself but remembered the only air around to breathe was poop-scented. I was smelling poo-pourri.

For the umpteenth time, he had painted himself head to toe in his own fecal matter. Oh, and did I mention his room was covered as well? He's a great finger painter. Too bad brown just isn't his color. His books, mattress, sheets, blankets, and whatever was in his room was either completely destroyed or meticulously painted in brown matter. It was always horrendous to clean. I remember feeling like there was no other choice, so I went in and slowly got the job done one poopy rag at a time. If you ever want to know how to clean a room of poop paint, give me a call. It's no wonder I'm known as the poop queen in my family. I've seen way too much of it.

This isn't just gross. It's taxing in every way. I couldn't raise my voice or get mad because it made it worse. If I yelled, Isaac would cry like a banshee and/or fight me, and believe me, you don't want to fight an unusually strong, poop-covered kid any more than you have to. It took all my patience and calm, along with angels, to get him into the tub for yet another shower. I stopped keeping track of when he had his last bath, because he usually got one, if not three baths a day because of the gross messes he constantly got into. The best thing we ever invested in is a detachable sprayer with different spray head functions for every shower in every house. The detachable sprayer made cleaning much easier. I highly recommend it! He still did the hand-flapping thing, though, flicking poop water all over me, my clothes, my hair, and my bathroom. What can I say? It isn't foolproof. Unfortunately, he did this multiple times a week. When I finally showed the social worker a picture of my son wearing nothing but poop is when talk of respite began.

I can't speak for anyone outside of the state, but here in Utah there is a waiting list for services, such as health care and respite—a *long* waiting list. And guess how you stop waiting and start getting services? There are a couple of key points. First, you have to whine like crazy and never even try to have it together. Second, experience an emergency involving police, an ambulance, and maybe child services. It takes extremes. People who stay silent rarely get the help they need. Too often parents (and others living in the home, such as siblings) drown in mental frailty, debt, physical abuse, and trauma before the child gets the help the whole family needs—if they ever get that help.

Too often in the news I hear of tragedies concerning parents who do not have the support they need and end up severely harming their special needs child. The knee-jerk reaction we have when we hear of such a case is to judge and talk about how awful that parent must be. After all, how could any parent do such a terrible thing? There is no question it is an awful crime that makes me sick to think about. When I hear these stories, though, I feel mostly sadness for everyone involved. As terrible as it sounds, I can understand how things get so bad. To even admit that is disturbing, but I know I'm not the only special needs parent that understands. I believe I can safely say that no sane parent would ever hurt a child, so the first thing I think is this: the parent(s) should have had help a long time ago. Next question: why didn't they have the help they needed before it was too late?

It takes a lot to get help. The instance I mentioned above is not the only reason Isaac has services today—it was just the last push. I made many honest and tear-filled phone calls pleading for help. Emails were sent, complaints submitted, loads of paperwork filled out, and time invested. My two youngest daughters are still on the waiting list, but I'm beginning to doubt if they will ever get the help they need, because a) Isaac has lots of help, so they assume I should be fine and don't need my girls to have help, and b) they are more high-functioning than Isaac. But their higher functioning does not mean they aren't still in diapers or need medical help. It doesn't mean *I* don't need help. In fact, a lot of times I have to be with Isaac at a doctor visit, school IEP, or other event where it's best to have me there as opposed to a transient staff member. At these times I really need help for my girls.

I should mention here that the services you fought for in your state won't follow you if you move to another. For example, we thought about moving from Utah to Florida until we found out if we did, there would be no more help for Isaac and we would be put on a waiting list that many say takes ten years to get the needed help. Without the help we get to pay for Isaac's medical needs, diapers and wipes, seat belt restraint, Convaid stroller, respite care, etc., we wouldn't make it. Now Isaac is bigger, he will soon receive a new wheelchair catered to his needs. I am grateful we decided to stay and didn't *have* to move.

It may sound like I am saying getting respite will solve all problems—it will not. It definitely can keep a struggling family afloat and in better mental health. Families should do whatever they can to obtain it for their child(ren). Parents need the respite as much as the child with special needs does. I am sorry to say, however, getting that respite and help comes with its own challenges.

The hardest problem we have is actually finding the right people to work—or any people at all. Here is a short list of some challenges we have encountered over the years with our respite and supported living as well as potential issues common in the field:

1. Transient individuals that only stay for a month or two: This is a problem because the paperwork required by the fiscal agent, such as a background check and legal documents needed to work in such a job, takes at least a month to get filled out and set in order. It is a lot of paperwork and effort to go through only to have the staff person on the job for only a week or a month. Not to mention the obvious fact that a child, especially one with special needs, needs consistency. But as parents we take whatever help we can get. Beggars can't be choosers, as the saying goes.

2. Inconsistent and unprofessional individuals: Many staff members do not treat this like a real job. They cancel whenever they feel like it, show up late, and sometimes friends and fun come before my son. In fact, after she had worked with Isaac for a week or two, one young woman said she would rather play soccer, so she quit and did that instead. I encourage you to be thorough in your interviews with potential staff workers. Ask the hard questions so you can get the best results.

3. A report has to be filed for any injuries caused by your child: This means paperwork and headache. If the injury is severe, courts and lawyers come into the picture. It is not pretty. In order to avoid this, I try to only hire people able to take on the task of my child, both physically and mentally. It is also important to give staff thorough training. One of my staff members had just had surgery around her abdomen and came to work only to get kicked in the stomach...not good.

4. Abuse: Yes, there is a required background check and I personally interview the people who come into my home, but it is impossible to always anticipate how even the kindest person will act under pressure. When someone has never been around things like constant screaming, defiant behavior, irritating habits, and huge, disgusting poopy diapers, you don't know how they will react. I am thankful nothing serious has occurred in my home, but I would be a fool to say my son has never been handled more roughly than I am comfortable with. We put cameras in almost every room in our home so nothing goes unnoticed that is harmful to our children. I suggest this for every home with a special needs child (as a bonus, these cameras are also good to track sleep habits, which is a huge key to the child's health and overall well-being).

5. Bad habits: Special needs children often copy the actions and habits of those around them. This can be a good thing *if* the action is positive and desired, but watch carefully. Something small, like nose-picking, may be a bad habit developed by your child, but too often other issues arise.

Although this has never happened to my children and I hope it never will, one example of a big issue is pornography. Special needs children are often at a younger age mentally and emotionally than they are physically. They cannot process such things. In my opinion, pornography will have an effect on every part of a user's life, no matter their age. If a trusted staff member exposes a child to pornography of any sort or uses the child's media device to indulge themselves, remove them immediately and file a report. I check my children's devices often, make sure they have all active parental controls in place, monitor the security cameras, and ask questions.

6. A stranger in my own home: Inviting someone new to come into our life and see every part of it was a whole new world. Suddenly, my husband and I couldn't walk around the house in our underwear! We had to be up early in the morning to answer the door for them and often what they saw on my face was no glamor shot. Sometimes families have to establish food rules if a staff member begins eating them out of house and home. Personal family moments suddenly become public. For example, holding our daily family prayer felt more awkward than sacred as the staff member played on her phone next to us.

7. Fiscal agents and paperwork: Working with government services to get help means also getting a fiscal agent so the staff get paid. It is unbelievable how much paperwork has to be done! I had to fill out page after page to become my own employer and then my employees had to fill out page after page to be hired on. Sometimes it takes months before they can even start working because of misunderstandings or glitches in the system. It is like having a full-time job just to keep track of time sheets, payments, paperwork, etc. It can really be overwhelming, especially when I have a thousand things clamoring for my attention and time.

8. Feeling replaced: Sometimes I have felt like the staff worker took away my position as a parent. Suddenly my oldest daughter was talking to them

more and they were having wonderful experiences I wanted to have. It hurt. I have learned to make sure I take those special moments with my kids no matter who is at the house. I have learned to teach the staff the way I discipline so even if I am not there, my children are growing up by my rules. Overall, it can be hard, but if getting this kind of help means I am still sane at the end of the day, then that is what matters most. My kids will always love their mommy best, even if the staff workers are more energetic and fun. No one can love my children the way that I love them. As long as they know that, I am content.

9. Keeping it professional: Maintaining a business relationship is challenging when the person coming into your home becomes a family friend. It can make for some awkward situations when you have to tell someone you think of as a friend or family member that they need to change your child's messy diaper, clean up vomit, or show up to work on time. Some individuals do not treat it like a normal job, so you are desperately at their mercy to accept whatever they are willing to do and whatever time they are willing to give, instead of a typical job where you as manager set the expectations and time commitments. After all, are you really going to fire them for being late when you will go crazy without their help right then and there? It truly is a balancing act of tactfulness and professionalism. I myself am not a very good manager, because I have a hard time saying anything that might be taken as confrontational, but sometimes you really do need to say what needs to be said. Your children and your sanity come first. It has been a learning process.

After reading this list, one might ask why in the world I would want respite anyway. Well, let me tell you. Despite the drawbacks, it is a need. I would not do it and go through the hassle if it was not necessary for my mental health, family life, and overall well-being. Getting respite helped me feel normal again. Before, I was depressed, overwhelmed, and tired. I did not want my depression to affect Millie, Isaac, or my marriage, but I could see it was. I noticed it most in Millie. I was so irritable and angry all the time. Instead of being the mom that played make-believe games with her each day, I was consumed by sadness and the burden of taking care of a newborn. One thing our respite workers do once the little kids are asleep is spend one-on-one time with Millie, usually playing board games, while Jeremy and I are out on a date.

Even though issues arise and I often have anxiety when someone else comes to my home, I have learned and am learning how to work through it so my family can get the help we need to thrive. No matter how comfortable I get with the people coming over, I always find some interesting adventures, whether fun, funny, interesting, or scary. Sometimes I just have to remember that, as William Shakespeare said, *"All's well that ends well."* And thankfully, things usually end well.

The most memorable time we had with a staff member was with Melina, who has since become a lifelong friend who I trust deeply. One day she took Isaac to the splash pad; I was happy he was going to have a good time and didn't think any more about it...until I got a phone call from the local police.

"Hello, ma'am," I heard a deep voice say.

"Hi," I replied tentatively since I didn't recognize it.

"Are you the mother of Isaac Fowler?" I immediately went into panic mode.

"Yes...is everything all right?"

"Do you know a young adult female named Melina?"

"Yes, she is a caregiver for my son," I said, confused. "Is something wrong?"

"There's been a situation. Your son is fine, but there's been an interaction between your son and Melina we need to address. Can you come to the splash pad immediately, please?"

"Um...oh. Uh, okay. I...yeah," I stammered. I had never had a phone call from the police and the fact that something was going on with my son that I didn't understand made me shaky. I didn't know what to do; I was in shock. My baby was asleep and I did not want to wake her (given the situation, this should be a clue to how important naptime and bedtime are with Fragile X kids. You just don't disturb them unless there's a fire in the room, because otherwise there will be a different kind of emotional fire in the house for the rest of the day). Also, getting my three girls into the van was often a nightmare. So I ran to a few neighbors to ask a last-minute favor of watching them at the house, but everyone was either gone or unavailable. I came into the house, trying to quickly decide on my best move when the phone rang again.

"We have been investigating the situation and we have all the information we need at this time. If you are comfortable with Melina bringing Isaac back home, we will let them go," said the police officer. "We have Melina's information if further investigation is needed."

I was relieved. I told the officer, "I trust Melina and I'm not concerned. Isaac has Fragile X Syndrome and I know how hard he can be, so yes, please, if you could send them back home that would be best, thank you."

As I hung up the phone I had the thought: I am surprised the police haven't been called on us because of Isaac's outbursts before this! In the meantime, I waited tensely for Melina to return. I honestly wasn't worried about Isaac's safety with Melina, but I wondered what would cause such a stir. I was worried about Melina. What a traumatic experience! When she finally came back, she looked shaken but okay. Apparently Isaac wanted a water squirter another boy had at the splash pad. We didn't know the other boy and Isaac could be aggressive, so Melina quickly decided it was time to leave. They walked there using his Convaid stroller with a five-point harness, and trying to get him back into it when he really didn't want to was proving more difficult than Melina thought. She did apologetically tell me that she did raise her voice as she was struggling to get him back into the stroller.

During this time, a bystander was recording with their phone the events between my son and Melina while another bystander called the local police department. Obviously, child abuse should not be taken lightly, so at least a half dozen police offers surrounded the park and splash pad area, slowly circling in on Melina and Isaac. At this point, Melina got nervous and was probably panicking a bit herself. I am not sure when Isaac was put in his stroller, but when the police got there, Melina was covered in scratches from Isaac and her hair was in disarray. If anything, she looked like the one in trouble.

I don't blame Melina for what happened. On a positive note, she learned from the event and it was helpful for her future career in special education. She never raised her voice with Isaac again, either. Unfortunately, this interaction threatened her job and career in any special education, as the situation was riding on whether this event would put a bad mark on her permanent record. After a week of waiting for the results of the investigation, there was nothing to put on her record. We were all grateful.

I feel blessed that at that time I had a staff member I truly trusted and one that *could* be trusted. I am grateful she continued to work for us and pursue her desired career in special education. Although I am grateful those bystanders put themselves out there to protect my son, I often wonder what happened to that video. Who knows what could be done with it. I cannot help but wonder if those individuals had no experience with autism or Fragile X; they could not see what was really happening and they did not go to help Melina.

One lesson I learned from this is to take my son's picture to the police department and explain our situation so if anything like this, or worse, happens in the future, the police will recognize my son and take appropriate measures. After hearing about so many troubles with autistc boys being shot or hurt by police officers, I want to do everything I can to protect my Isaac. It is a real fear for me and I am grateful more training has been implemented to help police officers deal with autistic or special needs kids and adults. I am grateful for the police and the sacrifices they make to keep us safe. I know not all cops are good cops, but I believe most are out there doing their best. I have many friends whose husbands are in law enforcement and I do not know how they do it. I am sure I could not be a policeman's wife—I would worry too much every day.

I cannot let this chapter end without sharing a few more experiences. At one point I had a young male staff person (I'll call him John) working in my home. He was the first caregiver we had and consequently dealt with some of the hardest moments with Isaac. He saw the worst of me, the dirtiest of my home, the strong will of Isaac, and more. We had many ups and downs, but remain friends and like to reminisce about the hard and funny times we experienced.

For example, one time I had him folding laundry while I spent time with my kids. Later, I realized that that particular batch of laundry included some lingerie. I wanted to die of embarrassment! I'm a very reserved person, but just thinking about it makes me laugh out loud. It was so awkward! Unfortunately, that was not the last time strangers folded underwear or other things. I always thought I got better at doing my own personal laundry, but it happened more than once and there were red-faced consequences for me.

But the story does not end there. John was around a lot helping me with Isaac. I was fairly new to the area and the schools, so when people saw us together helping Isaac with various things, they assumed he was my husband. It happened ALL. THE. TIME. Sometimes we had a chance to correct them and sometimes we didn't. One of Isaac's first bus drivers went almost the whole year assuming John was my husband until Jeremy put Isaac on the bus one day and the bus driver asked, "Hi. Who are you, an uncle? Family friend?" he asked.

"I'm his dad," Jeremy replied flatly. Awkward.

John was newly married at the time and I am sure both of our faces turned bright red every time something like this happened. Eventually, we learned to just laugh about it, but I'm not sure my actual husband appreciated it very much! I certainly would not like it much if someone thought a caregiver was Jeremy's wife!

Another funny thing happened when Melina came to work for us. For a whole school year, another one of Isaac's bus drivers thought Melina was my daughter. I didn't know this until the end of the year, so the next year I had to explain what happened to my "daughter" once she had married and moved away. Melina's thought was, "I'm not that young!" and my thought was, "I'm not that old!" But he was the best bus driver and I eventually explained she was a staff worker. Besides, he gave me, Isaac, and Millie candy every day, so I couldn't be offended, even if he did think I was ten years older than I really am.

Having respite taught me to let people in, let people help, not fear people's judgment, and laugh at myself sometimes. I am not perfect at doing these things, but I have definitely grown a lot. Because there is a high rate of staff turnover, I continually have to get used to new people and their quirks. But hey, if someone offers to help and they can, I let them. If I haven't done laundry in a week, I am completely frazzled, and my underwear needs cleaning, then I let them wash and fold it. If there's something unpleasant about those undies, then they are just going to have to deal with it, laugh, and think what they want, because at that point I am barely hanging on and taking life one hour at a time. Besides, who among us has never had an undy skid, right? The older I get the more I realize adults do all the things kids do, but it is more embarrassing because we are expected to be and do more. The truth is we all need a little help, no matter what our age or ability. Still, it is not always easy to be humble, let others in, and let go of your tight hold on everything.

This reminds me of a story my doctor once told me. It was a time when I was not feeling well and knew something was wrong in my body. I told him through tears, "I just cannot be sick. I *can't*. Everyone relies on me. Jeremy and the kids balance on me and what I do or feel." It seems unfair and difficult, but I often feel so much weight on my shoulders. I feel like Luisa in *Encanto* when she sings, "Who am I if I can't carry it all? Who am I if I don't have what it takes?" If anything serious were to happen—cancer, surgery, serious sickness, etc.—we would be in trouble. Our lives would crumble. But then my doctor shared a story from his life.

There once was a man who went camping with his two teenage sons. The father was an efficient swimmer and his sons had recently learned how to swim and even got their scout badges for it. There was a lake near them and in the lake was a small island about forty-five yards away.

"Can we swim to it?" one of the boys asked.

"Yeah, please?" asked the other.

The father looked back and forth between the two, debating in his mind if it was wise. *I am a good swimmer,* he thought. *If anything were to happen out in the water, surely I could help.*

The boys were so eager to try out their new skills and the father wanted to help them succeed, so he consented.

Out into the water they waded until it got deeper and deeper and they began to swim to the far-off island. They weren't quite three-quarters of the way there when the first boy cried out, "Father, help me! My legs are cramping up and I can't swim any more!" Obviously worried, the father swam over to his son and helped him while continuing to swim on to the island with one arm. Shortly after the second son cried out, "Father, help me! My legs are cramping up and I can't swim anymore!"

The father swam to his second son, grabbed him with the other arm. Floating on his back, holding one son in each arm, the father frog kicked backward toward the island. Being a more dense man, the father didn't easily float and holding his sons was now taking its toll. He could feel his body sinking, his breath growing shallow, and his own legs beginning to cramp. At that point, he knew all three of them were going under.

"Let go!" the father yelled out to his two sons with the little energy he had left.

"No, father!" said the first boy.

"No, father!" said the second boy.

"You have to or we will all drown. Let go and float on your back. Try to just relax as much as possible. We are almost to the island and you will get there safely," he said.

But he wasn't really sure if that was true. It was a desperate hope. He didn't want to let his sons go. He was afraid, but he knew there was no other way of survival.

The sons let go and drifted away from their father, floating on their backs. The father remained on his back, trying to relax and relieve his burdened muscles. Soon he felt the rocks and sand come up next to him and he looked around in relief to find his two sons sitting on the rocks, smiling and alive. They all had made it safely. But if the father would have kept holding on, they all likely would have drowned.

I sometimes feel like everything weighs on me, but I have discovered that Heavenly Father allows me to experience challenges in order to remind me to go to Him, who is really the one everyone can rely on. He and our Savior, Jesus Christ, can make the feeling of weight and burden feel light. The truth is, sometimes doing what is best means letting go. One thing I learn and continue to learn is to rely on the Lord, because it is through Him I make it day to day.

Sometimes letting go is in a big way and others it happens in little things. Maybe it means that even though someone helped load the dishwasher a little differently, I am just glad it got done. It means even though my child is dressed in a mismatched outfit, I am just glad he is dressed. It is accepting help when I don't want it, because I need it. Getting help made my burden lighter, my life more liveable, and my future more hopeful.

But getting help and relying on the Lord does not mean I do not have hard days, poor staff members, unwanted paperwork and stress, desires for more privacy, or complaints. I am human. I force myself to think of the positives and count my blessings. I am grateful for all the people that have come into my home—paid and unpaid—to help with my children and give me and my husband a break so we can continue to push on each day or even each hour.

Despite the many challenges, I still highly recommend getting this type of help as soon as possible. It is important to realize that getting help is better than dealing with going crazy, being overwhelmed, resenting your child, never getting time to do something fun, neglecting a child, or a whole slew of other problems. There is no shame in receiving help. The pros definitely outweigh the cons.

7

Hiring A "Nanny"

Diana and Eliza

"The simple act of caring is heroic."
–Edward Albert

A s Isaac gets older some things seem to get easier. However, as he gets bigger and stronger, in many ways life with him gets harder. Even though it is hard to accept and embrace help in various forms, I know it is what I and my family need. One of the best decisions I ever made was hiring a "nanny." I say "nanny" because she didn't live in our home or stay with my kids most of the day, but she had the option to get forty hours a week and became a great family friend. It wasn't always easy, but it was the best fit for us at the time. The trick is finding the right person for the job.

"Hi, I'm Diana," a woman replied over FaceTime as she relaxed in the passenger seat of a car.

"Thank you for meeting with me over the phone. This is just the best way for me right now," I said a bit apologetically.

"Oh, of course!" Diana replied. "I'm just driving with my husband right now. Hope you don't mind," she laughed.

"Not at all!" I replied with a smile. I liked her already. She was different from the other women I'd interviewed. She reminded me of my family—funny. She made me laugh the whole time. I don't know if I would have picked her out of the crowd and said, "She's the one!" I was so used to college students with trained professionalism, education in special needs, psychology, and therapy, and a sweet disposition, but this time I needed someone that would stick around, that was tough, and who would put up with a lot of crap—literally.

Over the years I interviewed many individuals, but not very thoroughly. Beggars can't be choosers, and I took what I could get. But I'd never done an official job listing before. There was a lot of word-of-mouth and sometimes contacts from previous university ties. Hiring through an official job posting and interview process worked really well in order to find the right person for the job. I received many resumes and interested people—more than I ever expected. I interviewed the top five. Here's an idea of what I put in the listing:

Job Title: Full-time Caregiver for Special Needs Children
Job Description:

I have four children ages ten, eight, five, and three. The youngest three have Fragile X Syndrome and one also has an autism diagnosis. I need someone that can provide the following:

- Assistance with daily living activities (diapering, dressing, showering, life skills, etc.)
- Encourage communication and appropriate social interaction
- Assist child to participate in activities they enjoy—not just watching TV
- Provide close supervision to keep children safe
- Attend school with eight-year-old as an aid/helper during the school year
- Transport in a safe vehicle to fun places, such as the rec center to swim, on a walk in the stroller, trampoline park, etc.

Your main responsibility will be taking care of my son, age eight. When he is not in need, cleaning (laundry, vacuuming, dishes, etc.) or playing with the other children is expected.

If you have special needs or nursing experience, this is a plus but not a requirement.

After receiving many applications, I put together a list of questions and scenarios I thought would help me weed out the unlikelies in the interview process:

Interview Questions:
1) Are you okay cleaning up vomit, pee, and poop on a regular basis?
2) How do you feel about changing the diapers of three children ages eight, five, and three?
3) Why did you apply?
4) What are your long-term plans?
5) What is your experience with disabled kids? Family members? Work experience?
6) Would you say you are compassionate and patient? Why or why not?
7) What is one strength and one weakness?
8) Do you like playing board games, pretend, and interactive games?

9) Do you feel comfortable with dog piles, deep pressure, and giving Isaac squishes?

10) Can you lift 100 pounds? This is how much Isaac weighs and once in a while you may need to carry him in difficult situations.

11) Would you be comfortable, qualified, and able to be an aide at school for Isaac if need be?

12) Are you flexible on hours? If I need you for an early shift at six a.m. or an overnight shift from six p.m.-twelve p.m., would that be feasible?

13) Are you willing to watch the kids at my house overnight or over multiple nights?

14) Do you have allergies or fear of cats or dogs?

15) Are you physically active and overall healthy?

16) Are you willing to take Isaac out for walks, swimming at the rec, and be with him in the trampoline park?

17) How do your friends describe you?

18) Do you feel comfortable coming with us weekly to church to be with Isaac and help him in the classes? This includes possibly taking him on a walk or home early.

19) Are you available for Friday nights six to eleven p.m. so my husband and I can go on a weekly date?

20) Do you feel comfortable traveling with us and going to larger family events with us?

Scenarios:

1) What would you do if Isaac doesn't want to do something and you're in a public place?

2) How do you react to situations where you feel powerless? Is it anger, physicality, fear?

3) Isaac has taken off his diaper, pooped, and smeared it everywhere. What do you do?

4) One child begins to cry and so all the others start crying and screaming loudly. What do you do?

5) Despite your best efforts, Isaac has escaped out the front door and is out on the road headed to the main street. What do you do?

6) Isaac has pooped and it is diarrhea. It is dripping down his leg and soiling his clothes. You need to get him into the shower ASAP, but he is resisting. What do you do?

7) You are at our house during dinner time. What do you do during the blessing? Do you plan to eat on your own time, eat with us, or help Isaac eat with us (I never did ask this, but it's something we had to figure out as we went)?

Basically I asked for a super person, but guess what? I found one! I've never had anyone fill out all the needed paperwork faster than Diana. That was amazing! She started soon after our interview. Another plus is that she lives near me, so before she officially started, she came to the house and met the kids. I think it was nerve-wracking for both of us.

The doorbell rang and immediately my dog, Luna, started barking. Millie answered the door with me right behind, holding Luna back. "Hi!" I said as I opened the door. "Come in!"

"Hi," Diana replied. "Thank you."

"Sorry about my dog. She acts scary, but she's just a goof," I apologized.

"Oh, it's okay, I have dogs at my house, too." Asking if she was okay with dogs in the interview was important!

"Come, have a seat," I motioned to the couch in our living room. Then it happened. The kids exploded—not literally, of course. Isaac flipped. He was hurting me, yelling, and trying to pull his younger sister's hair. I had to pull him to his room—with much effort—for a timeout. The little girls were all crying. I tried to act normal, cool, you know? It was not working.

"Don't worry," Diana said. "This doesn't bother me at all." My eyes opened wide as I thought, *Really?* "Seriously," she assured. "This won't scare me away. This is what I signed up for."

I was more than relieved and a bit surprised. Yes, I felt good about this one. She left shortly after all the craziness began and then I got a text from her:

Diana: Okay, now you have met me, do you still feel good about this? Be honest. I do have a tattoo on my foot and a little bumblebee on the inside of my wrist that I hope doesn't change how you feel.

Me: Of course we still want you! I didn't even notice, honestly, and it doesn't change a thing. I know you're a sweet and good person.

Diana: I just have this feeling that this was meant to be.

And so it was.

Then it came time to train her on the job, get used to each other in my home, and help the kids adjust. It was truly a crash course in the beginning. Diana was always so considerate and accommodating. She continually said, "This is your home. It's not all about everyone adjusting to me. I am here to adjust to you and the way things are in your home." She always reassured me through my anxieties and insecurities, and sooner than expected, we felt like she was part of the family. Her true initiation happened just days after she began working.

"Poop!" Evelyn yelled and laughed. "Poop!" Diana looked over from where she was sitting and suddenly Evelyn handed her a fresh, brown boulder. It was accompanied with a diaper with brown residue. Evelyn had never done that before—not even to me—and Diana just laughed about it. We decided Evelyn was just performing the initiation into the Fowler clan. I admit, though, I was surprised she had a run-in with Evelyn's poop fiascos before Isaac's. But then again, life around here is full of surprises, in all shapes, forms, and...smells.

As you can see, even though it was a good thing for everyone overall, we still have our challenges. Sometimes there is miscommunication and embarrassment or Isaac is too rough. Diana has been kicked, scratched, hit, jumped on, and more. She literally rolls with the punches. On my end, I sometimes feel guilty I am not with my kids twenty-four-seven. I have to remind myself that when I am mentally healthy and happy, my kids are better off, too. Although we sometimes have misunderstandings and differing opinions that make small bumps in the road, we keep moving forward and I am so very grateful. Since Diana has come into our lives, I feel less trapped. I work a little from home, do things I enjoy, and feel a bit of normalcy. I cherish my time with the kids more and want to make moments special. I thought I would get major mom jealousy, but she is just like a family friend or aunt. She calls me to talk and discuss what fun things we should do each day and spoils my kids with fun toys and treats while Jeremy and I are having fun on a date. We are so lucky to have her.

Our luck doubles when she brings her daughter along. It's like I got a two-for-one deal! She often brings her teenage daughter, Gracie, with her and my kids love to play with her. Even shy little Evelyn took to Gracie right away. Millie and Gracie will often get into giggling fits and have a blast together. Diana always makes sure that Millie gets special one-on-one time, given that *all* her siblings have special needs. They paint nails, play games, and watch girlie movies on Friday nights after the other kids are asleep when I am out with Jeremy. I remember in the interview I mentioned Millie and how important it is that she has one-on-one time. Diana totally understands and always keeps her in mind.

Somehow she just knows how to handle my children for the most part. She was never afraid to give Isaac the "squishies" he needed. Each day she plays Beast and Dinosaur games with Isaac, tickling him and letting him dogpile on her; not everyone is comfortable with that kind of interaction and not everyone can do it in a way that is appropriate and Isaac enjoys. I am continually surprised Diana keeps coming back after all she's gone through. In just the first month she changed dozens of nasty diapers, cleaned up vomit, was handed poop, got jumped on by half my kids, met my whole family, got scratched and bruised by Isaac, was hit by a stray frisbee, and spent way too much on Amazon for fun things to do at my house with the kids.

There are difficult things, too. Sometimes we all just need our space. Other times Jeremy and I have sadness, because she seems to have more of those happy moments with our kids than we get. I know my nephew and nieces will do things with their caretakers that they would never do with their parents. At times it just doesn't seem fair, but because we are their parents and we love them, we just do whatever it takes to make sure they get the most opportunities and best life possible.

One thing I have learned is letting people in does not show weakness or failure. It takes a lot of strength and humility to let someone in so fully. Inviting good people into our lives, whether it is an emotional connection, an opportunity to serve us, or any other means, is essential. As human beings we need connection. We learn from one another, teach one another, and help one another. I have made some wonderful connections over the years because of my children. I know Isaac alone has impacted the lives of dozens of people here in our home and as he has gone to school, summer camps, church, and other public places.

Too often I find myself hiding from the world. For one, I rarely feel accepted and invited in with open arms when my children are loud, disruptive, and just *different*; it is also just hard to leave my home. We have learned to enjoy ourselves at home as much as possible. And now I am trying to open up my heart and home to others to allow my children's sweet spirits to change their lives for the better and to help enrich my life as well.

With my children as one of my top priorities, when I feel they are safe and taken care of, I can relax and find time for myself. It is a balance, however, of finding joy along the journey and taking moments for yourself all along the way. I remember a time when I felt I never had fifteen minutes to myself. If anyone finds themselves in this same boat, I tell them to find help now. They need it. Their child needs it. Balance is key. It truly is a juggling act and it is a skill we learn over time and through trial and error. I am grateful there are times when my mental and physical health are up and my kids are doing well so I am more independent as a mother to take care of my children. I feel valued, loved, and a good mother no matter how much time I need someone else in my home to help. Either way, I have to remember to take care of myself or else I will not be able to take care of the ones I love. If that means locking myself in the bathroom while I eat a chocolate bar and listen to my favorite music for a few minutes while the kids watch a cartoon, it can make all the difference. It is okay, because after a refresher you can then better face the challenges, such as that third poop fiasco of the day.

8

Me Time & Marriage

Kirsten riding an adult trike/big wheel down the Provo bike trail on a date with Jeremy

"Me party! A party just for one."
–The Muppets

Doctors, scientists, friends, family, and other experts are always saying to get more "me time." Too often that felt impossible for me. It did not help that I always felt like I was not good enough anyway, so taking time for myself felt like taking away from my children or my husband. It felt selfish. Now I realize taking time away for myself is not selfish—it is necessary! In fact, it makes me a better wife and mother. Sometimes, when I am overwhelmed by the constant "Mom! Look at me!" or "Mom, I need to go potty!" or "Mom! Mom! MOM," a short break is what I need to reset and come back fresh. "Reset and fresh" means I don't yell, don't say things I don't mean, and don't feel trapped in my life.

It really hit me several years after my first child was born when a friend asked, "So, what do you like to do? What are your hobbies?" I didn't even know how to reply! I wanted to say, "My kids," because that is all my life was. I cooked, cleaned, made doctor appointments, took kids to the dentist, consulted with therapists, worked with kids on their goals, and went to IEPs. I ended up saying I watch movies and listen to books when I do laundry.

I realized everything had to have a dual purpose. If I was going to watch a show I liked, I had to do something productive or I would feel guilty. Later, when I became very depressed and my health was poor, I laid in bed and watched movies for hours. If I gave myself time to do other things I loved, maybe I would not have fallen into such a deep depression.

The truth is I lost myself. I forgot I am a fun and adventurous person. I forgot I have talents, even talents used for things other than taking care of my children. I love to go rock climbing, zip-lining, and visit rollercoaster parks. I play several instruments and I sing. Before my health declined, I loved to dance, especially doing stunts in couples dancing, country swing, ballroom, and triple swing. Just thinking about that makes me smile.

As a Carrier, there are certain symptoms that are a fact of life for me now. Things that used to bring me joy are no longer possible given the realities of life in my family and in my own body. But just because things look and feel differently than they used to does not mean I cannot find joy if I look for it. I found options online for dance classes of all kinds. Even with reduced flexibility or achy joints, there are thousands of possibilities for me out there, including yoga! I am grateful. I don't dance much anymore, because my joints protest, but on days I feel well enough I have been known to break out a few moves. Mostly I dance with my kids, or slow dance in the kitchen with my husband. I have accepted it is okay to find satisfaction in simple or more subdued things, like reading, watching movies, doing hand embroidery projects, painting my nails despite my tremor, and other activities that make me happy.

I still like the occasional adventure, but I learned the hard way that I have to listen to my body and its limits. If I push myself too hard, I pay for it later. Once Jeremy and I decided to visit the Olympic Oval in Salt Lake City, Utah to try out all the adventurous things. We went extreme tubing, ziplining, hiking, and did a ropes course. The next day I was out—I was tired, achy, and had a headache. I ended up getting sick for a few days after.

Even though I know I need personal time, I often find it difficult to come by. Sometimes five minutes of mindfulness in my room turns into a dog-pile fest with all the kids. From the bottom of the pile, I hear the calm lady saying, "Feel your breath as you breathe in slowly." At that point I usually get kneed in the gut, and my breath rushes out with a groan. Before we had helpers coming into our home, I felt like every waking moment was spent catering to my children and I had no time for myself at all, but I have since found that I *can* take some down time, even with the kids around. It is a different kind of recharging, but it can still help to do something I love. Sometimes sharing things I love with my children brings great memories and teaching moments.

My kids have noticed, however, that I am not too keen on doing a lot of strenuous activities or going outside a lot unless it is a nice temperature. If it's too hot or too cold, my body does weird things. Not too long ago, Millie talked about doing some fun outdoorsy thing, but said it was okay if I didn't want to do it. She said something like, "I know you don't like to go outside and do things a lot, so it's okay if you stay here and work on your computer." It made me sad and kind of mad at myself. It was another time to mourn the body I once had. I still feel like I can do a lot, however, despite all the issues

I face. I'm more grateful for my body today than I think I ever have been. I guess losing something makes you appreciate it that much more, but most days, thinking about going outside and running around with my kids being crazy makes me feel tired!

For me, being refreshed might include spending downtime with the kids, like watching a movie with them and eating popcorn, going outside and enjoying a popsicle, piling on the hammock, or listening to music while they dance around. Sometimes I just sit and let them brush my hair or lie face-down on the floor while they drive on my back with matchbox cars.

I don't always have the luxury of alone time, but I try to get a few minutes of downtime of some kind each day. Sometimes it is a few minutes here and there. My husband laughs because I will disappear for a little while and come back with some new funny picture or video I've taken of myself. You can see Nacho Madre on YouTube as an example. It just helps me to be goofy here and there to let off steam. I also try to make sure I get at least one day out a week with friends, family, or even solo. I love to have "Sister's Day," where my sisters and sisters-in-law all get together without kids or husbands to just be silly and do whatever we feel like. Sometimes Rachael and I get together at my mom's house to eat her homemade french fries and laugh our heads off.

I also feel refreshed when I date my spouse. I love this quote from *The Family: A Proclamation to the World:* "Successful marriages and families are established and maintained on principles of faith, prayer, repentance, forgiveness, respect, love, compassion, work, and wholesome recreational activities." I believe these principles are true no matter what religion an individual may follow: faith in a higher power is life-sustaining. We can have hope in an outcome or person. Prayer, affirmation, or meditation can focus our intentions on the positive. All of these can help a marriage be successful. When I feel whole and love myself, I can love others better. When I put selflessness and charity at the center of my marriage relationship, it is more likely to succeed. Of course, a successful relationship of any kind also includes a lot of forgiveness, respect, compassion, and work.

And activities—dating is a must! Someone once said dating is less expensive than divorce—and not just monetarily. Even though Jeremy and I have been married for years, it is important we still put effort into doing special things for one another. Jeremy and I try to go on a date every week. Respite care has saved us in that regard. Before that was an option, we got someone to come late at night when the kids were already asleep, or we would make some in-home date plans.

"What are we doing tonight? I've got Kathleen to come watch the kids after we put them to bed," I told Jeremy one Friday evening.

"I don't know. You usually plan that," he replied.

"I know, but I was busy this week. You're welcome to plan a date any time, you know," I said, annoyed.

"I have things I take care of and worry about and you have things you take care of and worry about. The things you take care of, I don't worry about. Date night is one of those things," he said.

I secretly rolled my eyes, but chose not to dwell on that comment.

"Well, my friend told me about this thing online called Dating Divas. They have a ton of date ideas. I think we should do the one where we go to the dollar store and buy each other five things in a specific category" (we didn't have a lot of money then and had to keep any date adventures low cost).

"Okay, I'm down," Jeremy replied. After Kathleen came later that night, we hopped into our minivan and drove to the nearest dollar store for a quick date night. Once there, we decided to do just three gifts.

"Let's say the first gift has to be something useful," I said as we walked into the store. "That way we get something worthwhile—as worthwhile as you can find at the dollar store, anyway."

"Okay, I like that," Jeremy said. "For the second item, what about something to eat? Like a treat or snack?"

"Ooo, yeah," I agreed, getting ideas. "And then let's choose something funny. That shouldn't be hard to find here," I said with a laugh.

"But not completely random. Like, it still has to be somewhat useful," Jeremy said thoughtfully. "I mean, I don't really want a rubber chicken or something."

I smiled, "What? It would be epic!" We laughed.

We split up and tried to hide from one another in the small store while shopping for three secret gifts for one another. For something useful, I got Jeremy seeds to plant because he loves planting and growing anything! Jeremy got me a kitchen utensil—the dollar store actually has some decent ones for a buck. For something funny, Jeremy got me a mug that said, "Bacon is the reason I get up in the morning." It's not far from the truth, because I really have a hard time getting up in the morning! I got him a grabber tool to pick up things without bending over or things that are high out of reach (that, my friends, *was* epic). For a treat, I gave him some off-brand brownies with sprinkles on top. He loves sweets. He got me a bag of Riesens for old times' sake, remembering a previous date where he told me "There is always a 'Riesen' to stop by." Cheesy, but I loved it. By the way, both treats were rock-hard, but we ate them anyway.

That date was memorable, simple, and definitely budget-friendly—meaningful dates do not have to be extravagant. In our experience, some of our silliest, most spontaneous dates have been more fun and memorable than intricately planned and expensive ones. Our dollar store date really made us think more about each other and we became closer as a couple.

Dating is an essential part of keeping the marriage alive, especially considering the extra stress children with special needs bring. Obviously, not all divorce can be avoided by dating your spouse, but the relationship we have developed through continuing to date has strengthened our marriage and gotten us through some rough times. Even during the COVID-19 quarantine, Jeremy and I found fun things to do at home without the children. In fact, we found we really enjoyed it—even more than going out! Sometimes we will go on a hike and find treasures, bird watch, or take pictures. Here are some of the fun, inexpensive dates a couple can do at home:

1. Put together a puzzle.

2. Get cheap canvases and some paint. Paint a picture together or side by side, even if you aren't artistic. You might look up some painting tutorials on YouTube.

3. Sit across from each other and draw pictures of each other. It can be serious or a simple, funny cartoon.

4. Play two-player games or have a game night with close friends. Don't forget snacks!

5. Play old computer games you find online that bring back childhood memories.

6. Play video games on your favorite console. My favorite is the old school Nintendo games, possibly because they are the only ones I can actually beat (for reference, I have beat Little Mermaid on Super Nintendo twice. Just sayin').

7. Have dinner delivered to your door. Light candles! During dinner, ask each other questions. Several lists like this are available online: https://coupletraveltheworld.com/fun-questions-for-married-couples/.

8. Cook dinner and/or bake a dessert together.

9. Pop some microwave popcorn and break out your candy stash, then sit back, relax, and watch a new (or old favorite) movie. Even home videos are fun. Jeremy and I like to relax in our adjustable bed and use our mini projector to watch movies on our wall.

10. Make a movie of your own. Maybe even start a Youtube channel for fun.

11. Write old school letters to friends and loved ones, then send them in the mail.

12. Video chat with friends and family or give a call to someone in need.

13. Service projects you can do at home and send off later, such as tying blankets, sewing, or putting together hygiene kits.

14. Online shop for each other and wait for your secret surprise in the mail in the coming days.

15. Give back rubs or leg massages to one another while listening to calming music.

The list can go on and on. Just get creative and be in tune with what you each like. Jeremy and I always wait until the kids are in bed (around eight p.m.) before starting the fun evening events. It doesn't always work out, depending on how the kids are, but if two people put in an effort, the rewards can be gratifying and joyful.

Before quarantine, and even more now that we have a nanny, we have been very blessed to have the opportunity to go on dates regularly—and often for more than just an hour! One night, Jeremy had been gone most of the week for work, so I was really looking forward to going on a date. We decided to go to Olive Garden for dinner, one of our favorites. Classic. Dinner was great and all, but the real fun came after.

We decided to find a mountain trail we could leisurely walk. We came upon an area we had been to before, but found a different trailhead we had no idea existed, so we took it! It was a short trail leading to an open spot with a great view over the valley. There were benches to sit on, too. We just talked and looked at the sky. Jeremy pointed out Venus and we talked about the stars, our kids, and everything in between (Jeremy has always been easy to talk to. It's nice). We were about to leave when Jeremy noticed some purple rock on the side of the mountain. We were there for like an hour looking at the different colors of rock and talking about it. I felt like such a nerd! Long story short, I felt like we were an engaged couple again. I love my Jeremy.

Now, this may sound like everything is hunky-dory in my marriage. Of course we have our troubles. Jeremy and I both make mistakes. All. The. Time. We are constantly asking for forgiveness and finding it in our hearts to forgive each other. Some things are harder to forgive than others, of course, but we both hate the feeling of discord between us when we argue or disagree. Learning how to communicate with each other is an ongoing process, and we are still learning, but the effort from both parties is so important. Being open, honest, and forgiving makes all the difference.

We talk a lot, but I confess sometimes that communication is not exactly pleasant. I, for example, communicate volumes through "the look." Jeremy knows he has done something wrong or I am in trouble if I give him the look. While I am not exactly proud of this imperfect skill, Jeremy says I am perfect at it. We usually laugh about it after the fact, but *never* during an incident. If he laughs at me when I am mad, he gets another look he refers to as "laser eyes."

Communication is a huge part of a successful marriage. A lot of problems arise because of simple communication errors (it is not that we don't talk to each other—we talk all the time about everything. We usually end up chatting way past bedtime at night, and these nightly chats have been one of our strongest bonding times throughout our marriage). But sometimes when Jeremy says something, my brain processes in a way his brain process did not intend. Sometimes I feel like we are speaking completely different languages. Men's brains and women's brains are very different from one another. One comedian, Mark Gungor, explains that we are simply wired differently. For example, he says, men have a "nothing box," while women do not. It is possible for men, he claims, to literally not think about anything. Nothing. As a woman, I cannot completely believe this, because that is not possible for me. Try asking your husband what he is thinking about, and he might say "nothing," and actually mean it. You will probably assume he just wasn't listening to you. Of course, this is greatly oversimplified, but the point is that communicating with your spouse in a way both of you understand is key to a healthy marriage. As John Gottman, author of *The Seven Principles for Making Marriage Work*, claims, "Successful long-term relationships are created through small words, small gestures, and small acts."

Many times little things make all the difference. A kiss before he leaves for work. A note to say *I love you* in his lunch box. An invitation to go on a walk together and talk. Praying together, even studying the gospel together. Jeremy and I are not perfect. Even after eleven years we are still figuring it out, and we probably will be for the next eleven years and beyond. Being open to listen to one another, putting yourself in their shoes, and feeling free to speak your mind is key. For a long time we thought keeping our mouths shut in order to prevent a fight was a good thing. Having a good marriage does *not* mean you never fight. So many young couples think that because they fight they should get a divorce. That is not true! It is normal to have disagreements, and it is normal to work together to find resolution to them. We grow closer through our challenges.

Although I believe not everything needs to be said, every healthy marriage has a bit of arguing. In fact, Jeremy told me about a friend of his who just got divorced—apparently he *never* fought with his wife. Sounds great, right? But if you never argue, you are likely not talking about things that really matter to you. It is vital to let your spouse know if you are hurting or if something is bothering you. Obviously I am not talking about having a yell fest over who ate the last chocolate truffle or the annoying way he eats his cereal—that rotten fruit can probably stay on the ground without picking it up to smear in his face. But sometimes you simply must talk about uncomfortable, hard things, and that can lead to hurt and offense. This is why learning to communicate effectively, forgiving one another, and having healthy boundaries are crucial skills in a partnership. Healthy marriage requires a lot of forgiveness and a lot of compromise.

Despite best efforts, I think every married person has thoughts of divorce at one time or another. Marriage is hard, but often when life gets difficult, it ends up bringing the biggest rewards. When I went to BYU, I had the opportunity to combine my background in journalism and my new study of Human Development/Family Studies. I worked with a professor building a new website for people considering divorce. I wrote several articles for the site, including a three-part series about how divorce is more common in families with special needs children. Here are some of the reasons we discussed:

- It is hard!
- You have little or no time for yourself, let alone for your spouse.
- Your child requires so much time, money, mental effort, etc. that it is hard to have any of the above left for your marriage.

Because I have three children with special needs, I have naturally worried that maybe I am disqualified from having a happy, long-term marriage, but this is not true! This is why I loved researching about divorce:

- I found hope that it does not have to happen to me.
- I learned so much about what it means to have a happy marriage.
- There is fabulous research, especially by Gottman. He is the true "love doctor!" I often suggest learning about him and his discovery about the Four Horsemen.

If you are thinking about divorce or if you want to gain some valuable insight about what a healthy marriage is, I recommend this website backed by great research: *yourdivorcequestions.org*. In addition to a few articles by yours truly, there are many great documents that can answer many questions.

Learning good communication skills can help navigate the small and huge challenges that come in any marriage. Here are some pointers I have learned:

1. Accept the tough things they tell you as a gift—a gift that will help you change for the better.

2. Pray before you speak. Pray for help to forgive.

3. Do not resort to low blows and attacks. Each of us knows to hit where it hurts, especially someone we know intimately, but we absolutely should not. We need to love and protect one another. Be an adult. Say how you

are feeling, but use "I feel...when..." statements to start out instead of accusatory "you never/always..." statements.

4. It is absolutely okay to go to bed angry. I have heard it said that one should "never let the sun set on an argument," but there have been so many times when I'm sucked into an argument because I am stressed and tired from the day. Sometimes a good night's sleep gives a restart and clarity. Often the next morning we laugh at how silly we were, give each other a hug, and move forward. Sometimes hashing it out before bed can lead to a long, drawn-out, exhausting fight that gets nowhere.

5. Try not to fight in front of your kids. Sometimes it happens, though, and when it does it is important you make up in front of the kids with kind words and hugs. Kids need to know that parents argue and it is okay—normal, even. And they deserve to see examples of how to make up. Children who never see their parents argue or fight, mistakenly believe the first argument in a relationship is the end of that relationship! Or they do not know how to swallow their pride and apologize. Be an example to your children of fighting fair and making up appropriately.

6. Take time to cool down. Sometimes I get really angry about something Jeremy did or did not do (I often expect him to read my mind), but instead of immediately yelling about it, I take a step back and allow myself to calm down before I do or say anything I will regret. This is a good time to pray for help, do some meditation, or read your favorite book. Just make sure you do not stew on it and make yourself more angry, which will just make you more liable to blow your top at the slightest provocation.

7. No one wants to walk on eggshells all the time. Being open, yet calm, about what bothers you is better than holding it in and walking around like a grump for weeks, making your partner guess what he or she did wrong this time.

8. Do not be afraid of feelings and emotions. We all have them and no one should be ashamed to let them show.

9. You and your partner both have needs. Help each other understand what your needs are and how to help each other obtain them in order to feel safe, loved, and secure.

10. Keep lines of communication open. Call them during lunch at work. Text them throughout the day. Marco Polo them to show them what your cute daughter did that day. By keeping communication open, you make it easier to talk about anything and everything at any time.

11. You cannot be everything to your spouse and they cannot be everything to you. You are both individuals that each needs personal time, time out with the guys or a girls' night. You have different likes and dislikes, but your spouse should still be your highest priority relationship.

12. Understand and come to agreement on expectations you have of one another day to day. Who takes care of what responsibilities? I have found many of our misunderstandings are over unvoiced, unfulfilled expectations. Also, be reasonable with your expectations and take into account their responsibilities, life, and desires.

I realize I am lucky to have a husband committed to me and to our marriage, despite the challenges of having three kids with disabilities and my own Carrier issues. We definitely have our issues individually and as a couple, but we work things out by communicating and forgiving. Jesus Christ is at the center of our marriage and I would not have it any other way. That thought is what gets us through. I have noticed positive little things really add up to create secure and safe feelings in love, such as when Jeremy drops what he is doing to listen, when he invites me along on his nightly walk so I can spend time with him, or when he sends me flowers on days he is away from home. Overall, I am grateful we share the same overarching desires in life as well. He is willing to meet me halfway and do his part in the team effort.

I cannot imagine the challenges faced by single parents. That is one realm I have not entered and do not wish to. My hat is off to those pulling through the journey of parenting special needs children alone and strong. Really, though, no one is alone on this journey. There are people everywhere that relate and love, so I have found I should never be afraid to reach out to others and let people help me in return. It is okay. Asking for help does not mean I am weak. It means I am strong.

No matter where you are in this journey—married, dating, single, divorced—do what you can to *make* time for you. Do things that make you happy. You may need some true "Me Time." Also, remember that good marriages are balanced between personal needs, couple needs, and responsibilities.

I now know it is important to remember who I am and what I love to do—this is part of taking care of me and it is essential to take care of my spiritual, physical, and emotional needs. One of my favorite speakers, Jeffrey R. Holland, once stated, "...slow down, rest up, replenish, and refill. Physicians promise us that if we do not take time to be well, we most assuredly will take time later on to be ill." Failing to take time now will mean taking time later in suffering. As a Carrier of Fragile X, I am no stranger to this principle.

More and more issues arise when I fail to take care of myself properly, especially in managing stress. I am constantly surprised to find that being a Carrier of FX is the culprit behind mental, emotional, and physical issues. Thankfully, the more I educate myself on the subject, the more capable I am at caring for myself in a way that is helpful and conducive to my needs.

9

Fragile X Carriers

Kirsten with her two older sisters who are also Carriers

"Jesus Christ is the source of all healing, peace, and eternal progress."
−Jean B. Bingham

For the first eight years of our marriage, Jeremy was enrolled in college pursuing his Master's degree in Civil Engineering. Of course, he also worked various jobs. Because he was so fully occupied, I often felt alone. Not only literally, but on this journey of raising children. With Millie, my first child, things were simple. Sure, it was hard to be a parent and adjust to a new life, but overall I was happy once I got the hang of things. On the other hand, after Isaac was born, I just couldn't find a happy rhythm.

As time went on, despite my best efforts, my depression became unmanageable. The last thing I wanted was for my family to be hurt by it, but I could see my depression was negatively affecting my marriage and children. I noticed it most in Millie. I was irritable and angry all the time. Instead of being a mom that played make-believe and games with her each day, I was consumed by sadness and by taking care of a baby with disabilities. I finally admitted to myself that I needed help. I scheduled an appointment with my doctor and had Jeremy come along for support and input.

"Okay, Kirsten," the doctor said after reading over my depression test. "Can you tell me a little bit about what is going on?"

"Well, I have two kids and one has a disability," I started, staring at the floor. "It's been really hard on everyone," I said, tears forming while my voice shook, but I continued. "Sometimes...sometimes I just feel like Jeremy would be happier if I left or if he married someone else. I just want him to be happy and I don't think that is possible with me in our circumstances."

"I see," the doctor said through sad eyes. "Kirsten, it looks like you are struggling with depression, but there *is* help. There are some different treatments and medications we can look at."

I just stared down at the floor, ashamed, and cried. I felt so broken. For the first time in my life I really felt like something was wrong with me. I was going to be one of those people on regular medication. That wasn't me! I had never taken any medication longer than it took to get rid of strep throat. All of these feelings added to the overarching thoughts I continually had of *you're not good enough*, but I knew I had to do something. I began medication and got lucky with the first one I tried. It actually helped. I felt like I processed and handled things better. But I still was not ready to go to therapy. In my mind, therapy was for weird people who were half crazy and could not get a handle on their lives. That was not me. Nope. Never. I decided to take matters into my own hands—I went back to school.

I needed to find something to occupy my thoughts and actions besides full-time mothering, so I went back to something I always enjoyed: school. I enrolled in the school of Family Life at BYU. I thought if I could learn more to help Isaac, it would make me a better parent and help me feel like I was really doing something worthwhile. This may sound strange, but I love school. I love learning, being around students excited about their futures, and pushing myself to do more than I thought I could. For some reason I wasn't finding purpose in motherhood at that time, so I looked for another purpose and went back to earn my Bachelor's degree. It was not an easy task and I did most of my work online. It took a lot of love and coordination with Jeremy, but we worked it out. In 2015 we graduated together with our Bachelor's degrees.

After Isaac was born in 2011, odd things began to happen to me physically. One day while I was shaving my legs I went over an area that felt funny. It felt like I was wearing a rubber sock. Other areas of my legs were numb, too, to varying degrees. Of course, I immediately got out my Google doctor and found some pretty terrifying stuff, so I did not hesitate to set up an appointment with a real doctor, who ran a series of blood tests. We learned there was something off in my blood samples, but nothing definitive. The doctor was worried it could be Lupus, but there was not enough evidence. We considered Lyme's, Diabetes, Multiple Sclerosis (MS), and various other issues, but nothing really fit the results. My doctor finally sent me to a neurologist.

The neurologist was certain I had MS, which was devastating and frightening.

"Your life is going to change drastically and you need to prepare for the future," she said. "I advise you not to have any more children." I sat in the chair trying not to panic and cry. After our little chat, she ordered a series of MRIs and other tests to confirm her diagnosis, but when I returned for a follow-up appointment, I found a very confused doctor. The tests showed I did not have

MS, but didn't allude to any possible reason why I was having numbness in my legs. Nevertheless, she simply prescribed medication and sent me on my way. That was it!

I had no answers. I had no idea what the medication was or what it should do. My sense was that she wanted me gone so she could move to her next appointment, as if she did not want to admit she had been wrong, so she just wanted me out of the office. Sometimes I feel doctors give you medication just to placate you. It was so strange, and I left her office in a daze. I was grateful I did not have MS, but I still had no idea what was going on with my body. Not knowing what else to do, I filled the prescription on my way home. However, a quick online search taught me the medication was likely prescribed for pain, which I thankfully did not have, and it could potentially cause even worse problems than I was currently experiencing. So I disposed of the pills and never went back to that neurologist. I was so frustrated, I decided to just ignore the numbness, chalk it up to a weird Carrier issue, and move on with my life. No one could find anything wrong with me, I reasoned, so why should I worry?

Life went on. I did eventually go to a therapist to help with my mental struggles, but it was expensive and I did not find it helpful, so I stopped after a few months. Throughout this time of virtually ignoring my symptoms, I went on to have my next two FX children.

In June 2019, however, I really hit a wall—I noticed more and more odd symptoms that no one could explain. I believed I really did have MS and it was now going to take control of my life. I pictured all the worst possible outcomes for me, my kids, and my husband, and these thoughts did not help when I was already struggling with so much stress and responsibility for four children. I felt like I was caring for triplets, since all three young ones were in diapers and constantly needing me, and I never had a moment to myself.

We pushed along as normally as possible until that summer. Jeremy went on an overnight backpacking trip with his friend. I had been struggling with my mental health, but I did want Jeremy to go and have fun and take some time for himself. That night, however, was another turning point in our lives.

After Jeremy left that Friday evening, I became very overwhelmed with my kids and responsibilities. At this point I cannot remember why I did not simply call someone to come help me—maybe I did not want to be a burden. Maybe I just could not think what I would say if I did call someone. I do know I felt like I was going crazy. I made a quick decision to just get out of the house.

"Okay, everyone!" I shouted, exasperated. "Let's go for a drive." The kids usually did pretty good in the car, and sometimes that was a good way to get a restart. "Don't worry about shoes. We aren't getting out," I said to everyone. "Let's just get in the car."

Of course there was crying and whining, and the usual difficulty getting them into the car and buckled before leaving the house. At first I tried playing music to calm them down, but they were still being loud and yelling, and Evelyn, the baby, was crying. I started to shut down inside—even getting out of the house and going for a ride wasn't changing the feeling I had of being trapped and alone. I kept praying, but it was really just a plea for help over and over.

"Okay, how about we watch a movie?" I tried, annoyed that I had to fall back on this crutch, even outside the house. But I turned the movie on in hopes that there would be peace for even a few minutes. Unfortunately, when they finally quieted down, I found myself lost in the thoughts of my own dark mind. I began having thoughts that scare me to think about today.

Maybe I can run the van off the bank in the canyon. Maybe I'll swerve just before the diesel truck passes by me in the opposite direction. Surprisingly, these thoughts did not seem that bad at the time. In fact, I felt like these actions might provide relief and greater joy for Jeremy until another thought came. *If I die, Jeremy would be left with all the kids. That wouldn't make him happy. It's better if I take the kids with me. Then he can move on and have a better life.* And so I found myself planning how I could ensure that none of us came home that night.

I drove around nearby towns and cities for what seemed like hours before I found my way back home. In the end, I just could not do it. Thank goodness. I hope I could never go through with something like that in the end. My children had no idea the awful thoughts playing in my mind. For the rest of the evening, I wrestled to manage the children until finally it was time for bed. Bed was the relief I needed. When the kids were safe in bed, I finally relaxed and enjoyed Me Time, but that night the depression still weighed heavy on my heart and mind.

The next day, Jeremy came home and I put a smile on my face. I listened to him talk about the great time he had on his adventure and I was happy he had gone and had fun. It was clear to me I should not hide the feelings and thoughts I had experienced, so later that day I opened up to him, finding the courage to tell him everything. He was surprised, worried, and hurt. The experience terrified him so badly that he did not go anywhere overnight for the next two years unless it was absolutely unavoidable. When Diana came to help, she made it possible for us to start getting back to normal again.

A few days after this terrifying experience, just a few days before my thirtieth birthday, we asked our religious leaders to pay us a visit. Jeremy and I both broke down and told them how much we were struggling. Even though I did not want to tell a soul except Jeremy, it came out that I had suicidal thoughts and often felt that life was not worth living. I was worried I would be judged and viewed as incapable or weak. I felt responsible and guilty when Jeremy was released from his leadership position over the teenage boys in our church congregation so we could focus on us and our kids. For the first time, we started going to therapy together and focused more exclusively on our family. When COVID-19 hit a year later, we were already in the mode of staying at home and focusing on us, so it was actually a relief to know no one expected us to do otherwise.

While my mental health deteriorated through the years, my physical health went along with it, but I did not start to believe something was seriously wrong until that summer of 2019. I now believe the high levels of stress I experienced and the depression my pride would not allow me to address were contributing to increasingly serious issues that threatened to encroach on my fundamental abilities as a mother and wife.

It now became imperative that I find doctors to help me deal with my physical health. Unfortunately, I found what William McAdoo said to be true: "*It is impossible to defeat an ignorant man by argument.*"

When my oldest brother was little, his kitten died. His confident response was, "It's okay. Daddy can fix it." It was a hard lesson for him to learn his parent wasn't all-powerful. In many ways, that childish naivete also characterized the faith I had in medical professionals when I was a young wife and a new mother. I have since, of course, learned many valuable lessons about this. I was in my mid-twenties when I realized doctors are not infallible or all-knowing, and they cannot fix everything, even though many medical professionals are amazing and gifted and most are determined and well-meaning. Some of you may be thinking, *Well, duh!* Navigating the world of Fragile X has opened my eyes in many ways.

Put that way, it is clear we often expect too much from doctors. Why do we do that? Hope. Longing for answers, understanding, reasons, or something to blame. Clearly we are all just trying to do our best as parents, caregivers, medical professionals, and individuals—but we still have to find the best help there is to fit our needs.

In my opinion, what separates a great doctor from a mediocre doctor is that the great doctor is humble and willing to learn, listens to patients, cares about patients as individuals, and keeps up on research. I have been fortunate to find two doctors who fall into this category on my journey of finding out what is going on with me physically and mentally.

As I mentioned before, my first encounters in the neurologist's office were memorable in unhappy ways. This exchange will illustrate: after telling the doctor about some of my symptoms, I asked, "Could these be connected to being a Carrier of Fragile X Syndrome?"

"You have Fragile X Syndrome?" he asked.

"No, I have three children with Fragile X. I'm just a Carrier," I replied.

"So...you and your husband are related?" he asked, trying not to look judgmental. I did not understand why he asked this at first, so I looked completely confused as I replied, "No...." Then I realized he thought if we have children with Fragile X, Jeremy and I must be related, as if it were an issue caused by inbreeding. First of all, that is not how Fragile X works, and second of all, who do you think I am? Honestly, it was the weirdest question I had ever been asked. None of this sank in until I got home, though. I told Jeremy about it and we laughed. We just thought, *Wow...he is clueless.* I had other issues with that doctor and his office, but the bottom line was I could not trust his medical opinion or his judgment.

My faith in doctors was restored when I finally found Dr. West at the Rocky Mountain MS Clinic in Salt Lake City. He treated me like a person, thoughtfully considered my questions and opinions, and he ran what I felt like was an extremely thorough battery of tests, including an MRI, in an attempt to get a completely clear picture of what was going on in my body. When I returned to follow up on the test results, I was extremely nervous. Following the nurse to the examination room, I felt like I was going in for a life sentence. Dr. West came in and said hello, and we chatted as he pulled up my files, lab results, and images. I sat stiff in my chair with my hands fidgeting in my lap.

"Well, the good news is you don't have MS. However, your blood work is showing a lot of different issues. I've never seen anything like it!" Dr. West stated.

"Uh, that's probably not a good thing?" I asked, joking, and he chuckled.

"You for sure have Hashimoto's, that much is clear."

"Hashimoto's?" I said, confused.

"Yes, Hashimoto's Disease is an autoimmune disorder where your body attacks your thyroid. And your thyroid affects your entire body. It could be the reason behind several of your symptoms, actually," he said. "By your blood work alone, though, it looks like you have other things going on too. When you have one autoimmune disorder, it is not uncommon to have two or three others. They like to come in groups."

"Oh. I didn't know that," I said, a little shocked, trying to absorb everything he said. "What other things are you seeing in the results?"

"Honestly, it's hard to say. I'm going to refer you to a rheumatologist. They will be the ones that can really help you from here on out. My expertise isn't in that area and I want to give you what you really need."

"Oh," I said, disappointed. "I hope I can find one that listens."

"It has been a joy to work with you for this short time," he said. "I really hope that you find answers and get the help you need." I smiled and nodded and he went on. "Do you watch *X-Men?* Are you familiar with the stories?"

I laughed. "Not really. I think I've seen a few."

He laughed, too. "I promise I have a point. I'm a nerd, so you'll have to bear with me." He went on to explain that in the comic adventures, Charles Xavier (the bald guy in the wheelchair) has the ability of telepathy and uses it to help others. In one comic, his body is healed and he can walk again. The downside is the healing depletes his powers, and that has dire consequences for his friends. Ultimately, Xavier chooses to return to his wheelchair and his disability in order to regain his superpowers so he can help others.

"Sometimes in life we are given challenges that we just want to go away, but often those challenges are exactly what makes us who we are," Dr. West said. "Sometimes we are able to help more people in our 'broken' state, so we should not view our limitations as burdens or weaknesses, but as superpowers."

I stared at him, trying to grasp what he was telling me, because I certainly felt broken at that point, in more ways than one.

He continued, "I have noticed that often people who suffer the most from fibromyalgia and the other issues you are experiencing are also very empathic individuals. For some reason there is a documented connection to the mental and physical pain these individuals face. But, if you take away one side of the equation, you take away the other. If you look, you will see it in the people you know."

That was the last conversation I had with Dr. West, and I will never forget it. He helped me realize that even though there are things I struggle with and *cannot* change, I also have greater compassion, understanding, and love because of them. And that I *would* not change. Dr. West was one of the doctors who made a real difference for me, even though I was only in his office twice.

I left there feeling hopeful and made my first appointment with the rheumatologist, hoping to get further answers. Sadly, this was not the case. After they tested my blood (yet again), I returned for a consultation.

"Well," the rheumatologist started, "Your blood work looks okay for the most part. Nothing is off the charts really. I mean, you're kind of teetering on things here and there."

"Okay, so I don't have Lupus or anything else?" I asked. "I mean, I have Hashimoto's, right? Is that the only thing causing issues?"

"Your bloodwork shows that you possibly have Lupus, but I would have to see more symptoms to diagnose you. Even if you did have Lupus, I wouldn't give you that diagnosis, because that can make things complicated with insurance and it can affect what they will pay for things."

Now I was really confused. So many things were happening in my body that scared me, such as blackouts, nausea, numbness, muscle weakness, and more. But I could not *force* the rheumatologist to give me a diagnosis. I did not *want* something to be wrong with me, but there was, and I needed to put a name to it so a) I would know it was not all in my head, b) I could figure out how to treat symptoms, and c) I could stop worrying about some unknown impending health-related doom. This doctor's refusal to give me a diagnosis communicated to me, *We are going to just wait until you are practically dying and then maybe we will believe you and tell you have Lupus (or whatever else).*

Later, I asked my insurance about what the doctor had said and learned they cannot withhold coverage just because of a Lupus diagnosis. Besides, I had hoped he could prescribe something that would help with my strange symptoms. He gave me nothing. I walked away from that appointment having made no progress, except now I had a concern that I *might* have Lupus.

Not long after this fruitless appointment I started developing more serious, obvious symptoms of Lupus, such as mouth and nose sores, sun rash, swollen lymph nodes visible through the skin, chronic fatigue, trouble breathing, a night cough, muscle pain, aching joints, racing heartbeat, and more. I kept trying to get other tests done to find answers, but over and over the rheumatologist just told me I was fine.

One day I called the rheumatologist's office in a panic because I was having shortness of breath and chest pain. The nurse said she would call me back after talking to the doctor. Hours later (thank goodness it wasn't a heart attack), the nurse called me back and said this was not a concern for the rheumatologist, that it was out of his jurisdiction, and I should contact my regular doctor. I asked, "But this could be related to Lupus, right?" and I was told very bluntly I don't have Lupus—as if it had never even been brought up before.

At this point I knew it was time to find someone else to help me, but I didn't know where to go. I did end up going to my regular doctor to be checked over, but two things got in the way of getting help. First, when I came for my appointment, I informed them I have anxiety. Now, I know anxiety can cause a myriad of physical manifestations and problems, but too often doctors dismiss anything going on with your body because you have anxiety. Also, once again, she could not find anything specifically "wrong" with me. Second, this happened in the middle of the COVID-19 pandemic, and some of my symptoms looked like Coronavirus. I asked the doctor if these symptoms could be caused by Lupus. She simply looked at me and said, "Maybe." Then she tested me for COVID-19, because she was sure that was it. Of course, that test came back negative.

Thankfully, I have since found a doctor who listens and cares about me. He diagnosed me with Lupus in the blink of an eye due to my many symptoms and crazy bloodwork. I am especially grateful he helped me find the right medication and supplements to assist me in my journey. He prescribed me a medication called low dose Naltrexone, which has helped a great deal with most of my symptoms. Many doctors refuse to prescribe it because it does not bring in pharmaceutical money, even though there is a lot of research backing up positive results. I also take several helpful supplements, depending on personal needs and my body.

My current doctor respects me, even when I am plagued with anxieties, and he always wants to make sure I am okay. Here are a few key characteristics of a good doctor:

1. Humble and teachable – No doctor can ever know all the answers, so he or she must be willing to learn from you as well. Because it is not very common, Fragile X is often something doctors learn about alongside the patient, especially when the patient is a Carrier.

2. Kind and patient – A doctor should never treat your anxiety, depression, or feelings as if they do not matter. You deserve to be validated in your feelings and in your desire for good health.

3. Great listening skills – Your medical provider must be a good listener and take what you say seriously. If you think something is wrong, the doctor should check it out. If it really is nothing to worry about, the doctor should explain this in a non-condescending way.

4. Determined – The doctors I have come to love most are those that want answers as badly as I do, so they line up tests and schedule check-ups to figure things out until we find answers and direction.

5. Careful and understanding concerning financial burdens – I appreciate providers who are aware of my time and money, especially when they see me often. Many doctors have billed for less time when I didn't have insurance or contacted me over the phone for quick check-ins until insurance came through.

It was worth asking around, trying new places, and traveling extra miles to find doctors that will give me the care I need. I wish there was a miracle drug to solve all my problems, but of course there is not. It takes a combination of many things, such as medication, supplements, stress management/mindfulness, diet, and exercise, and I am still experimenting to figure out the right combination that works best for me. Logically, every individual's needs are different in all of these areas. Many of my friends like the HIIT workouts, but if I do a lot of strenuous cardio, I get really sick and end up being in bed all the next day. I have found I require a balanced approach. Being too strict on a diet, for example, negatively impacts my mental health, so I still have a donut now and again. Ya gotta live!

It is difficult to care for children with disabilities, but when I struggle with health issues, physical issues, and mental issues, it is so much more difficult. It feels unfair to be in pain each day and still be expected to do all that is required to take care of my children. That's life, though. When I was diagnosed with small fiber neuropathy, fibromyalgia, Hashimoto's, and Lupus (and there is probably more), I realized that no matter who you are, what you do, or what choices you make, life will be hard. Jenkins Lloyd Jones once said, "Anyone who imagines that bliss is normal is going to waste a lot of time running around shouting that he has been robbed." I try not to think of my life as one big robbery...but sometimes I let my pity flow.

It is probably normal to mourn for the life you used to have (or thought you had)—the old you. Sometimes I get overwhelmed by things that have not even happened yet. I catch myself wondering, *what if I can't walk in a few years?* or *what if I can no longer take care of the kids?* Yes, these are possible outcomes, but I have to remember that right now—today—things are going okay. I strive to eat better, exercise as much as I can, and continue using mindfulness strategies to manage stress.

One day I decided to make a bucket list of things I want to do on the good days I have in the near future to help me focus on positive things and goals. I want to ride in a hot air balloon, go to Six Flags, act in a play, go to Universal Studios, visit Europe, and so much more! I do not know yet how I will make some of them work, but they are always there as aspirations. When I have good days, I try to do all I can. On bad days, when I feel sick and don't leave the house, I let myself rest and enjoy cuddles and movies with my kids. At the end of the day I am glad I have a loving Father in Heaven and a Savior to make the burdens feel lighter; it is the only way I make it through each day. Many times a prayer has brought strength to get me through another day when I did not think it was possible. My trials bring me closer to my Savior and for that I am grateful.

I admit it is hard to be grateful for trials, especially when I am smack dab in the middle of them. As I learn more about being a Carrier of FXS, I also learn how to accept future possibilities and problems while still finding joy in the journey. Knowing I am a Carrier is helpful, but it is kind of like knowing part of your future. As we learn in the movies, "knowing" the future does not always yield the best results. On the other hand, being informed can help improve the end result. Sometimes knowing all about your gene pool can be frightening, like knowing cancer runs in the family, or heart problems, or Fragile X Syndrome, but the possibilities that open up to have the best life and get the best help you need is beneficial.

I have let my anxiety run away with me on occasion as I discover more and more about the issues Carriers endure, but in the long run, I prefer to be informed so I can make better decisions and get the right care I need early on. Because I have autoimmune disorders and other health problems, I regularly get checked for various cancers. When my body is constantly off balance, it mimics breast cancer, ovarian cancer, Lymphoma, and other life-threatening illnesses that I try my best not to freak out over. Unfortunately, given my background, I have health anxiety that often leads me to the worst conclusions. Despite all the cancer, autoimmune, and other health issues I and other Carriers endure, there are a few reserved just for Carriers of Fragile X.

There are three main issues Carriers face (how lucky are we?): Fragile X-Associated Tremor Ataxia Syndrome (FXTAS), Fragile X-Associated Premature Ovarian Insufficiency (FXPOI), and Fragile X-Associated Neuropsychiatric Disorder (FXAND). More in-depth information on each of these can be found by going to *www.fragilex.org*. I have also heard many good things about a new book called *The Carriers* that is very helpful.

So far, FXAND has been the most difficult for me to deal with and one that has affected me most. Basically, it is a conglomeration of symptoms including anxiety, depression, ADHD, fatigue, and autoimmune disorders. In my personal experience, I feel like stress is a huge factor determining whether these issues will manifest and how extreme they will be. As Carriers, we are genetically predisposed to these symptoms. Many professionals and researchers of Fragile X say Carriers need to manage our stress, but I always laugh, because having children with special needs is so stressful! How in the world do we *not* let it affect us? It is difficult to find respite and help, and sometimes relaxing just is not an option, but we need to make our health a priority or we will pay the price later.

I am currently working with my doctor to discover whether I am now dealing with FXPOI. Irregular periods and feeling like early menopause is not fun, but it is not the hardest thing I deal with. Many others have dealt with FXPOI for most of their lives and it has made it difficult, if not impossible, to have children naturally. It is possible many women with fertility issues have undiagnosed FXPOI. In fact, statistics show one in 250 women are Carriers! It is amazing to think that so few people have heard about FXS or the consequences of being a Carrier when it is, in fact, so common. Although a diagnosis can bring a lot of confusion and heartache, knowing the reason behind your health conditions can be helpful and bring peace and understanding.

FXTAS is probably the issue that scares me the most, though, for my dad and sisters as well as myself. I imagine it as a combination of Alzheimer's and Parkinson's Disease. It occurs most often in older males, but it is now being identified more often in women. It commonly manifests in those fifty or older, but has been seen in much younger individuals. As I watch my older Carrier family members, I worry about every little issue they have. I find myself quizzing my dad. "Dad, your hands are shaking," I say. "Is it getting worse?" or "Dad, you just asked that question, don't you remember?" And then I stew over it. I buy him workbooks to help with memory and brain function. I encourage him to go get checked out at the doctor. Then I realize if he does have FXTAS, my chance of having it is much higher. I already worry because I am constantly looking at the symptoms and signs of FXTAS and finding similarities in myself, such as neuropathy and tremors. I also have times when sedation is needed, but that can accelerate the disease. One helpful document I found on *fragilex.org* shows definite and probable indicators of FXTAS. Oftentimes FXTAS patients are misdiagnosed with Multiple Sclerosis (MS), so it is important their doctors understand what it means to be a Carrier. One day I hope to find a good movement disorder specialist I can see that knows about FXTAS, because then I would feel more confident about getting the care I need if anything worsens.

Clearly Fragile X is no small diagnosis. Perhaps the largest difference between FX and autism is the genetic component; as a genetic disability, it affects individuals across generations. When I am asked about the difference between autism and Fragile X, I always emphasize the genetic factor, and the fact that Carriers have problems, too; however, as do all disabilities, Fragile X affects the lives of many more than just the person with the full mutation, or even the Carrier—it impacts the lives of everyone it touches: spouses, siblings, grandparents, aunts and uncles, nieces and nephews, and even family friends. Over time, it becomes a familial journey.

10

Siblings, Family, & Caregivers

Grandma Judy and little Isaac

The greatness of a community is most accurately
measured by the compassionate actions of its members."
–Coretta Scott King

Fragile X changes the lives of siblings, Carrier and non-Carrier parents, extended family, and even the community—it takes all of those people to raise a child with special needs. After Isaac was born, many young women came to help me do physical therapy with him. After Evelyn was born, several women in my church volunteered their time to come play with my other kids and help out where they could. There have been so many times when my neighbors have texted or called me when one of my kids snuck outside the gate or they come when they see I am in need of an extra hand. I feel lucky to have such great friends and neighbors around. Admittedly, there are times when I feel like people are judging me. In the darkness of my mind I feel their eyes and hear what they think about my parenting, but it's important to think positive and know you are doing what you can. I am really grateful that even inside my home, I have a little helper. As I have mentioned before, I have four children and only one of them is a neurotypical child. She is also the oldest. There are many challenges that come with her role in the family, but there are also some wonderful things. I decided no one could describe it better than her, so the following is an insert from my daughter, Millie, who was ten when she wrote this:

Life with all Fragile X siblings is pretty tough. There's constantly screaming, fighting, crying, and not being able to go places (we have gone places, but there are stressful times). There are also those times when you're grateful for what they have, in fact, I helped Isaac climb the rock wall out in our backyard; he always wants to climb on it now! Isaac, having both autism and Fragile X, you might think he's the most stressful. He is sometimes, but we all have our times when we're the most stressful, not just him. Sometimes I cry because I'm bored, Eliza doesn't want to go to the potty and instead does it in her pants, Evelyn is constantly screaming, we all yell, and contention can be strong. But overall, Eliza is becoming a very smart, loving young woman, she's ahead of her grade, and is always willing to help. Evelyn always brings a smile to my face, her laugh is like a bell, and she's flexible and funny. I just know that she'll help many people. Isaac is always ready for a dogpile or squishies. I love when he's happy. I never would've met so many great people if it weren't for him, and when he's in the mood he can be very caring, loving, and willing to share.

Every day I see the struggle that my parents have and I love how they are still with us.

One day during scripture study, I asked my parents why they were still staying with us, despite our challenges, and they said, "We have hope." I will always remember that, even as I grow into an adult. Another day, my parents' anniversary, we were all going to sleep over at somebody's house. I was going to sleep over at my cousin's house, but the mom wasn't feeling well, so I went over to my grandma's with Eliza and the dog. Then, Rachael got sick, so Isaac had to come with us, too, but Grandma couldn't take care of all of us, so my mom and dad only got to do stuff for one day. I worked hard to help Grandma and Grandpa take care of the kids, and when we got home, I was just so worn out and tired I cried. There are happy times and sad times. But overall, I am super duper whooper happy that I was born into this wonderful family!

I am so proud of my Millie. She continues to amaze me each day. I've always wanted her to feel that I love her, want to spend time with her, and cherish her. She is talented, funny, and kind. I do not expect her to take over the task of caring for any of her siblings, because I want her to have her own life, unburdened by my choices. I also know that because of the person she is, she will always be there for her siblings in one way or another. It's always her choice, however. I hope in the future, her husband loves and accepts her siblings as much as we do.

Although I've never been a sibling to an individual with special needs, I have watched Millie and tried to do my best to give her the best. There are a few things I've found that help her the most.

1. One-on-one time: This can come in many different forms. I feel like the most important thing is her one-on-one time with me and Jeremy. We have open conversations about anything and everything, we play games, or even just watch a movie of her choice. Sometimes when we have to come home early from events with my family, we let her stay back and my mom or sister will bring her home later so she can still have fun. After I

had Evelyn and Melina was at the house a lot, Millie became attached to her and loved every minute spent with her. She even has solo sleepovers at both of her grandparents' houses sometimes.

2. SibShops: There are several different companies here in Utah that do a weekly or monthly gathering of individuals who have siblings with special needs. Having a safe, fun environment for them to come together and talk about what it's like—for good and bad—is a blessing. Sometimes they do fun activities and other times it's more introspective to help their mental health. Whether or not there is an organization putting these together, several parents can come together in a community to put something like this on for their neurotypical child(ren).

3. Individual space and time: I made sure Millie had her own room where she could feel safe and at peace. That's been a huge help. She also goes to her friends' houses pretty much any time to play and get a break from the home chaos and expectations concerning her siblings. We rarely have her friends here, mostly because Isaac often strips down naked and pees on the floor. I don't think most parents would appreciate their young daughter seeing a stark naked boy just a year and a half younger than they are. Honestly, for various reasons, I think it stresses Millie out unless she locks herself in her room to play, and even then her sisters are banging on the door. I also make sure she gets to participate in plays, take piano lessons, and do other things she enjoys that are just hers.

4. Connecting with others with FX siblings: I connected with another mom who has a child with FX and other children. She has a girl Millie's age and they've connected on Messenger Kids to chat, talk, and vent about their frustrations. They help give each other ideas and empathy. I hope to connect with more kids her age in the future and find Facebook groups when she is older that she can connect with. I ended up making a FB group called Siblings of Fragile X to help in this area, so feel free to join!

Now, I would be missing out if I did not also have the viewpoint of my husband, Jeremy. He is a non-Carrier parent of these children and has had many difficult and rewarding moments of his own. Too often fathers don't get enough time and credit in such circumstances, so I want to give him this opportunity to share with the world:

A lot of the things that have affected Kirsten over the years with our kids haven't had the same impact on me from an emotional standpoint. I tend to be more mellow when it comes to emotions. When I first learned that Isaac had Fragile X, it didn't change much for me. I figured he was still our son and it didn't matter if he had a disability or not. We would treat and care for him all the same. It wasn't until later that the gravity of the situation settled into my heart and mind. I think for me it was gradual, happening over the last eight or so years. The moments when I would feel the impact the most were when the needs of my children would alter plans, such as going backpacking or camping.

You might ask me, "How do you get up day after day?" I would say I haven't finished my course yet, but up until now, it's been hope. Truly having a hope in Christ. This hope in Christ, in His resurrection and life after death, gives me courage and strength to tackle one day at a time. From a worldly and financial perspective, we were crazy to knowingly have children with special needs. The road has been long and difficult so far and I don't anticipate it becoming any easier. Having hope of the resurrection makes dealing with the anxiety, fear, affliction, pain, and resentment much easier. Even on the most difficult of days, I know it will pass and the end result will be much better. I believe that one day my children and I will be resurrected and made perfect in Christ. All our sicknesses, disabilities, and heartache will be over. I will be able to speak with Isaac as the man he will be. My kids will be able to express themselves appropriately. I know some mothers yearn to hear the words, "I love you." That will come. Right now, the difficult task is finding joy in enduring the trials and afflictions.

Life isn't all sad and hard—we definitely have our happy moments. These moments give us renewed strength and life to go another day; perhaps these are the Lord's tender mercies for me. As Kirsten and I plunge ahead, I love the promise in a book of scripture called the Doctrine and Covenants. It talks about what we in our church believe is the "oath and covenant of the priesthood." It is that as we magnify our callings, our bodies will be renewed. This is a true promise. We fail each day, but I think we try and each time we do, I believe the Lord blesses us with physical strength enough for the day ahead. Like light shining after the dark night, the spiritually renewing power of Jesus Christ shines upon us each day. There is no way I could work with my children each day without my Savior.

I have not been so angry in my life with anything or anyone more than I have my children. They know how to push every button. I remember a moment during the "Blue Period" that I think I broke. I was done. I was tired of Isaac's relentless moaning and crying and the physical injury he was inflicting on my wife, my kids, and sometimes me. I often say my kids bring out the worst in me. We tried to find a place for him to no avail. There weren't any options and we had to continue forward one step at a time. Somehow we made it through. Somehow.

It hurts to think about situations when others talk about their children leaving home and going on missions or off to school, someday fleeing the nest and making a family of their own. When I think of my son, Isaac, I only see a lifetime of pain and work, but then he'll say something like, " I love you" in his own little way and it somehow seems okay. He'll be my little buddy for the rest of my life.

I consider the future and I have thought of ways I can be prepared for those days to come. I will need to provide for my wife and I, but also my kids for the duration of their lives. This means finances will be very important. I believe the Lord knows my needs and we try our best. Our family motto is taken from Proverbs 3:5-6: "Trust in the Lord."

Sometimes all I can do is find alone time on the toilet or just make it through to the night time when the kids go to bed. We are constantly trying new things to help our kids and sometimes we are pleasantly surprised. Sometimes others suggest things or offer their time and we are again pleasantly surprised. Sometimes, we thought things would work out and they didn't. The kids freak out, we lose our cool, and we find ourselves apologizing later. I think Millie has seen my wife and I in our worst moments and our best. I just hope she learns from both.

As hard as it is with kids with disabilities, even harder still is seeing my wife, my love and life, break down in tears or be so depressed that she doesn't want to do anything. It's in these moments I fear. There is no way I could physically do this each day without my wife by my side. The hope in Christ gets us both through, but the day-to-day mechanics are unthinkable if something were to happen to my wife. I pray most often for her—for her well-being, both mental and physical. I pray she and I will have strength to rise to the challenges each day. I pray for safety and guardian angels. I'm sure other fathers have challenges; in fact, I know we all do.

I feel like having children with special needs has brought me closer to my wife and my Savior. It's easy to fall into the trap of complacency in the particular duties a husband or wife performs each day. Oftentimes, this is challenged because of the roller coaster ride we enter into each day. Many times I tell Millie that she needs to be flexible and go with the flow since this is what is required of me as a parent. There are days where you simply must change what you had planned to make it peaceful for everyone. Sometimes when I come off work, I immediately take up household chores to ease the burden of my wife, who regularly lifts the heavy weights of caring for the children during the day. I think my wife appreciates this, though sometimes I ask myself what task does she really need me to perform at this time. This is something I learned from a book I read back in college. Taking a break when

I get home from work isn't always possible and so being flexible and rolling with the punches is necessary to mitigate getting impatient or angry.

It's difficult to hear comments like, "Oh I just love your kids. They are angels sent from above." I tend to see the little devils inside of them wreaking havoc on each day and event we try to attend or schedule.

My parental awareness goes on overkill when we are out in public. We never know when Isaac or Evelyn will lose their cool and have a meltdown. You could say we are always on the alert for a way out, a back door, or the escape route. I can't tell you how many times we have to use the exit door fast. Even today at church, we had to leave in the middle of the services because both Isaac and Evelyn were done. In the past I've had to hold onto Isaac's hands as we navigated a crowded hallway to keep him from grabbing and scratching passersby. I remember one time at Lagoon trying to find a place to change Isaac's diaper only to see the only handicap stall was occupied or otherwise rendered useless. As I tried to go back out, Isaac, in his anger and tantrum, grabbed another boy's shorts and nearly stripped him there in the bathroom. Totally embarrassing to say the least.

So what's it like? It's tough and sometimes we are ready to quit. Sometimes we don't want to do the work anymore. Sometimes we just sit in our room and pout. Sometimes, we look forward with too much happiness to the time when the kids are in bed so we don't have to deal with it anymore. Sometimes we are too eager to go on a night out. And sometimes events that should be rewarding or uplifting are actually tormenting and create a lot of anxiety. Sometimes it is easier to stay at home than brave the world with our kids.

We find success in the little things and hold on to the simple pleasures. Laughter is a key go-to when things get tough. We try to laugh often and will watch funny movies just to lighten the mood. We give each other breaks.

At the end of the day, the hope in Christ carries us through.

Having children with FX has been different for Jeremy and I. There is one thing I have discovered that is needed and that is his personal time. I've come to realize I cannot be everything to him. He needs to do things he enjoys that maybe I don't. He should be able to go out with friends or on a hike. His newest Me Time is playing computer games. It gets him away from the world and makes him so happy, especially when he gets to chat and play with his friends online. It takes a special balance as a parent, but I feel like Jeremy spends so much time with our kids both to meet their physical needs but also to just have fun and play.

I am so grateful for my husband. I'm grateful for his honesty, love, patience, support, and perseverance. I would be lost without him. I know in a time of feminist views that may sound weak to some, but I believe a man and woman are two pieces of the same puzzle. We are each different, but each equally important in our family. My parents have stayed together for thirty-nine years, and although they make mistakes, they are a wonderful example of sticking together through difficult times despite each other's imperfections. Here are some of my parents' thoughts on the subject of my children. First, this is from my mom, Judy:

I love that since Eliza was just little, she always loved my homemade mac 'n cheese. I love singing with her on my guitar. Evelyn and Millie also love to sing and dance to my songs on the guitar. Millie is one amazing child. She always tries to help where she can. I know it is hard on her sometimes, being the oldest and trying to help mom the best she can, but her mom sees that and lets her do other things, like being in plays, hanging out with friends, or just having alone time. Millie has grown up faster than most girls her age, because she saw the hard things, especially with Isaac. I've seen how frustrated the kids get because they can't get through what they are thinking and they have such a hard time with crowds. They don't know what to do, so they kind of just crash!

I can't count the many things the parents have faced. The challenges of getting used to Fragile X and learning, growing, and trying their best to make it better from food and toys to play equipment and sleeping arrangements. I see the parents worked together to see what plan worked best. Jeremy could see he needed to help more. He would get up early with Isaac before he went to work. They learned what parents with special needs kids do: work together, play together, and get a surrey bike for the family to do something fun!

We have all grown more compassionate for others and learned that love can be so big! I also learned to pray very hard. Sometimes my heart would break watching the parents struggling for survival and staying above water, but our family is a team. We made a team effort to take care of one another and I'm so thankful Rachael was able to take Isaac once a week and help so much. I would also try to help Kirsten once a week by taking Isaac for a day when things were really hard. His favorite thing was to go for a ride in the car and go around the farms to see the pigs, cows, and horses. Every time when we would leave the animals, he would say, "Bye! Happy Halloween!" That's his favorite holiday. He said it to everyone when his family went trick-or-treating on the surrey bike. I'm so thankful we have a close family, we love each other so much, and other family members are stepping in and trying to help the best we can. Now I am so thankful Diana is here to help us all.

I have enjoyed every minute having these children in our home. They bring such joy to my heart. I love them so much. They have strong spirits and have love in their hearts. They are like having a piece of Heaven in our home when they come. These children have taught me more than I even imagined! I'm better because of them. Together as a family, we have learned to endure, appreciate, love unconditionally, have compassion, patience, hope, faith, and a kind of love I never knew I had. I love them so much!

I am very thankful that my family is close. I don't know what I would have done without their help in tough times. My mom and dad are truly some of my best friends who are always there for me, encouraging me along, even in the darkest times. My dad, James, also shared his view:

I have many good memories with each of the grandchildren. Millie and I like to read books and we talk about things for hours—if Judy lets me. I can give Isaac a hug or squish if he's in that kind of mood. I know the pressure helps him. He chooses who and when he is going to hug and that's okay. I do more playing on the trampoline with him. My best time with him, I think, was the school track meet. He really enjoyed it when I pushed him in his stroller down the track. Then there's Eliza. She is a fun girl. Trying to keep up with her is something! She is a busy, high energy kid. I think that helps her. Evelyn, on the other hand, is more quiet, but she isn't as shy with me anymore. I like to do things with her and now she seems more willing to interact with me. Judy and I have been busy lately, though, and I have not integrated with the kids as much. Plus, Kirsten has more help and that has changed the dynamics of visiting and such. The way things are at this stage with Isaac, Eliza, and Evelyn, I think they will struggle with a lot of things, but they are smart. I am amazed by them! I cannot see them overcoming the complexity of their environment at this point. I want to wave my magic wand and change things. Nonetheless, "make it so!" (Star Trek), but I think over time Eliza and Evelyn can learn how to solve and cope with some of their own problems as well as find ways to accomplish things, even if it's in their own way. This will help in caring for them, but the parents have a game plan: they work together and are committed. Sometimes they get overwhelmed, but they have good resources and support.

I worry about Millie who sees herself as a resource. Millie helps her parents a lot, because sometimes they are outgunned, but I do not want her to burn out. She is like an older sister on overdrive. She is on top of so many things and Eliza follows her good example. But she still needs to be a kid, have friends, and pursue her own goals and dreams. She needs to set up her own perimeters. I think Millie sees that she could be fenced in and I would say she will be her own girl. She will make choices to help her siblings, but they will be informed choices.

My dad has always been a rock and someone I can talk to and trust. He is full of knowledge and loves to share history, and I think that is so needed in this world today. I don't think my parents ever could've imagined what trials their children would go through and how heartwrenching the journey would be for them to watch and try to help. What I do know is that without them, Jeremy and I would be lost, because they have come to our aid in every way throughout our entire marriage and love our children unconditionally.

Jeremy's family is also involved in our lives, but they live a little farther away and see us a bit less. His youngest sister, Autumn, has spent the most time around us as she grew up. She has seen us in the best and worst times, so I am glad she could share this with us:

When I think of this family, love and understanding come to mind. In all the challenges I'ves faced, Jeremy and Kirsten have shown me nothing but love and understanding. Even if they don't fully understand how I feel or what I'm going through, they try their best, keep an open mind and an eternal point of view, or offer a weekend getaway full of nail painting, movie watching, and cookie baking. I see nothing but love in how Jeremy and Kirsten interact with their kids, family, friends, and the community.

I think the biggest challenge they have as parents is getting help and feeling accepted. It's hard asking for volunteers all the time, but it's expensive to always have nurses on hand. I know they appreciate any and all help, but sometimes it's just not enough. I also feel like they feel the need to apologize or be sorry on their kids behalf. This is not true in any way, shape, or form! When they visit family, I see the way they follow their kids around and clean up after them to keep them from getting into things. On a level, this is necessary, but not to the point where they should feel like they have to in order to be welcome. I know it's hard traveling with Isaac, but we do love having all of them around at family gatherings.

Some of the other challenges I've seen are primarily communication-based. I believe on a day-to-day, moment-to-moment basis it doesn't bother the kids, because they're in their own happy little bubble, but when they don't understand a situation and can't communicate effectively, they have a meltdown of sorts and it is hard to watch because neither side knows how to communicate with the other at times.

I'm not going to lie—I've only stayed the whole time at church with their family a few times and it is hard. I get distracted easily and Isaac is a huge distraction for me. He in no way takes from the spirit I feel while I'm there, just distracting me from what is being said. Outside of church, there's moments I get frustrated at family gatherings and such, but they are such sweet additions to any event that the frustration does melt away about as fast as it comes. I love the little bubble they live in and it's so stinkin' special when they let you in for squishies and tickles.

I think my best memory with Isaac and Eliza was when my mom and I helped babysit them. I picked up the two of them and Mom and I tag-teamed it. That was the first time I experienced Isaac being able to communicate bathroom needs that I understood. It was one of the first times Isaac and I actually played. We wrestled on the floor and laughed and snuggled and afterward he'd go off and come running back when he saw me.

Some of the attributes I've seen in Millie is her unconditional love, her undying ability to show empathy, and her dedication to helping. Every chance she gets, she draws the most darling pictures and always adds a joke to brighten your day and, more often than not, they are her own jokes. She never leaves without giving you a big old bear hug and telling you she loves you and she can't wait to see you again. And most of the time she asks if there's something she can do to help when she sees you're in the middle of something. I believe Millie is as strong as she is because of the challenges she faces. I know she loves her siblings and her family, but they do require more attention on a day-to-day basis. I can see how she could feel like she's being left out, ignored, or excluded at times because of her siblings, like at doctor appointments or a rough day that keeps her from other activities she wants to do.

I know not all families have such positive or hopeful views, but I am grateful for mine. Even my church community is very helpful and supportive. They have often told me how Isaac has brought the spirit to touch them during services, despite us feeling embarrassed about how loud he is. It really depends how others choose to view our children and if they come from an angle of compassion and love. Of course, not all are always so kind to us. We have had many hard conversations, misunderstandings, and heartbreaking words said, but we continue to move forward and lean on those that choose to love and support us no matter what. That love has been shown in many ways.

I can recall many times family, friends, neighbors, and even strangers have shown kindness and been touched by my children. I recall one day in the early years of my Fragile X journey when I was crying on the steps outside of my church because I felt my burden was too much to bear. Then a friend of mine came up to me, sat with me, and spoke comforting words. They weren't empty words or cliche, either. I felt so loved and felt everything would be okay. God had sent her to be His arms around me that afternoon. Later in life, for almost two years, two women in my neighborhood came in the morning to clean my kitchen. That made so much difference when I felt so overwhelmed. There's something special about a clean kitchen that makes the rest of your house feel okay. These women were busy, older women with grandkids, but they still made time to help me. At one time I had half a dozen women who volunteered to come watch my other kids after my fourth child was born and my life became extremely hectic. They would take Millie to do something special, take all the kids on a walk, or just play with the kids out back while I took a nap with the baby. Sometimes it was stressful having others in my home, but I will never forget their love and kindness that meant so much to me and my family. During that time, I believe those serving me were blessed as well. Some of them experienced some difficult days with Isaac and in return grew in patience, understanding, and compassion.

During the summer months, Isaac touched even more lives through summer camp. People that were once strangers quickly became close with him. I had so many individuals tell me how much they loved him, despite how difficult he could be at times. He changed their lives for the better in ways I'll never fully understand. And, of course, the staff members that came to our home through Supported Living were greatly impacted. Even though they are responsible for Isaac, they end up knowing all of my kids and playing with them. Some worked with our family for years. John was our first respite worker and went through a lot as we navigated how to maneuver life with a new helper in the home. He was also here when Isaac went through some of the toughest years and spread poop more than ever. He was there when we tried to potty train (that was six years ago). There have been so many staff members that have come to our home and we have touched each other's lives forever. Melina also spent a lot of time with my children in our home and shared these thoughts with me:

I had been caregiving for two different families, each with an adult with a disability. These men I worked with were practicing job and independent living skills and they were my friends. I got a call to come meet a family who needed another caregiver, but this client was five years old. I knew it would be very different from my other jobs, but how different I was about to find out!

I was not supposed to start working until I met Isaac and had some training, but shortly after signing paperwork, Kirsten was in the hospital giving birth to Evelyn and I received a text message asking if I could watch Isaac. I showed up for the first time in their new house, never having met Isaac, to find his grandmother desperately trying to calm him down. His phone had run out of charge. He was throwing himself onto the ground and banging his head into the floor as hard as he could—the kind of skull-crushing bang that would make anyone cringe. Neither his grandmother nor I had any idea what to do. I tried my best to shield his head from the blows. Eventually, I got Isaac outside to play with his bubble machine and things calmed down a little. It was a bit of an intimidating first day on the job!

Honestly, Isaac was and still is the most difficult client I have ever had, physically and emotionally. Isaac had a very hard time communicating, but even more so he had a hard time handling his emotions. When he was not getting what he wanted, he would scratch, bite, kick, shove, etc. Since I was trying not to be a pushover and be a good caregiver, I would not always give him what he wanted (usually TV). We were also attempting to potty train, which was often not what he wanted either. Trying to balance keeping Isaac happy and having some peace with being responsible by enforcing potty training, outside time, and a variety of activities was like a precarious see-saw with hot coals underneath each side. Too much giving him his way or too much enforcing rules he didn't like would swing the teeter-totter too far one way or the other resulting in burns.

Hurting was one of his ways of trying to communicate. I got scratched just trying to pull his pants back up or help him wash his hands. One of my friends saw a big red scratch across my face and told me I needed to either talk to his mom or quit. I tried to explain to her the difficulty of the situation and I wanted to just keep working through it, but I don't think she really understood. Maybe that was because Isaac was not just a high-risk job for me—he was my little Isaac! I loved him and wanted to help, especially since I knew many others would not.

Despite many difficulties, I felt I formed a friendly bond with Isaac. He learned to feel comfortable with me around and I loved him. Sometimes he would fall asleep in my lap, give me a hug, or grab my hand to show me what he wanted to do. I felt so much peace in those moments. He learned I was there to try to help and take care of him.

I loved Isaac, but I also really loved the entire family. Millie loved having me around to have someone to talk to. I think she thought of me as a friend. She could not always play or converse with her younger siblings in the way she wanted and her mom had a new baby to take care of, so she sometimes used me to fulfill that need. She loved to teach me Spanish and play games with me. Millie was and I am sure still is an amazingly patient older sister. She understood the fact that Isaac had a disability which made it hard for him to treat her with gentleness. She did not hit back when she was shoved or get too worked up about it, though she did ask for help from whatever adult was closest. I saw the struggle it was for her to sacrifice time with her parents or time with her favorite shows on TV, etc. in order to cater to a sibling with a greater need. I know she did not like to sacrifice those things, but she did it anyway. I also have observed the care her parents took to help her feel important even though she needed less of their attention. Millie participated in a play while I was there and even joined a club for siblings of those with disabilities. These things helped her feel supported and important.

The family member I was always most impressed with was Kirsten. She had to manage all the caregivers' schedules and training, oversee their work, and help when needed as well as manage the rest of her household! I could see she cared so much about each of her children. She tried to give each of them her time, love, and attention. I was impressed with the way she allowed less important tasks to slide (dishes, laundry, cleaning, etc.) in order to use the time caring for and loving her children. She would probably claim that when you have four kids, three of which with a disability, you do not really have the luxury of keeping house. But I did witness plenty of moments when kids behaved well and were occupied, but she chose to spend time with them rather than catching up on chores. Additionally, I worked with the family for almost two years and I never once heard her raise her voice or lose her temper, though there were plenty of opportunities to do so. Not only was she a dedicated mom, but she was a down-to-earth, honest person and I really enjoyed talking to her and becoming friends with her. She probably felt pretty alone with some of the trials that came her way, as there are not a lot of other women in the world with three kiddos who have Fragile X. Despite her being in a unique situation, she was such a relatable and kind person. She took the time to talk about and support me through my struggles and successes even though her own family was enough to occupy her entire attention.

Though the family has their hands full all the time, there was a period of a few weeks when it seemed especially difficult for them. I was not there during the conversations and decisions about sending Isaac away, but I knew they were exploring the options and I saw how intensely it caused pain for all of them. Kirsten especially seemed to be in a lot of pain. I could tell she was hurting over how difficult Isaac's aggression was at the time, especially against his younger sisters. I could also see the intense pain she felt when she thought about having to send him away. I can never understand the emotions she must have been enduring, but I saw she was unbearably tired and worn completely out, emotionally and physically.

Though I do not envy the Fowler family's struggles, I look to them as an example of sacrifice and love pulling through. I love and miss this wonderful and fun family!

We have had many different caregivers over the years. We have changed each other's lives. Our current staff member is Diana. She has become like family and desired to share this about my family:

Coming into this family was one of the biggest blessings I have ever had. I believe the Lord knew I needed them more than they even needed me. The Fowler family is the true meaning of strength. Kirsten is the true meaning of strength as a mother. For all that she goes through, she does it with the most grace I have ever seen. Jeremy is a quiet guy who helps hold it all together. There has never been a time I have felt so much love for a family as Kirsten and Jeremy have in their home. I was hired for Isaac, but I take care of all of them. They truly are my second family.

Isaac has given me so much love. I didn't know going into this job how much love I would feel with someone with autism. Isaac is one special boy. He doesn't say a lot, so when he does, it makes it all the more special, from

"I love you" to "miss you" and "goodnight." Those words are all I need from him...even when he calls me Beast.

Millie is the little mommy of the family. She is a big sister everyone needs. I love when I have time to hang with her one-on-one. Eliza is the stubborn one and the hardest to crack. If she says no, then game on. Once she lets you in, you're done for because she is the best snuggler.

Evelyn is the sassy one. I love when she is so mad because she will go from three to sixteen in minutes. She is full of spunk and there is nothing better than to be put in shape by her. She is going to give us all lots of gray hair in the years to come.

The Fowler family has been a gift in my family's lives. They are stuck with their Diana for as long as they will have me. The whole family is a gift that keeps on giving.

It is for all this and so many more experiences that show me my children are meant to be here just the way they are. They teach us, help us become better, and bring a love we never knew we could possess. I know my husband and I continually learn from our children and it has led to a change in our viewpoint, doing our best to make choices to be happy no matter our circumstances. This includes changing the way we have fun family time together.

11

Specialized Vacations & Activities

Kirsten and Isaac riding Dumbo in Disneyland

"Let us relish life as we live it, find joy in the journey, and share our love with friends and family."
–Thomas S. Monson

Finding joy in the journey has been a huge theme in my life, especially since having children with FXS. Unfortunately, from the moment I found out Isaac had FXS, subconsciously I compared my life and future to the typical family, especially those "perfect" ones found so readily on social media. Of course, I tell myself there is Photoshop being used and professional photographers that get only the best moments, or the picture was just a tiny second of life shown to portray everyday normalcy; still, many times I look at some families and think how perfect and happy they are. Sometimes it seems that even without photo editing and special setups, some families are seriously perfect! Everyone has something, though, and I'm learning not to compare. It's true that as parents, we desire to make the best life for our child and spend special time as a family, but social pressures come in and we want to do it a certain way with a certain look that we can share on social media—just the happy, perfect parts, though. We dream of those epic family vacations and picture-perfect outings to share. Well, guess what? It's not always perfect, special needs or not.

However, it was quite a wakeup call for me when I visited my brother in Florida. I realized that, although no one person or family is perfect, it is a lot easier to have fun family time without wheelchairs and strollers, diapers and wipes, extra clothes and snacks, and medication and tablets everywhere you go. I often feel like I have to carry my whole house in one bag wherever I go out somewhere. In fact, I once saw a meme of a person carrying a backpack as big as a car. It said something like, "Only the essentials for my special needs child." And just think—I have to multiply that by three! Not to mention their need for constant attention, assistance, and calming.

As I looked around at my brother and his family, I compared them to mine. My brother, Daniel, has a wife and five children. All of their kids are healthy, smart, neurotypical individuals. Sure, there is crying or fighting here and there. No one is perfect. But their craziness and difficulties compared to my life look like a really great day to me. I remember one day in particular while staying with Daniel. I looked around at the happy family enjoying an evening together outside in the pool and asked my sister-in-law, "Is this how it always is around your house? Like, is this pretty normal?" She looked at me surprised and said, a little confused, "Yeah, this is pretty normal." So I replied, confused,

"So...they usually just play together and kids aren't constantly crying and screaming all the time?" Because now I saw the reality of another family, not just an Instagram picture. This really was...real. And...well...it kind of hurts.

Now, that really isn't fair to either of our families to compare. It's like apples to oranges really. It is important to recognize that everyone has trials and no matter what they have going on, it is just as difficult for them. But sometimes our emotions don't match our logic, so there I was, watching all the family play in the pool and hot tub having a great time. No one was fighting, yelling, crying, screaming, or scratching. It was just some simple everyday fun. No biggie for them. That was their normal.

Going to Disney World whenever with whomever is normal. Flying on a plane together, going out to eat together, having friends over, being out in the front yard—all the simple things I can't easily do with my family, if at all, are *their* normal. Once I got home from Florida and faced my own reality, I shamefully admit I felt shortchanged. Again I imagined that bliss was normal, running around shouting I'd been robbed, like Jones said. But then I remembered that he also said that "the trick is to thank the Lord for letting you have the ride." "the trick is to thank the Lord for letting you have the ride." So despite the challenges and heartache, I choose to take the ride given me and do my best. Besides, I'm figuring out what Elizabeth Moon said is true: "'Normal' is a dryer setting." It's all about accepting what is normal for us as a family and going along for the ride. Therefore, we have tried our hand at many vacations and activities.

Our first big vacation as a family was Disneyland. Neither Jeremy nor I had ever been. At the time, Millie was six, Isaac was five, and Eliza had just turned two. Autumn, Jeremy's sister, came along. We figured we could use her help and she would get a free ride to Disney as her first time also. We didn't really know how it was all going to turn out, but we did our best to pack and plan things out to a tee. Then we said many, many prayers. Honestly, I think the prayers of family and friends helped us get through more than anything. There were some really tough times. Because going on a plane seemed practically impossible, we chose to take a twelve-hour car ride to California. Thankfully we broke it up into smaller intervals by stopping at Jeremy's sister's house halfway through.

On the last half of our ride to Disneyland, Isaac had *another* blowout of no small proportion. This was his second or third of the journey thus far, I believe.

"Uh oh," I said, looking wide-eyed at Jeremy from the passenger seat. "Do you smell that?"

He looked at me and sniffed a few times, his eyebrows furrowing as he replied, "Yeah," and shook his head in dismay.

"Isaac poop," I said matter-of-factly. There is a certain smell, especially when it's more loose than his normal loose stool. "Do you think we can wait until the next stop?"

"I dunno. The next stop is miles away and we're kind of in the middle of nowhere right now," Jeremy replied, showing me the empty land before us and a long stretch of road.

"Mom!" I heard Millie pipe up in the back seat of the van. "I think Isaac's poopy," she said, making a face. She was forming into that motherly big sister.

"Hey, Autumn?" I called behind me to where she sat in a bucket seat with a space between and Isaac in the next bucket seat. Thank goodness there was space there. "Do you see any poop on Isaac?"

Nothing.

"Autumn?" I repeated. I looked behind me and she was looking out the window with earphones in her ears. Our kids had been so loud and cried so much, I didn't blame her. In fact, I envied her aloofness. "Autumn!" I said louder. She finally turned and pulled out her earphones.

"Yeah?" she asked, eyebrows raised. She finally smelled something in that instant and looked over instinctively at Isaac. "Whoa!" her eyes widened in surprise and a little terror. I felt the dread sink in my stomach, because I already knew the problem. "Uh, Isaac has poop coming out the back of his pants or something." Apparently Isaac was rocking back and forth in his seat, squishing poop out on each backward bump.

"Okay, hon, we need to pull over or something," I said, starting to panic a little.

"Uh, okay, let me find a better spot to pull off," Jeremy said, a bit nervous. "This is going to be interesting."

"Mom! *Mom*!" Millie yelled. "Isaac has poop all over." She backed as far away as possible in the tight space, bringing her legs into her chest like that will stop poop from flying. "Ew, Mom! Mom!"

"I know, Millie!" I called over my shoulder. "We'll take care of it, okay? Just don't yell. We're going to clean it up." I reassured her and myself things were going to be just fine. Thankfully, it didn't take long to go from eighty to zero on the side of the road, though it was a bit disconcerting.

I got out of the car and whipped open Isaac's door behind me while Jeremy safely navigated his way out of the driver's seat with cars intermittently passing by. I grabbed the wipes, a diaper, some grocery sacks, and got to work. I cleaned up all I could with Isaac still buckled, since he is a runner and we were next to a highway. Wipe after wipe I scraped poop off the seat. Thankfully, we had taken the soft covering off the booster seat on the first blowout of the trip and now just plastic remained. I'm sure it wasn't the most comfortable, but we had to make do and, unfortunately, Isaac required us to make cozy things not so cozy just for the sake of sanitation. He wasn't too happy and threatened to shower us in poop with flapping hands, flailing arms, and an arched back.

"Okay, we gotta get him out," Jeremy said.

"You'll have to hold him the best you can so he doesn't run off, though," I said, worried. We unbuckled him and quickly wrestled until we got his clothes off and into a bag. I then ripped the diaper off, trying not to get more poop everywhere, and gave him a wet wipe bath, not without getting poop on my hands in the meantime. That was becoming the norm.

"Here, let's put him in the passenger seat for now," Jeremy said after Isaac was as clean as he was going to get and crying from all the commotion. I quickly slipped a diaper on his kicking feet and wondered how much stranger passersby thought of the whole fiasco. As Jeremy got him to sit in front without destroying anything or finding DVDs to bite, I wiped down the seat and surrounding areas. I used wipes, water bottles, and hand sanitizer to clean myself as much as possible. I tied up poopy clothes into a bag and a poopy diaper with almost a full package of used, poopy wipes into another and tossed it in the back of the van, even though I really wanted to leave everything there on the side of the road. Jeremy washed as well and we got Isaac into his seat again with some kicking and whining.

When we got back in the car, we looked at each other and around at what had just happened. We vented and laughed while getting our seatbelts on.

"I can't believe we just did that on the side of the road," I said, shaking my head.

"Yeah, we had a little poopy streaker on our hands," Jeremy laughed.

"Oh my goodness, why do we do these things? It's after stuff like this I wonder why we even try!"

"I know! But we can't turn back now. Besides, it will make a good story and Autumn will never forget this trip!" We looked back at her and I could tell this was all new to her—she was taken aback by everything.

"Let's get on the road so we can throw out these stinky bags and really wash our hands!" I said, pleading with Jeremy to get going. "Actually, we are going to need to buy more wipes now. With all the blowouts, we won't have enough to last us the rest of our trip."

That memory is more vivid than some of the rides at Disney. The whole car ride was quite memorable. Eliza cried most of the way there. We all probably had colds and she was coming down with something. She was often inconsolable. Thankfully, there were some fun times, too. Those are the things that keep us going and trying.

I spent more on a hotel room with several rooms, bathrooms, and living areas in hopes Isaac would do better. Everyone sleeping in the same area wasn't ideal at the time, so it was worth the extra money. I also made sure it had a kitchen so I could save money making meals and storing items Isaac would actually eat. Besides, I doubt he would've eaten anything in the park except popcorn and water. It was also really important that the hotel was close to the park. Isaac doesn't do well with transitions, so it was nice to put him in the special stroller while still in the hotel room and walk all the way to the parks without having to get in and out of a car and his chair. It was also nice, because our kids lasted only in short intervals. We made the best of our time, came back to the hotel for swimming, movies, and eating, then went back for another round. I made sure to get at least three days so we didn't feel we had to rush everything.

One of the biggest game changers for Disneyland was getting a disability pass, though having a special stroller for Isaac was enough proof. With this special pass, you don't have to wait in long lines. You get put in a totally different line or sent up to the front immediately. It was a nice perk and necessary for impatient, anxious kids. It made me sad to see people abusing this power, however. I don't think people realize the true needs of special needs children. They use the swings at the park for larger children with disabilities, use the handicap stall when others are vacant, and give accusing looks if a child cries or makes a loud noise. It takes tolerance on both ends.

I think, overall, it was a good experience, but there were some difficult times. I made the mistake of taking Isaac on a *Finding Nemo* underwater submarine ride. It was dark and claustrophobic and Isaac screamed and cried, making it miserable for everyone. His favorite ride was Dumbo. It gave me such joy and made everything worth it to see him smile and enjoy those little moments "flying" high and going around in circles. He also enjoyed going to Radiator Springs at California Adventure to see Lightning McQueen and Mater. One of the most surprising moments is when we went to see the *Frozen* play and he actually did well through the entire thing. Unfortunately, Jeremy was out with crying Eliza the whole time, but Isaac enjoyed it without much moaning or whining. Of course, we made sure to have popcorn and water. Every little thing was a big thing and we really relied on all those little wins to make it through our adventure.

We haven't been to Disneyland again, but hope to go again one day as well as go to Disney World. Now we have four kids and they are bigger, which can mean bigger problems and meltdowns, but it can also mean longer stays in the park, fewer diaper changes, and little perks like that. Maybe one day I'll get the courage to go on a plane with the whole family to Disney World, but today is not that day. In the meantime, we have found other things to have fun.

One of our best investments has been a surrey bike. It's a bike with four wheels and can fit six people with two additional little kids in front. We even bought a little bell and a horn to go along with it. After all, we already feel like we are in a parade when we ride in it, so we might as well embrace it! I just love seeing people's big smiles when we pass by them. It makes it all worth it. This has been such a great purchase for our family, because most of my kids can't ride bikes and there seems so little we can do together out of the house. Eventually, we had to buy Isaac a special five-point harness so he wouldn't try to get off or do something to get hurt. Since doing so, I can tell he feels safe and secure and is always happy to be on it. He doesn't even try to pull his sisters' hair in front of him like he did before. Sometimes the simplest things make life so much better. In fact, we even made it into a Halloween mobile to go trick-or-treating together. It lasted a short while, but it was the best trick-or-treating experience as a family yet. We have taken our bike to many different trails, including Bear Lake, the Provo River, and Utah Lake. It's become quite the iconic ride and has brought us so much joy, including when I see the faces of passersby. They have the best reactions. We almost caused a wreck on Main Street once because a guy driving a truck stared at us instead of the road. Whoops!

More recently, we decided to try a road trip to St. George to stay at an Airbnb and go rent a six-seater side-by-side. It turns out all the kids love the side-by-side, especially the wind blowing in their face, so we decided to purchase one later after saving up. The Airbnb was horrible the first night as everyone adjusted, but by the second night, things improved. I had to get an Airbnb with separate rooms for Eliza, Evelyn, and Isaac for peace and sleeping arrangements. Often when we go on such adventures, we ask ourselves, "Why do we even try?" It is so hard and often leaves little reward compared to the pain. There is always a lot of crying, adjusting, and coaxing, but we try because we want to find out if we really can do it. We want to have fun as a family. We want to believe hard things are possible and maybe one day our kids will *want* to go on an adventure with us; however, it is also important to realize limits, too. Taking all four kids on a plane ride, for example, isn't feasible right now. I hope one day we can all go.

Jeremy often liked to take Isaac for rides in his 4Runner or camping. We ended up selling the 4Runner to help pay for side-by-side. No matter what outing we are on, Isaac needs one-on-one supervision and engagement. As a family, we tried camping in a tent and it is always a disaster. When we got a tent camper, I thought it would be better. It was a little. We fixed it up and customized it so one end had an enclosed, screened and zippered area where Isaac could be. It was quite the contraption and it served its purpose, but it just didn't quite work for us. We ended up getting a toy hauler camper many years later. This has been a godsend. We can finally go places and have a center place of familiarity and comfort for the kids. There is even room to set up Isaac's bed tent so he has his special, safe place. The best part is we can take our surrey bike or side-by-side in the trailer. One of our first adventures in the toy hauler was up to a place with a large bike trail by a river, covered by trees. We brought our surrey bike and rode the whole trail, then into the city to buy 7-11 slushies.

Our second trip with our trailer was to Bear Lake. The kids *loved* it. We went to the north side where there is a nice sandy beach and shallow water. It was a perfect combination for our kids. Besides getting sunburned, it was a really great trip. Sometimes we watched a movie in the trailer, colored together, or gathered rocks to make rock art pictures for the next campers to find. We also rode the bike trail with our surrey bike and got takeout from the local restaurants. We learned a few lessons along the way for next time we go there. First, apply sunscreen *all the time* and make sure it is SPF 100! Second, showers are needed after playing in sand and mud for hours, so make sure your water heater works. We all took ice cold showers—if you call splashing water a few seconds at a time on your body a shower. Third, never pay five dollars for a grilled cheese made of cheap, thin whitebread and plastic-looking cheese. There's a reason why there wasn't a long line at that restaurant. Those things are small compared to the major meltdowns, scream fests, and blowouts that typically happen, so I'll take it!

In the end, we try to do what our kids can do. We do what is fun for us all. Maybe this means we don't get to do all the fun adventures we want to as a family, but maybe we can at least do something adventurous on a date night. Overall, successful activities and vacations with special needs kids is about the kids and spending time with them. Part of making this happen includes planning ahead, being over-prepared, basically packing your whole house, and keeping in mind the needs and likes of all your children. Sometimes I'm not mentally or physically where I need to be to do something big and that's okay. We also do things at home and adapt our environment to meet our needs. For example, I can't safely take the children to the park by myself, so we have a fun playground in our fenced backyard. We also have a tramp and various ride-on cars. Most of the time, we just bring the fun to our house because it is so hard to go to other places. We have a bouncy house with plastic balls to play in, a portable water sprayer made of pipes that makes for an at-home splash pad experience, swing sets catered for our kids' needs, and lots of adaptive toys and things to do inside. It's been a learning experience and I am continually understanding new things. Things change as our children get older: possibilities open up and with some closed doors come opened windows. Jeremy and I simply choose to accept what we have and do what we can. It's about finding our own rhythm. It takes trial and error, bravery, planning, and sometimes spontaneity.

So maybe a family trip to Hawaii isn't in our future, but a fun night playing a simple game of Twister might be and that may be what brings the family closer together, brings a smile to my child's face, and takes us away from our worries just for a moment. Besides, sleeping in your own bed, spending less money, and not stressing out about the itinerary is a plus, right? Maybe it's not what I always dreamed, but sometimes dreams change. It's my decision whether or not to enjoy the ride and what perspective to have. The truth is, our family vacations and activities may not look like other families', but we do things our way and have fun. We keep trying and keep going. It's about us. It's about finding our own joy in our own way as a family unit.

12

Extracurricular Activities

Eliza and Evelyn in dance class together

"I hope you know you're capable and brave and significant.
Even when it feels like you're not."
–Unknown

A s individuals, I want each of my children to find something they enjoy, whether it is in music, art, dance, sports, or gymnastics. I've decided Isaac's past-time will always be watching shows on his tablet. Eliza, on the other hand, is my tricky one. I say that because she is high-functioning and yet has her obstacles. Oftentimes I feel like she doesn't belong in either world: special needs or neurotypical. She struggles in regular activities but is over-the-top in special needs activities. One example that opened my eyes to this interesting debacle was a summer of dance.

"I want to enroll Eliza and Evelyn in a dance class together," I told Jeremy as we laid in bed one night. "I think they would do better together and I really think both of them would enjoy it. I just think we should expose them to different things and see what they find joy in."

"I think the girls would really enjoy dance class. Is there one that would work for them?" Jeremy asked.

"I have a few in mind, but they are just regular classes. I'm just not sure if I should make a big deal that they have special needs, but maybe we should just enroll them in a special needs class," I said, thinking about the options I had searched earlier that day.

"You never know, they are still young and it might be good for them to be in a regular class," Jeremy said.

"Except if they are some serious competition team. I don't want to deal with that," I said.

The next day I continued to search and found a local dance class I felt would be good for my girls. It was for ages three to five. Evelyn had just turned three and Eliza was five. It was a small class and sounded like it would just be exploring movement and introducing the girls to dance. Perfect. Soon the day came around for the girls to start. I got them dressed in their dancing outfits my sister had passed down to us and put them in their dancing shoes. They would be doing ballet and tap. I didn't know how it would go, but I decided not to tell the teacher that my girls had special needs yet, because I wanted to see how they did without any prejudices. Besides, I felt like they would do well and wouldn't need extra help anyway.

"Okay, guess what girls?" I said excitedly. "Today is your first dance class!" Their eyes lit up and Eliza jumped up and down.

"A dance class?" Eliza said. "Wow."

"Yeah, we need to get dressed in our special dance clothes and shoes before we go. Can you help me?"

"Yeah, let's go to dance!" Eliza said, running downstairs to her room.

"Yeah," Evelyn echoed and followed behind.

We hopped in the car all ready to go. My girls were excited and I was a little nervous. It was a small studio and when we walked in, there were two or three other parents there. I believe there were a total of four or five girls in the class. I chatted with the parents and we watched our little girls have fun out on the floor.

"Is that your little girl?" A woman asked me, pointing to Evelyn.

"Yes," I said and gave a little laugh. "This is her very first dance class and she just turned three."

"She's so cute. It reminds me of when my girl started," she said, smiling. "I'm just glad they are here to have some fun."

"Yeah, I like that it is a small class and there's no pressure," I said. We continued to peek in and watch our girls flit around. Eliza did well and followed directions. I was so proud of Evelyn. This was her first time in anything. She hadn't even started preschool yet. She did amazing, though. I thought she was going to hide under her blanket and cry, but she was excited to go out there and dance the second we got there. Her anxiety didn't inhibit her at all. I was so, so happy. She wasn't following directions as well as the older girls, but that was understandable and no one seemed to mind, because all the girls were just having fun.

Once the class was over, Eliza and Evelyn came up to me all smiles. All the other parents were leaving past me when the teacher came up to me.

"Hi, you're Evelyn's mom, right?" she asked.

"Hi, yeah," I said, smiling.

"She just barely turned three, right?"

"Yeah, just last month," I replied.

"Okay, I just don't know if she's quite ready. I feel like she's still a little young," she said.

"Oh," I replied. My face reddened as parents walked by, pretending not to listen.

"I just don't think she's ready and I can't run a class with her distracting the other girls," she said. I was tongue-tied. Was this really happening? We were in a dance class for little girls three to five. It wasn't a competition. It was a small class. The parents didn't seem to care and were happy alongside me watching their girls. She continued, "Maybe we can try next week where she sits in this other room with a one-way mirror. That way she can still dance without getting in the way of the other girls."

"Oh. Um....oh...yeah, okay," I said, trying not to cry. "We can try something different." Unfortunately, in situations like this, I never say what I want to say in the moment, but later as I'm driving home and fuming, I have lots to say! The other parents in the room didn't say anything. I don't know if they sided with her or if they were as shocked and embarrassed about what the teacher was doing as I was. I found out later the teacher was kind of a snob and treated the tiny, simple class as some start of her world champion dance company.

Later that day, I emailed the teacher to explain that my girls have special needs and I wanted them to be in a class together. I apologized for not telling her from the beginning, but I thought it was a simple class meant for learning and growth. I told her I believed my girls did wonderful and had fun, which I thought was one of the main purposes of the class. We emailed back and forth for a bit and I ended up dropping the class for both of my girls and she made me pay for the one class we went to with no remorse for what happened. I never went back. Never will. Not with anyone. I think I could've handled the situation better overall, but so could she. After this experience, I didn't give up, so I contacted another woman I'd had good experiences with before for Eliza. She had gone to a regular class a few years back and liked it. There was a new class specifically for special needs children of all ages. This is somewhere I knew my kids wouldn't be unwanted or kicked out.

The first day we went to this new dance class, Evelyn was terrified. She wouldn't even dance. She wouldn't leave my side. The room was big, cold, and loud and I don't think that helped. There were more kids there as well. Eliza, who bloomed in the other class a few weeks back, now reverted back to some bad habits and followed the hyperness of the children around her. I was so sad. The first class was so good for my girls but I got the feeling the teacher did not want them. This new teacher wanted them, but it just wasn't good for either of my girls. I ended up taking them out after two classes, feeling defeated.

It was at this time I realized my daughters may not have that obvious place Isaac does. They didn't fit in the regular world or the special needs world. They needed somewhere in the middle. Even in school, Eliza needs to be in the regular Kindergarten but with help in place. I felt lost; Eliza has been the trickiest to figure out how to lead her to success and joy in life.

Later I found a gymnastics/tumbling opportunity for both of the girls. I was nervous and didn't know what to expect because of my experience with dance and also because I know nothing about gymnastics. I emailed the business manager and explained our situation. They didn't even respond about their special needs, signed them up, and we went on our way. The first day went pretty well. They were in separate classes but I could watch both in the gym. The coaches were great with both of them and afterward, Eliza's teacher asked what she could do to help Eliza not be so scared of the bars. Neither of the coaches were told about the girls' special needs. Both coaches told me how great my girls did. Still, I was nervous that maybe my girls would need more attention than the other kids and the other parents wouldn't appreciate that.

I wasn't sure if we were going to continue until I talked on the phone with the manager again. She said she would tell the coaches about their needs, but she didn't want the first impression to be changed by this information and give the girls a chance to just shine. The coaches were happy to have them and help where needed. As I talked to one of the parents later, she told me her child has OCD and this child was also in the class to learn social skills, motor skills, and just gain experience. The manager reassured me that no one was in the class to make their children olympic stars, so we were totally fine. I felt welcomed, so of course we kept going!

A few times after going to tumbling classes, though, I realized a pattern. The girls loved the thought of going, got excited when we were there, but afterward the anxiety of the event took over. One day it was too much for everyone. I walked out after Evelyn screamed, "Stop it!" for ten minutes. She kicked, hit and scratched me, cried, and I was done. I was embarrassed, I was sad, I was frustrated. She cried loud all the way home and wouldn't stop when we came in the door. It was so bad and I couldn't comfort her. She finally had to stay in her room and take a long time out, but came out with scratches and red marks on her head. That day I canceled tumbling for the girls. I just cried. I hate that she does that to herself. It breaks my heart. After she has calmed down she is happy, but says, "Ow," and touches her head.

It's so hard to be a special needs parent. I try to do things for them but it often backfires. Keeping them home makes me feel guilty. Finding the right medication, activities, teachers, time of day, and every little thing so that the stars align as I try to give my kids the best life often feels impossible. But I just keep trying. Things change day by day, week by week, and year by year. I feel that my extracurricular activity is riding this roller coaster of life. Sometimes it's fun and exciting, and other times I'd do anything just to get off. I try to make my life and my kids' lives the best I can with who I am and what I've got at the time.

I don't think people realize how they can make such a difference by being kind. The right teachers have made all the difference for each of my kids. It matters. I will continue to find things the kids enjoy doing. I want to see their skills grow, no matter how big or small that growth is. I also want to find places where they are welcomed. Not every parent or teacher will always be and that's okay. They don't understand, but thank you to all that make the extra effort to be kind and inclusive. My kids appreciate it and I love you for it.

13

Media Time, Noise, & Unseen Expenses

Isaac sitting in his favorite position watching his tablet with blanket and water

*"The great thing about social media was how
it gave a voice to voiceless people."*
–Jon Ronson

W hat kid doesn't love iPads, tablets, TV shows, music, and movies? But there is something about kids with Fragile X and other special needs that seem to gain a unique attachment to these things. For example, when Isaac finds something he likes, it really sticks. The thing is, he usually only likes the beginning theme song to his favorite shows. I know every word to theme songs from the old *Strawberry Shortcake*, the original *Bob the Builder*, *Little Einsteins*, *Cyberchase*, and others. I also know various clips from many different shows and movies he watches over and over, like *Peter Pan*, *A Goofy Movie*, and *The Emperor's New Groove*. There are these little golden nuggets he gets such a kick out of. I love what a great sense of humor he has and how he laughs. It goes to show there's more to him than meets the eye.

One thing I find funny is all the different theme songs he listens to in Spanish, German, French, and many other languages. I may even have *Little Einsteins* memorized in Spanish. But a few things that drive me bonkers is when he puts the tablet in my face a million times wanting me to change it to something else or when he plays the theme songs people make on their own with Satanic undertones, creepy colors, and kaleidoscopic pictures. I can't help but think, *who makes this crap?* Yet, I look and they have hundreds of thousands of views. Most of those are probably from Isaac. I used to try and stop or filter these ones out, but eventually I found other priorities. Besides, Isaac is referred to as "The Boss," not just at home, so he basically rules the roost for most things.

Something surprising is how well he learns from educational shows and their music. One of my favorite things on YouTube is Preschool Prep Company. Isaac has learned over fifty sight words from these programs along with numbers, shapes, and colors. I use them for all my kids. Before they were on YouTube, I'd check out the DVDs from the library. When I started homeschool during COVID-19, I bought flashcards, workbooks, sight-reading books, and other items from their website. Even though I love to teach my kids, Isaac learns really well through the media, so I let him watch educational shows whenever he wants. Leapfrog also has some great learning shows, like the *Letter Factory*. Eliza has also learned dozens of sight words this way. Evelyn knew the basic shapes, many colors, and some letters when she was just two. Some other favorites my kids enjoy and learn from are Super Simple Songs, Storybots, and Badanamu.

Of course, YouTube and lots of other media outlets can be damaging and harmful in many ways to children. Monitoring their usage, creating rules, using time limits, and using a reward system can all be part of creating healthy media habits in the home. I'm not perfect at keeping my children off the TV, but being aware is at least something. I used to wonder why my sister would let her children watch so much TV and be on their iPods so much, but now that I have three with FXS, I totally get it. No more judgment here! Sometimes that's the only way to catch a break, gain some peace, and/or get something done.

Different types of media can have different benefits and drawbacks. I know for Isaac, DVDs didn't work, because he bit them, scratched them, and ruined them before we could watch them twice. We did away with all DVDs and slowly went only to digital where nothing could get ruined by sticky fingers and bite marks. We occasionally use old VHS tapes that seem unbreakable (as long as the film doesn't get stuck in the machine), but those definitely have drawbacks. Thankfully, technology has come a long way in assisting special needs children with communication, for example. In school and at home, Isaac has used various different communication boards to help express himself. Although he can talk, it is very limited and he has difficulty forming words in his mouth. Such devices and apps can be a huge help to some children with disabilities. For Isaac, it helped a bit, but mostly it caused frustration because of his obsession with tablets and iPads. It was hard for him to differentiate between playing on the iPad and working on the iPad, even if we used different ones. He is averse to schoolwork anyway, but we always try new things. I try anything to help my son, even if I feel there is a small chance of success.

Sometimes the iPad or TV show was used as a bribe or reward for Isaac, especially when trying to get him potty trained at school. This caused unforetold issues. He would strip down or go sit on the toilet without going and expect media time. When he didn't get it, a giant meltdown could ensue. At the same time, we couldn't give him a reward for just going through the motions, especially after months of trying. He knew what to do. Sometimes we would give him a tablet time limit and as soon as it was over he'd want to go to the potty. It was quite a frustrating game. The same thing happened with award systems and bribing with chips. It just didn't work for him.

Overall, I have a love-hate relationship with tablets and such. It has caused a lot of contention, fighting, and tantrums, but it has also created a lot of possibilities, peace, and opportunity. I do feel that committing time to teach and play with my children is always the best route, but I also know I can't do that every hour of every day. Sometimes Isaac watches his tablet for most of the day, because that is what keeps him happy, brings peace, and overall allows family life to be somewhat normal. Overall, though, I find it is about balance, following the needs of my children, and sometimes saying things like, "It's okay if they watch a movie now so I can get a break, refresh myself, and be a better, more available mother later." Unfortunately, the never-ending songs and repeats can get on my nerves and disturb everyone in the house. I am reminded of the Grinch when he says, *"Oh the noise! Oh the noise, noise, noise, noise!"* Sometimes it's enough to want to pull your hair out before Isaac does it.

My girls could almost never take naps because Isaac was so loud. If it's not a movie, it's his own "singing," wailing, bouncing, pounding, and laughing. He literally yells randomly and sometimes for no apparent reason. You'll just be sitting there and suddenly BAM! He's yelling at the top of his lungs for a five-second interval. I think I and my family, if we don't already, will have some serious hearing loss due to the volume and frequency of his yelling, but my two FX girls also have some good lungs. They scream—*really* scream. You pick the wrong show to watch or look at them the wrong way (I'm not joking) and it sounds like they stepped on a nail or are being kidnapped. Funnily enough, there are times when they actually get hurt and hardly make a sound. Go figure.

In my house, we constantly try to keep the peace as much as possible. This has led to many different expenditures—some good, some worthless. Over the years I've realized how much money we pour into our children as we try to make things better for them, for us, for everyone; trying this or that for one reason or another to help in any way. I resonate with Elena Delle Donne who said, "It's expensive to raise a child with special needs, which people don't even think about. Emotionally it can be a struggle, but financially it's really rough." As I thought more on this, I realized how much we have purchased over the years. I've compiled a list of all the things Jeremy and I have bought in hopes of helping one or all of my children to maybe give someone else inspiration or lend another to understanding. I've listed many items in the following pages, but for a more comprehensive list with links to the products, please visit kirstenfowler.com.

Cleaning/Home

- Air Fresheners of all kinds throughout the house
- Bed pads, reusable mattress underpad, and protective sheets. I like to use the reusable pads with the soft, vinyl lined protective sheets to protect the mattress. The small mattress bed pads that are like doggy pee pads move around too much and always miss the mark
- Blink or other security cameras for indoor/ outdoor, both battery and plug in options
- Bulk amount of their favorite foods
- Calming clipper haircutting kit (although this didn't work for my son, it may work for your child. I personally like these quiet, cordless hair clippers. You can even use it in the tub, if necessary-wherever they will let me cut their hair!
- Carpet cleaner and spot carpet cleaner that I prefer. We've taken out most of our carpet, though.
- Cleaners and rags in bulk
- Couches and chairs that are easy to clean/ wipe off, such as wood or leather.
- Cupboard, drawer, and handle locks of various kinds to meet your needs. Also locks for nail polish, cleaners, and maybe the fridge
- Diaper bag backpack that can attach to a stroller or wheelchair that's always packed with snacks, extra clothes, diapers, water, and bags for dirty diapers and dirty clothes
- Diapers of various sizes, pad inserts, and wipes/disposable washcloths.
- Extra clothing due to more accidents and messes
- Extra laundry detergent for all the surplus of laundry. I tried the cheap stuff, but Tide is the only one that really gets out the smells and stains
- Extra sheets and blankets as well
- Hand soap for dry hands
- Hard floors, like rubber, wood, tile, or laminate. Keep in mind possible head banging on the floor, however.

- Heavy duty, large capacity washer and dryer
- Lamination machine, printer, and paper for all those picture schedules and more
- Lume deodorant and other products to help with body odor
- Machine washable rugs, such as Ruggables
- Non-contact forehead thermometer because the kids won't let me take their temperature any other way
- Onesie pajamas turned backwards or specialty onesie clothes and pajamas that zip in the back. These can also be found on Amazon.
- Period Underwear
- Plastic cups, plates, and utensils to cut down on overwhelming dishes
- Shop vacuum or vacuum mop that can clean up wet/dry messes
- Special car seat with a five point harness with items to help them not slip out or get out easily
- Special harnesses for various rides, such as the surrey bike, side by side, etc. I like a five point harness that can easily be installed to meet your needs
- Special needs chair, booster, or harness for the dinner table that has straps and weight bearing capacities, may be needed for years
- Special needs stroller/wheelchair. This stroller saved us for years
- Special shoes, like ones that have no laces and are easily slipped on
- Special toothbrushes (I like the three sided kind)
- Street signs in front of your home for safety
- Swim diapers and plastic pants
- Trash cans with lids
- Tvs
- Vacuum, heavy duty and bagless. I like ones that give access to the hoses, because something always gets sucked up that shouldn't
- Vacuum, small and bagless for kids to use that really works. A light stick vacuum with detachable hand vacuums work great

Educational Items/Toys

- 123 Numbers- Count and Tracing App (free)
- ABC cookies game
- ABC Kids-Tracing and Phonics App (free)
- Blocks- Various sizes, textures, and materials
- Boom Cards App (free)
- Bead maze, including this travel sized one
- Bean bag games- Shapes, expressions, sensory, alphabet, or numbers themes
- Counting and sorting items
- Dab and Dot Markers or Do A Dot Art markers
- Egg shape matching toy
- Fine motor tools set or these ones that make it a game- Water beads, Gator, Avalanche Fruit Stand
- Fine motor munch ball using a cut tennis ball or the official game that uses the same skills.
- Gear toy with music and lights.
- Hot Dots
- LCD Writing Tablets of different sizes
- Leapfrog Magical Adventures Globe
- Learning clock
- Mathlink cubes or Numberblocks (also has a fun YouTube channel)
- Multiple shape sorters- Simple, intricate, and ones that make sounds
- Nesting Cups
- Nesting dolls the kids can paint
- Peg boards- Various shapes and sizes
- Preschool Prep bundles- Books, Flash cards, Easy Reader Books, Movies, Work books
- Puzzles- Various sizes, materials, and difficulty
- See and Spell learning toy
- Stacking rings- Geometric stacker, multiple peg shape stacker, Rainbow spinning wheel toy
- Stringing beads
- Tablets/IPads with screen protector and almost indestructible case. I like the Fire tablet or iPad. Use parental controls, locks, and time limits
- Teachers Pay Teachers website- Lots of free and inexpensive learning worksheets
- Water Wow books, such as ABC and numbers, Blue's Clues, or others

Books
(There's so many good ones, but here's a few)

- An Early Start for Your Child with Autism
- Becoming Mrs. Rogers
- Best Behavior Series board books (The boardbooks are more condensed and more heavy duty) or you can buy them individually on Amazon in different formats.
- Beyond Behaviors
- Chicka Chicka Boom Boom
- Coloring books with simple, large drawings and thick lines
- DBT Workbook for Adults
- Dr. Seuss collections
- Easy Phonics books, such as Bob Book sets, phonics books, and Preschool Prep sight word books
- Elephant and Piggie Books
- Engaging Autism
- Fairytales Take Along Storyteller
- Feelings and choices flip book
- Fire Truck
- First 100 Board Book Set or other books with simple pictures to talk about
- Fragile X, Fragile Hope
- Fragile X Fred
- If You Give a Mouse a Cookie
- Improving Speech and Eating Skills in Children with Autism Spectrum Disorders Hardcover or boardbooks. You can also laminate softcover books
- Leapfrog Scout and Violet 100 Words Book
- Magic Ink copybooks for kids, reusable
- Pigeon Books
- Pirates Wear Underpants
- Positive Discipline for Children with Special Needs
- Sound button books
- The Accessible Church
- The Carriers
- The Child with Special Needs
- The Color Monster: A Story About Emotions
- This Train

Sensory Items and Engaging Toys

- Adult full back swing seat with sturdy frame (we made ours out of 2x4s).
- Animal squeeze popper toy
- Ball pit of various sizes
- Bath toys, squirters, bubbles, motorized sprayer, etc.
- Bean bag seats of various sizes. I recommend leather ones used with a blanket or making your own cover that can be easily removed and washed
- Blankets-my kids each have a favorite and it's best to have two of them. When they are babies, swaddle blankets and swaddling sacks were really helpful and provided deep pressure sensory
- Body sox
- Bounce house
- Bumble ball
- Car tracks to watch cars go down
- Cars that go when you shake it or make sounds
- Chairs for adults and children. Extra large bouncer chair, rocking chairs, egg shaped, etc.
- Chewy tubes and chewelry with various shapes, sizes, and textures
- Collapsible tunnels
- Compression back brace (Because it is cheaper than a compression vest)
- Compression sheets
- Disco Party ball lights. Of course, be careful with this one, depending on the needs of your child
- Fake, lighted fish tank. Here's a cheaper option and the more expensive option I wish we had
- Fidget spinners
- Foam swords
- Giant outdoor Connect Four game
- Half yoga balls and full yoga balls
- Hammock
- Hammock swing seat
- Hooded jackets
- Hopper balls
- Imagine Ink coloring books
- Inflatable lounger
- Inflatable peapod
- Kinetic sand
- Koosh ball
- Lava lamp
- Light up spinner wand
- Liquid floor tiles of various colors
- Liquid timer
- Magnetic blocks/cubes
- Magnetic drawing boards
- Magnetic tiles
- Many different types of bubble machines: Bubble gun, rechargeable, battery powered
- Marble run
- Mini flashlights and projector flashlights
- Music players with simple buttons, various kinds
- Musical instruments
- Orbeez of various sizes
- Paint with water books or paint outside on the sidewalk with water on a sunny day
- Platform tree swing
- Play doh with cutters and rollers. I also like these pieces you can just stick in easily like a play doh potato head
- Pop it stress ball
- Pop up tents for fun and sensory
- Pop toys fidget
- Pop tubes
- Press and spin dome
- Pretend play items, such as kitchen toys, dolls, and cars
- Rocking horses
- Sand and water table
- Seat chair band to help restless legs
- Sensory balls of various sizes and textures
- Sensory swing seat with stretchy material
- Sensory teardrop pod swing with inflatable pillow seat
- Sidewalk chalk- I like to use this for practicing their handwriting skills and learning ABCs, numbers, and shapes.
- Slides
- Spikey rings
- SpinAgain stacking toy
- Spinning tops- Stationary, light up and sound, motorized
- Sticker mosaics
- Stretchy strings fidget toys
- Suction Squigz toys
- Sunglasses
- Squeeze machine
- Squishy stress balls with various textures and fills
- Therapressure brush
- Trains with motors, like VTech GoGo train, Thomas the Train motorized engines with tracks, or my favorite, Thomas the Train Minis Playset
- Tramps- With and without enclosed net of various sizes to meet needs.
- Vibrating pillow
- Wacky Tracks fidgets
- Wacky Waving Inflatable Tube Guy Mini
- Water Doodle Mat
- Water squirters of various types (not water guns where you have to use fine motor to pull the trigger-unless that's what your child needs and is ready for). Ones from the dollar store work but just don't last as long.
- Water Wubbles and water balloons. My kids like to fill them up as big as they can and bounce them on the tramp until they pop or all the water comes out. For easy, safe water fun you can also use reusable water balls.
- Weighted blanket- You can buy all kinds of different kinds now like furry, slick, Minky, sherpa, or fleece in the right size and weight you desire. They are much more available and affordable than they used to be.
- Weighted stuffed animal or lap animal
- Weighted vest

Specialized Fun/Other

- 8-seat Surrey bike with gears and pedal assist or a Pedal Kart
- Camping Trailer/toy hauler
- Combining items for a calming corner or space at home to help your child calm down using things like a bean bag chair, emotion books, sensory toys, etc.
- Electric scooter with seat and baby seat in the back to take a few kids on a ride
- Headphones that go over the ears, bluetooth
- If your child needs glasses, I recommend rubber frames
- Large parachute with handles
- Movies (VHS, DVD, Digital)
- Noise canceling earmuffs
- Pool passes
- Pop up tent bed or other enclosed bed options
- Service Dog and everything that comes with it
- Side by side
- Swing sets/playgrounds
- Tandem bikes, three wheeled bikes, and other custom bikes to meet needs.
- Trampoline Park tickets
- Wagons to tote kids around, especially ones with seatbelts

Our Surrey bike is a family favorite. This is us dressed as characters from Mary Poppins for Halloween

For my children, some items were total flops and some were a total godsend. Oftentimes what would be great for Eliza wouldn't work at all for Isaac, and what would work for Isaac didn't work for Evelyn. It really depends on the child and if they are hypo- or hyper-sensitive. Sometimes even the setting changed the success rate of an item. For example, Isaac loved the weighted blanket at school but would not have anything to do with it at home. That is one thing that often puzzles parents: home and school are two very different places for a lot of these kids struggling with various special needs. They might do puzzles at school and not at home. They might be really well-behaved at school and then a complete fireball at home. Overall, I try to be happy in whatever triumphs come and ride out the inevitable disappointments.

I'm sure there are more things I've bought than I could ever remember, and I have made many DIY sensory items, but I bring this up for two reasons: first, to show having a special needs child means more time and money spent that you typically wouldn't spend on a neurotypical child. Sure, there are obviously things every child needs, wants, and could use, but having to purchase diapers and wipes for years on end and special items to assist your child in daily living adds up. Many people take for granted all the little things their child can do, like use a spoon, go potty, regulate their emotions, talk, self soothe, pretend-play, and more. Second, I thought some of these items could spark some ideas in other parents to help along the journey. I know I like to join Facebook groups and see what kinds of tools parents are using, or even what toys they buy for Christmas and birthdays that their children like. It's also helpful to join these groups for support.

Be cautious, however. What worked wonders for so-and-so's child does not necessarily guarantee the same result for you. Do what works for you and your child. I cannot emphasize this enough. Sometimes things worked out and sometimes they were a disaster. You have to find the flow of your own family life. As parents, I've found we will do just about anything for our kids, because we want what's best for them—I guess that is one reason why it is so hard to see them fail, hurt themselves, or make mistakes, especially when you feel so hopeless to help.

14

Other Self-Harm & Aggression

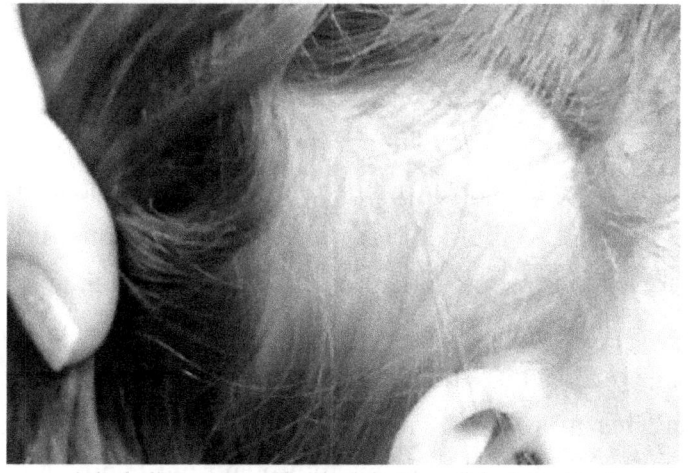

A chunk of hair missing on Eliza's head after Isaac pulled and ripped it out

"No one ever told me that grief felt so like fear."
−C.S. Lewis, A Grief Observed

T here are a lot of difficult things I've been through as a special needs mom, but one of the hardest things is watching your child physically hurt themselves and feeling powerless. When Isaac was just one year old, I noticed something I'd never really seen before. I later had a name for it:

"self-harm." There my baby was, punching himself on the side of the head or banging the back of his head hard over and over, even on cement. There was a time when we tried new medication where things got worse rather than better and he caused bruises near his temples. He gave himself a scar by scratching his cheek and you can still see it now, nearly eight years later. It was scary and awful.

Everyone, including myself, was always surprised that despite Isaac's skinny, tall little body, he was stronger than a typical adult and could overpower you easily when he was angry or frightened. With all his jumping, his thin legs unnaturally bulged with hard muscle. Many outsiders didn't realize that a three-year-old could be dangerous. Sometimes when all the kids were home from school and Jeremy was still at work, I was afraid. Before, when Isaac had constant tantrums, meltdowns, or harmful behavior, I put him in his room and locked the door for the safety of everyone. It often led to destroyed items in his rooms, like ripped books and broken toys, or a "poop fiasco" where he painted with fecal matter. Eventually he'd calm down and I'd talk to him, give him a hug, then let him out. Now I can no longer physically control Isaac because of his increasing strength and mass. I'm amazed how strong he can be. The thought of his future and our family grew very dim. The only thing I could do to protect everyone was to rush all the girls into a room and lock the door. Isaac would yell, cry, hit the wall, bang his head, and whine. I'd try to be strong and happy for my girls. Outside the door, Isaac would slowly calm down and get quieter. Then I knew we were probably safe to come out. I still kept an eye on Isaac, though, because without warning he would grab at one of his sisters and hurt them.

Sometimes we can't get him on the bus in the morning for school and he has to stay home. Just recently, Jeremy and I were giving it our all to coax him out the door, into his stroller, and onto the bus.

"Come on, Isaac. It's time to go to school," I said sweetly. "We get to go play with your friends and see your teacher!" He looked at me and out came the screeching and whining that gnaws at my nerves.

"It's okay, buddy," I said and tried to keep him and me calm. "I packed you some yummy pretzels in your lunch for later. You can keep your tablet with you, too."

More whining, hitting his head on the floor, and swiping at me.

"No, don't hurt us, bud," Jeremy piped in. "We're trying to help you."

He kicked at us both and screeched again, then threw his tablet across the room. I switched tactics and tried to tickle him into submission. It got him up the stairs, but then he resisted again. Jeremy finally grabbed hold of his arm and leaned Isaac up against his body to coerce him into the direction of the door, but Isaac flailed and screamed more.

By the time we got him out the door, the bus had been sitting there for at least five minutes waiting. This is why we usually give ourselves 10-20 minutes to get him to the bus before it even arrives. But Isaac still wouldn't get in his seat and proceeded to charge at me aggressively. I put my hands out defensively and asked him nicely to get in his seat. He swiped at me to scratch. Jeremy came up from behind with the wheelchair and Isaac fell back into the chair. He used his feet to push back, so then we chased him backward as he beat into the bikes and water bottles stacked in the garage behind him. All the while, we spoke calmly to him and outwardly stayed cool. The bus driver and assistant watched us. I had fear, embarrassment, sorrow, and PTSD all bubbling up inside me. We finally got him buckled and rolled him over to the bus.

"Watch his hands!" I said to the bus driver as we put him on the wheelchair lift.

"Isaac," she said, "we aren't going to act like this on the bus."

He screamed and swiped at the air fruitlessly like a caged animal trying to break free from his captors. In situations like this he doesn't understand we are trying to help him do what's best—send him to school!

By then I'm crying; crying because I don't want him to hurt anyone; crying because I want him to show his beautiful sweet side I know; crying because I'm trying to love and help him but he's hurting me; crying because it brings back memories and realizations he may not be able to stay with us in our home. The bus driver hugged me and told me it will be okay.

"Did he get you?" she asked, looking down at my hand. I didn't realize I was bleeding from his scratches.

"Oh, yeah. I guess he did a little," I said, not really hearing my own voice.

The door of the bus shut and I walked back into the house, tears streaming my face. I turned to wave goodbye as the bus pulled away.

Dozens of moments like these and more wear me and my family down. Usually this calls for an adjustment of medications, but it only prolongs the next episode.

When I first had Evelyn, which I'm sure exacerbated Isaac's anxiety and misbehavior at the time, I worried about her the most. I couldn't leave her on the floor for tummy time if Isaac was anywhere nearby. I worried about Eliza, too, but Isaac wasn't as big then. I never knew when a stray kick would come our way or he might suddenly become upset and violent. Even when he is just happy and in a good mood, he is unaware of his body in space and could have easily squashed her with one happy cross-legged butt bounce on the floor (I don't know how he does this without pain). I worried even when I was pregnant, because I thought I might lose her early from the stress, his physical demands, and his kicks or occasional head butts to my stomach.

There was one time when I put Evelyn down for a nap in her pack 'n play in my room. I would usually lock the doors, but apparently I forgot a few times. Isaac is quite sneaky and quick when he wants to be, so I didn't realize he had snuck into my room—the last place in the house I wanted him to be! When I heard his giggles and her cries, I realized where he was and rushed to Evelyn's bedside. There I found Isaac curled up next to her in the bed. Although this was cute and I loved that he wanted to be by her, I couldn't stop thinking of what could have happened. I wondered if he had hurt her while getting in the bed, but she looked okay despite being upset from waking up. I took a picture because it was cute and didn't get angry with him, because he was innocent, but I took him away quickly and tried not to think what could have happened. All I can say is angels must've been watching over us.

Evelyn wasn't the only target of Isaac's harm and behavior issues. When Millie was the only other child around, Isaac scratched her and pulled her hair. She was afraid of her own brother and it took years for them to finally trust each other enough to coexist. Once the other girls were born, Isaac had someone younger than him to tease and pick on. I'll never forget one day when Isaac and Eliza were in disagreement over some toy or puzzle. Jeremy and Millie were out at the neighbor's for a moment and I was taking care of the baby, but suddenly I heard a commotion and a loud scream from Eliza. When I got downstairs, I was horrified. No, there was no blood and gore, but it still scarred me. There was a large tuft of Eliza's hair on the floor with strands seeping through Isaac's fisted hand. As I looked closer at Eliza's head, there was a round bald patch on the side that made me feel sick. I admit I yelled at Isaac. He began bawling right alongside Eliza. I was shocked and angry.

I ran and called out to Jeremy to come home and he took the baby while I tended to Eliza and gathered up the strewn hair. We got Isaac into his room to cool down and eventually things calmed down again, but I kept that wad of hair in my bathroom for a long time. It made me sick to look at it, but for some reason I just couldn't throw it away. Weeks or maybe months later I forced myself to throw the hair in the trash. I didn't want it to be tucked away in a baggy labeled "Eliza's first hair pull-out from Isaac." I didn't want to remember it. Obviously there's no forgetting such traumatic things.

Sometimes I got calls from Isaac's teacher saying Isaac intentionally went up to the brick walls of the school and hit his head against it hard. He did this sort of thing at home as well. He even purposely found the stove when a wall wasn't available to bang his head against. Then he'd look at you and say, "Ohhh," like it hurt, but it was an attention thing. The hard part is you couldn't completely ignore it or else he would hurt himself badly.

Along with head banging, hair pulling, scratching, etc. I also classify bolting or elopement as self-harm, because by running away, they put themselves in great harm. Sometimes the teachers spent most of their time keeping Isaac in the class or at least in the school. At home, we have to lock all our doors and gates so he doesn't run out on the road in front of traffic or get lost. We can't often do anything as a family in the front yard because it is not fenced and he just walks off. Of course he always goes toward the busiest road! There was a time he kept escaping to the front yard and all I could do was get his 100 pounds on my back and make it a game to get him back home. It wasn't good on my body, I can tell you that. One time I decided to go on an adventure to JoAnne's fabric store. Millie was at school but I still had Isaac and Eliza. At the time, Eliza was still in a carrier car seat and we didn't have a stroller to transport Isaac. I'll never forget hefting Eliza with one arm and running after Isaac as he bolted toward a stoplight on Main Street. I couldn't set Eliza down, so I just ran as fast as I could with her until I caught up with Isaac and grabbed him around the waist. I was a total Hulk Mama as I turned away from all the onlookers with two crying kids hefted in each arm. Thank goodness for adrenaline or else I don't know how I would've done that!

Many years later, Isaac very rarely hits his head on the floor and doesn't self-harm much at all, thanks mostly to the right medications. Unfortunately, when Evelyn was born and got to about two years old, we noticed she was beginning to self-harm. At age three, when she gets frustrated or goes into a full meltdown, she will pull her own hair out, scratch her face and body until it bleeds, and punch her head so much and so hard that she regularly has at least one bruise. There have been times I tried to lie over her to give deep pressure, hold her arms so she can't hurt herself, and do anything to stop her. I've sat with her for hours as she screams at the top of her lungs and won't let me help. I'm afraid to leave her in the room like I did Isaac, because she doesn't stop screaming and injuring herself. There have been a few times I haven't known what else to do, especially when I am mentally and emotionally spent. She is slowly getting better at calming herself, but parents don't realize the preciousness of self-soothing that typical children naturally learn. It's a skill my kids have to really work on.

Another skill is coping with going into a grocery store or public place. Most parents just take their kids grocery shopping or bring them wherever they go. I have to get a babysitter or shop online, which is thankfully so much better and easier now. I think I have PTSD from going to the store so many times with my special needs kids—mostly Isaac. There was a time I really needed to get groceries and I felt pretty good that day, so I decided I would take all four of my children to Costco. They have big carts, so it was going to be fine! I planned it all out in my mind where each of the kids could sit. Eliza in one of the front seats of the cart. Evelyn in the big basket while still in her car seat with the shade pulled up. Millie would walk beside me, holding onto the cart. Isaac would go wherever he would be happy. He was being so good and I prayed he would not hurt the baby. Well, I got to Costco and parked near the carts. I got out of the car, grabbed a cart, brought it over to my mini van, and opened the sliding door. I had Eliza and Millie get out of the car first and hefted Eliza into the little seats. Of course, she stiffened her legs, so it made it nearly impossible to get her in and she grabbed at my head and my hair was all over the place. Then I grabbed Evelyn and placed her in the cart. Isaac started whining and I knew already he didn't want to go, which wasn't a good sign. I got him out of his seat and started to wrestle with him to get in the cart. Soon he was yelling, people were looking, I looked a mess, and Isaac began reaching for the baby and Eliza to scratch or pull their hair. Needless to say, I never even made it into the store before I threw in the towel and came home with no food and crying children. That was the very last time I ever went alone with all my kids to a public place.

Compared to what other special needs families have been through, though, this is nothing. I'm thankful for that. At these different points in time, however, I wondered, as I had many times before and many times after, what terrible thing would happen before we placed Isaac in another home? Did we just wait until something really awful occurred before we took action to protect our girls? Even ourselves? It wasn't uncommon for Isaac to literally push me around, pull my hair, shove his tablet in my face, or scratch me and Jeremy. He hurt others, too, and I felt so completely helpless to stop it. I tried to figure out how to make things right with the whole family.

15

Trying to Help

Roxy practicing her service dog skills for Isaac

*"Sometimes letting things go is an act of far greater power than
defending or hanging on."*
–Eckhart Tolle

W e were getting desperate to try and help Isaac. I wanted to do anything
and everything possible. I never wanted to be accused of not trying
something or doing A, B, or C to help him. The idea of a service dog had been
in the back of my mind for a while, but Jeremy was opposed to getting a dog

in general. He likes dogs, but we had a dog from the pound that caused more stress than anything.

"Isaac loves dogs, hon," I argued one night. "I really think this could be a huge help. Maybe we could go to more places. Maybe he wouldn't have so many meltdowns."

"I just don't want another dog. It only adds more stress," Jeremy replied. "The cost of food, the poop scooping, and everything else. I just can't right now."

"Then I'll worry about the details," I said, pleading for him to reconsider. "I'll poop scoop and be the main caretaker."

He looked at me in surprise, wondering if I'd really do that.

"Look. I just can't stand by and not do everything I can to help our son. If there's something we can do, I want to do it. I have to try everything as a mother to help him."

"I just don't think it's a good idea. I know you love him and are trying to help him, but I just don't know if this is the solution."

However, I was determined, and so one day I saw a cute labradoodle puppy online and I took the kids to get it. When I told Jeremy, he wasn't happy, but he didn't want to tell me no. He also knew when I set my mind to something I am very stubborn, so I went and picked up that cutie and named her Roxy. The dog was adorable, but it was hard. I think my stubbornness fueled me and I potty trained it, taught her not to chew on everything, and did my best to hold up my promise. But the truth is, we all came to love her—even Jeremy. Still, having a new puppy, especially in our situation, wasn't easy.

Getting a service dog trained is *so* expensive, so in order to make things happen, I went to work contacting businesses and individuals to donate to the cause. I also put together a GoFundMe page. My cousin and I even came together to make a music video to help promote the page and gain new donations. I sang a song my mom wrote called, "Super Mom," but I changed some words to make a fun spin-off called "Service Dog." Roxy was featured in it with a super cape on coming to Isaac's rescue. I was very thankful and blown away by all the generous donations we received.

Once Roxy was old enough and vaccinated, we went through a dog training company in Salt Lake City. We dropped her off for bootcamp and awaited the results with anticipation. Unfortunately, Roxy didn't pass the test. Apparently, she wasn't meant to be a service dog.

"She's too aggressive. She tried to bite my hand," one of the trainers claimed.

"That doesn't sound like our Roxy. She is so mellow with children and just needs a lot of love. What was going on when she apparently tried to bite your hand?" I asked, skeptical and shocked.

"She wasn't listening, so I did what we do with all our dogs. I bopped her on the nose. But she wouldn't listen even after that and continued to get more aggressive."

Well, gee, I wonder why. I never hit Roxy. Maybe this can work for other dogs, but for Roxy, I knew for a fact this wasn't how she would learn. I knew she had many bad behaviors as a young lab, but what she needed was love and kindness, especially since she was put in a new, strange place, kenneled, and reprimanded for things she didn't understand. I felt so bad leaving her there without her understanding we'd come back and we loved her, but I felt so much worse finding out how she was treated. Needless to say, I brought her home, not knowing what to do. We had a dog we loved, we had put money into this company, and already signed contracts, but I felt at a loss.

On top of all this, not long after we found out Roxy caught Kennel Cough while staying her short duration in boot camp at this company's facility. I've never seen a sick dog like that before, especially with a terrible runny nose. It was so sad and I was disappointed with the company and the whole situation we were now in. I'm not even sure why we continued to work with them, but I didn't know what to do next. We ended up finding a new dog to train with the company's guidance and approval. It was another black lab mix we named Daisy. At this point, we had two rambunctious labs in the house with three children, two with special needs, and I was pregnant with Evelyn. It was getting wild.

"This is so crazy, but I don't know what to do at this point. We love Roxy. I can't just sell her," I said one afternoon with Jeremy.

"I know I didn't want her at first, but she's the coolest dog," he replied. "I've had a lot of dogs growing up, but she's definitely my favorite." It was true. Despite the fact that I was taking care of her and training her, Jeremy was the fun parent and she attached to him. She also listened to him better. She was never very happy being a service dog like I've seen other dogs enjoy and feel loyalty to their person. She just wanted to play, but was obedient out of duty and we all loved her. Even with all that and the chaos we were in, we just couldn't get rid of her, but also needed to go through with our original plan of training a service dog for Isaac; yet, how could we deal with two dogs? The truth is, we couldn't. After a short time, we realized Daisy just wasn't for us; there was no attachment with her and Isaac or any of the family for that matter. If we were going to have a service dog for Isaac, it would have to be Roxy, because everyone had such a great attachment and love for her. We sold Daisy to an army veteran to finish her service training for his benefit and I believe it was a better fit for everyone...especially after Daisy chewed a hole through Isaac's mattress.

I approached the professional trainers again and it was decided that if we wanted Roxy to be trained, they would not do it in-house and I would have to train her at home. This was because they saw her as unfit and aggressive. The good news was it would be much cheaper, because we hadn't quite raised all the money we needed for the training anyway. The bad news is I was very pregnant, already stressed, and had limited time. I was so determined to see this through no matter what, though, so I said yes and we moved forward.

Training Roxy meant traveling an hour away from home once a week or so to get the training I needed to then train Roxy. Sometimes I had to take Eliza, barely two, along with me. Sometimes Millie would come. I only brought Isaac when I had to do a pick up or drop off where he didn't need to get out of the car. There were times I had to cancel because I couldn't find someone to watch Isaac. Nowadays we probably could've done this through Zoom, but it was helpful to have one-on-one help. As she got better, I went with Roxy and a trainer to different public places for practice. It was a really cool experience, but a lot of work. Toward the end, the trainers teaching me got impatient with me and Roxy, feeling like I was wasting their time and not worth the money we'd paid them. Apparently they couldn't see I was training this dog by *myself* for my son *with special needs*, bringing my toddler with me an hour away for training sessions each week, and was just weeks away from having a baby. I really was doing my best.

The big test came up to qualify her for official service dog status, but I didn't feel like either of us were ready; however, I felt if she didn't pass, I'd be a failure, that everything up to that point was for nothing, and the people who paid and helped me so much would be let down. Unfortunately, Roxy and I didn't pass the first service dog test we took together, but we were close! I just hadn't put in the necessary time. It required thirty minutes a day and time out in public to practice various commands and appropriate behaviors. I found it so hard to find time to take her in public without my kids so I could focus and train her, but I wouldn't be defeated! In fact, I distinctly remember singing "The Fight Song" by Rachael Platten on my ride home from the failed test: "And I don't really care if nobody else believes. 'Cause I've still got a lot of fight left in me!" I sang at the top of my lungs while Roxy looked at me like, *Lady, what are you doing?*

Finally, around a month later, we took the test again after I really kicked it into high gear. I wanted to get this done before the baby came or it would never happen. The day we received the go-ahead and Roxy officially became Isaac's service dog, I cried. We did it! I got on my family's Marco Polo and said, "You're looking at the newest service dog and her *trainer!*" I had to tell everyone. It was such a triumph. After that I called my mom and we met up at Wendy's. I took Roxy in with me and my mom made sure to buy her a hamburger patty to eat later. I bought Roxy an official service dog harness with a handle for Isaac on the back. I even got special IDs with her picture and info on it and made sure to study up on the laws and rights of my son and Roxy when out in public. So yeah, I felt pretty awesome. I was proud of Roxy and myself. There I was, almost ready to have my fourth baby, and I had trained this dog for Isaac. It just goes to show the determination parents have to help their children.

I'll never forget our first trip out with Isaac and Roxy in her official capacities. We went to what I felt was a safe spot: a store called Dollar Tree. I figured if everything's a dollar in here, I could afford to buy something if we broke it. The stress and anxiety was definitely there, but replaced with gratitude and amazement for Roxy's abilities and proving the original trainer wrong. Besides, I gained a great education through it all: how to train a service dog. How cool is that? Not many people can say that.

I learned a lot from this experience. First of all, if you go through a professional trainer, be sure to pick the dog with the trainer or at least run the idea by them first. This will ensure you pick a great dog the trainer feels comfortable working with. Be sure you picked a good trainer or company as well! Second, unless you want to become a trainer yourself, I suggest letting someone else do all the work and you learn some tricks to keep things in balance when the dog returns home. Third, research dogs to see what is the best fit for your child. For example, a lab is very energetic and can play or work for hours. A labradoodle is typically very snuggly. Fourth, if you don't want a dog, then don't get a service dog, because it still requires all the same needs and attention. I know some of these may seem obvious, but just trust me. You have to be willing to take the dog everywhere with you and spend the money to take care of them. Fifth, save up. I've owned a lot of mutts in my life and loved them, but buying them from a high-end breeder will likely get you better results. Also, professional training costs thousands of dollars, depending on the company or individual.

If you know a lot about dogs and are confident in training them in general, you can likely do the training yourself with lots of time, effort, discipline, dog treats, and how-to YouTube videos. It really depends on what you are looking for. I know of people who bought a dog they liked and it naturally fits the needs of their special needs child in areas such as sensory needs. Also, remember that even after all the hard work you put in, a special needs child will still need other things to help them through their life, like medication, therapy, etc. A service dog is not a cure-all. In fact, nothing is, no matter how bad we want it. It takes a whole village and more to raise a child with special needs. I think that's what Jeremy tried to tell me to help me realize that getting a dog or doing this, that, or the other is not a miracle pill that will make it all go away. Still, I had to try *something*.

So, even after getting Roxy trained to be a service dog for Isaac, there were still many times when we wondered if Isaac would need to be placed in another home or residential area because of his self-harm, aggression toward the family, and school problems. There was one time in particular, now referred to as "the Blue Period" in which we actively sought, with the help of our angel support coordinator, somewhere Isaac could live outside of our home. It felt awful to even think of it, but every day felt like hell. There was endless fighting between the kids, yelling from everyone, Isaac constantly tried to go after me or the girls, and the whole feeling of the home was toxic. The only happiness we found felt more like we were going crazy in the head. Despite my faith and knowing God was there for me, I felt forsaken.

Then why was it so hard to even think about letting him live somewhere else? Because he is my son. *My son.* I love him no matter what. I want him to live with us and be with us whenever and wherever possible—but what was I to do? There were times when others would ask if there was any way he could stay with us and if I had considered doing A, B, or C. I know it was all to help, but I felt a little offended thinking, *Don't you think I have already tried everything else I know so he can stay with us? Do you think I just decided one day raising a child is hard so I was going to give up?*

Others said things alluding to the feeling he would not really care to go to another place anyway. Like he doesn't know I am his mom or that home is his safe place to be cared for and he wouldn't cry for me or want me there. I think these kinds of comments hurt the worst. I know they meant well, trying to soften the blow of Isaac leaving, but I'll always be his mama and I hope he always knows that. When I hear him want to come home from school or a family member watching him I feel happy, even if it is because he could then watch his tablet or eat snacks. Like every parent, I want my children to want to come home, but I also couldn't shake the feeling that, no matter what I thought or others said, I was just giving up on my son. I've never had to give a child up for adoption, but I wondered if this is similar to how it feels to give your child to someone else to care for. The guilt, shame, and embarrassment seemed to surround me, especially when I talked to others about it. Any time I spent doing something frivolous, like watching a movie, I felt guilty that I wasn't doing something to help Isaac or somehow help our family. At the same time, I was trying to make it through the day and movies and books were pleasant escapes.

On that same note, I felt guilty and couldn't bear to "give Isaac away" if I was going to keep the service dog I trained. I thought, *I can't keep a dog if I'm going to send my son somewhere else. They either both go or both stay.* So I sold Roxy. I've never cried so hard over an animal in my entire life. I put so much into that dog and to sell her was heart wrenching. We still think of her and miss her. The family that bought her is such a perfect fit and have enjoyed the hard training I put into her. Unfortunately, I put a lot more money into her than I ended up getting out of her, but the most important thing was that she went with the right family. For years I kept in contact and the new owners sent pictures and videos of Roxy, happy in her new environment. In fact, I think she is happier being their pet than our service dog.

Through all of this, we tried to figure out where to place Isaac. Our support coordinator worked with us, but we couldn't find any residential places to take anyone at such a young age. We looked into professional parents, but no one willing could because they had other children in the home and that was one stipulation based on Isaac's harming and aggressive behavior. I also didn't want him to go out of state. In fact, I didn't want him to go more than an hour away. I also didn't want to give up my parental rights in any way, so looking at the various types of care was extremely difficult. I bawled my eyes out thinking of letting someone else take over the rights of my own child, but I was assured I could still maintain rights and also visit him whenever I wanted if we found the right situation. He could even come home on weekends if things got better, but there was no one to take him. My sister even offered to take him on, but she was taking care of three children with disabilities of her own and it didn't seem fair to ask her to take on a fourth. Besides, that would be complicated and emotionally charged; yet, what were we going to do? I felt so hopeless, lost, miserable, helpless, and in despair.

Then we found a ray of hope I didn't expect. Isaac's psychologist gave him a new prescription that changed things for good. It helped get us through. Shortly after, our support coordinator helped get Isaac into a place in Salt Lake City called the University of Utah Neurobehavior Home Program. They take more extreme cases and, after the trauma we went through, Isaac was a perfect candidate. It was there we felt like things got under control. Psychologists, therapists, and doctors worked together in the same place to give the best overall care.

This whole experience, even though it was so hard, taught me many things. There have been and will be times in life where I honestly don't think I will make it through to the next day, the next hour, or even the next minute, but I can and I will. There are three main things that always help me: my Savior, my husband, and my family. I wouldn't make it without them. Others may have other people or things they trust and hope in, but the point is we can make it through. As much as I love to laugh and find joy in the difficulties, I admit there are times when I just need to cry, be angry, and deal with the pain. Some things are just hard and I need to take some time for self-pity. Once I've given myself that space, it's time to rise up and move forward, because there is a reason I am here and purpose for my life. There is a reason my children are my children and they also have a purpose.

Even though Isaac is still in our home, it doesn't mean everything has been easy, but it is better. He is very much like a roller coaster: sometimes for months he will be peachy and we can do many things as a family. Other times he does nothing but scream and cry, making life seem impossible to live peacefully and happily. We must remember that those times will pass. We find much hope in future days and possibilities. We take things one day at a time and treasure the good days. I still wonder if one day Isaac will not be able to stay in our home; it's a reality we face. So when I put him to bed, I thank God I'm the one that gets to read him that same book for the fiftieth time, give him hugs, and hear him say, "Happy Halloween" to wish me goodnight and sometimes "Love you." I treasure the good and am grateful for what I have. I push through the hard to find what there is to learn. Oftentimes I don't see it right away, but given time, that gratitude and learning comes as I allow it to become a part of who I am and what makes me, me. Through it all, we continue to try new things to help our kids. In the beginning, one of the first things that gave us some hope is medication, but it was a scary thing to start.

16
Doctors, Medication, & Oils

Isaac playing with the exam table paper at the doctor's office before the doctor came in

"Was eye of newt not already natural enough?"
—Studio C sketch, "Essential Oils MLM for Witches"

B efore Isaac was three years old, we didn't feel comfortable giving him prescription medicine. I'm not sure why three was the magic number for us, but we waited until then before taking him to the doctor to help him with various issues. Even at the age of one, however, he didn't sleep, hurt himself, and could never sit still. He seriously needed *something* to help him and our family survive day to day, so that's when I started looking at essential oils and melatonin, which were just booming at the time. I heard from other parents the wonders it was doing for their children, so I decided we should try some with Isaac. It felt safer to try something natural on my child. I liked that idea more than pumping my son full of prescription drugs, so I figured there was nothing to lose.

I got a diffuser, hooked up with all the necessary oils, and mixed and meddled with all my new products. I mostly used Vetiver, Serenity, and Balance from doTERRA. Vetiver may have been the most helpful, but Isaac wouldn't wear anything on his wrist or around his neck, so all I could do was diffuse it in the air. It didn't help him while he was at school and he needed it there, too. His poor teachers were in for a whirlwind when my boy came in. Overall, I thought maybe oils helped to take the edge off his ADHD, but not enough to convince me to stick with *only* oils. In my opinion, oils can be a good companion to medication and can help with some of the more common and mild maladies, such as motion sickness or stress. I don't believe solely using oils will cure autism, Fragile X, or cancer, however.

For the first three years, though, we did what we could with melatonin, natural oils, and behavior strategies from various therapists to help us make it through another day. As much as I wish there was a magic pill to cure FXS, there isn't right now. In the meantime, I do my best to give my kids the best treatment to help them succeed in the world, but at times it seems such a difficult burden to bear. People are often of the opinion that medication is "the easy way." In reality, it is difficult to find the right medication, the right dose, and stick with that as your child grows. It's full of trial and error, tears, and triumphs.

I told myself I would wait until Isaac was three before trying prescription medicine; those were the longest three years! The week he turned three, I made sure to have an appointment set up with a doctor to prescribe Isaac medication, but he refused to treat my son due to his young age and liability. I understood, but I was also going out of my mind, and he could see Isaac needed help to control his own body to succeed and function in life. We were at our wits end. I finally went to a family doctor Rachael recommended. He was more understanding of my situation and willing to help. He prescribed Isaac various medications for his ADHD, ODD, anxiety, insomnia, and so forth. It took years to find something that really worked. It took trial and error trying different medications in various doses. Sometimes it helped and other times it made it worse. When we finally found the right fit, though, it changed our family's life for the better.

Unfortunately, this took a lot of doctor visits and Isaac *hated* going to the doctor. I can't blame him. Because he was always so against being there and cooperating, it made for even worse experiences for him where nurses and everyone tried to hold him just to look in his ears. It was all so traumatic. Just taking Isaac into the doctor to get the medication can be a nightmare. Taking him anywhere is quite a circus, but taking him to see any medical professional makes it look like an exorcism.

Thankfully, my children have no major health issues, but there are many things that come up all the time. One concern we had was about his breathing, especially during sleep. He snored and sometimes sounded like he had Apnea. We took him in to one of the best pediatric nose and throat doctors, and boy did the doctor feel he was the best. When we came into the room, Isaac did his typical refusal and screaming. We had to turn his stroller backward to get him into the room, otherwise he would stick his legs out and stop us at the door jam. As I sat by him and tried my best to calm him, I could tell he was agitated and I knew not to get too close or else I'd get scratched or with less hair on my head. Jeremy and I spoke with the doctor about Isaac and shared our concerns about how he reacted to this invasion of his space in his most tender area: the nose, mouth, and ears. Thankfully, we forwent the ears, but I'll never forget what the doctor said.

"Well, we handle lots of kids like this and I've personally had a lot of experience. I have my ways and I don't think it will be a problem," he said. Jeremy and I just looked at each other with eyebrows raised. *Oh really?*

Jeremy piped up. "I don't know. He's really strong, especially in situations like this. He goes into a fight or flight mode and acts like someone is going to kill him."

"Really. I'm not too worried. Like I said, I've dealt with this before. Besides, I have ways of aiding in the process," the doctor replied confidently. *Okay, we'll see,* I thought and I knew Jeremy was on the same page. The doctor's idea of safe holding for Isaac was putting both of his arms in a pillowcase behind his back and lying him down so he couldn't move them. Well, he moved them. The doctor took a pause and called in a nurse. It took the nurse, the doctor, me, and Jeremy doing everything we could to hold his legs, arms, and head while the doctor tried to look up Isaac's nose and into his throat. To no surprise, the doctor barely got to look up his nose and never got a chance to look in his mouth before giving up. I didn't want to say I told you so, but it was tempting.

"Well, I wasn't able to look into his throat and barely got to see into his nose, but there is definitely a lot of inflammation there. For now, I'm going to prescribe a nasal spray, much like allergy medication, that should help with the inflammation which will then help in breathing and hopefully a better sleep."

"Okay," I said, trying to hear over Isaac's crying. I did my best to comfort him, but I knew we needed to get out of there and then he'd be okay. When we did come home, we realized we were expected to put nasal spray up his nose all the time after the doctor couldn't even look inside. It was pretty ridiculous, so that didn't last long!

Unfortunately, some of the tactics used in the doctor's offices, such as the pillowcase in this instance, make me feel like special needs kids get treated inhumanely; however, when you need to accomplish something for health reasons, what other choice do we have but to do whatever it takes? When Isaac got stitches, we had to put him to sleep, but just to do that was like roping a calf! You can't just let him bleed out! I feel awful, because Isaac just doesn't understand. He doesn't see we are trying to help him out of love.

Another such instance happened during COVID-19. Isaac was scheduled to go to the hospital for sedation for a routine dental exam and cleaning as well as blood work to find out if there were issues causing bowel problems and other things. In order to do that, they needed a confirmed negative COVID-19 test. He had no symptoms, but it was protocol. The whole thing was a joke. We couldn't even look up his nose without a fight or look in his teeth without violence—we needed a miracle.

I showed up at our designated testing place and they gave me a saliva test tube. He can't spit into that, of course, so for forty-five minutes, I tried to get two mL of spit into this tube while trying to not upset him and let him watch his tablet linked to my phone's hotspot. Eventually he got tired of me poking in his mouth and the tube was compressed at the top from him biting it so hard. I took the tube back (this was a drive-thru testing place) and explained to the worker that I tried, showing him a blob of spit at the bottom of a chewed and flattened tube. He then said we'd do a nasal swab. I hoped it was one of the easy ones that don't get stuck into your brains, but, of course, it was not. We parked and the nightmare ensued. I'd done stuff like this too many times and it triggered me to cry no matter what. I was a mess in front of a stranger. It wasn't the first or last time.

I got out of the driver's seat and knelt down in front of him. He still had his five-point harness on, so I felt good and the guy doing the test waited at the open window. At first we tried to be calm, gentle, and allow Isaac to help. He soon began a total meltdown. I finally tried to hold him down as best as my little arms could against his. At one point, he pulled my hair and my head was sideways and down toward the ground as I cried and spoke softly, "It's okay, buddy. Please let go of Mommy's hair. Don't hurt Mommy, okay? We just need to do this swab and touch your nose. It's going to be okay," I said over and over, trying to calm myself as much as him. I told Isaac I was sorry, then held him down with all my might as my last push while the guy got the best swab of Isaac's nose that he could in a matter of seconds.

Afterward, I looked like I'd been in a car wreck. My hair was a frizzed-out mess, I had bloody scratches on my arms, and I was crying. It felt like it took an eternity, but by some miracle, we did it. I say "we," because it was a team effort with me and the guy in his hazmat suit doing the test. I was scratched, pinched, and kicked. I got my hair pulled and pulled out. I had to hold my son down by force while he shoved me and used his feet to push my head up against the roof of the van. Isaac was constrained the whole time by his five-point harness seat, but it wasn't near enough.

Do you know what it feels like to restrain your child? Or to have doctors and nurses try to do so alongside you? It's awful and traumatizing. So why am I sharing it? Because most parents don't tell anyone, but this is what we go through all the time. This is our normal. Our reality. We stay silent because we are afraid or embarrassed. We don't want to be pitied or shamed. We don't talk about what life is really like behind the scenes. That's why I'm writing. And I guess it's one way I get my therapy to deal with life.

After the COVID-19 test was finally over, I told Isaac we were done. He immediately stopped fighting and was totally fine. I told him to tell the man "thank you" and he did. Isaac got a sucker and the man said I could have one, too (since I was bawling and looked like I'd been through a tornado). We both apologized and asked if the other was okay. Let's just say that that young college kid will never forget that day.

But most of all, I hope that young man remembers this: I didn't yell at my son. I didn't fight back. I told him he did a great job after it was all over and gave him a big hug. I said, "Love you, bud," and everything was okay again. I want people to know that despite the pain, there is love and compassion. Isaac gets scared and doesn't fully understand. These kids deserve to be loved and cared for. They are not less than anyone—I would say they are more. Because I love each of my children so much, I think it hurts that much more when they go through hard things or don't realize I am trying to help them; instead, they go to fight or flight and often people get hurt. It's times like these I am afraid of having to let Isaac go one day, and I don't know whether that shows more love or the lack of love.

After the COVID-19 test, I think Isaac was more fine than I was once everything was said and done. I couldn't stop crying, but I had a dentist appointment to go to and Jeremy was taking time off already to watch the girls. I wanted to get the tiny filling over with, so I dropped off Isaac and went to my appointment looking like a fool with my eyes red and puffy. I kept telling them I was okay and I just wanted to go ahead and get this done. I knew I was totally fine, but my mind couldn't stop repeating the hard day. It took everything in me to be strong.

My dentist had compassion, because he knows I have three children with disabilities. He was kind and said enough but not too much. If anything, going to the dentist was just what I needed! I could be alone, lay down, and "relax." It's places like the dentist getting a filling that special needs parents get a break. Sad, but true. At least then I had enough time to calm down so my children didn't have to see me crying...again.

But as I got into my car after the dentist that day, I cried for a whole different reason. I saw many kind texts and voicemails on my phone. My husband had reached out to family members on my behalf and I was flooded with texts, pictures, stories, and love by many. I knew this was started from the love of my husband, even though he didn't say a word about it. I'm so grateful. I'm grateful for all the people around me that continually reach out and have always been there for me and my family. Some people think I'm superhuman, but oftentimes I feel as fragile as glass; one little tap could make me shatter. Honestly, I've shattered many times, but my friends and family put me back together and the atonement of my Savior Jesus Christ is the glue. I am "like a broken vessel," as Jeffrey R. Holland says. At the end of that day, it was time to go home, take a quick break, and proceed to change a couple of poopy bums, get snacks for the kids, and then make dinner. All in the life of the FX mom.

Once the trials are over, I'm grateful for them, because they help me be more compassionate and understanding. It reminds me of the formation of a rainbow. There are two parts: the light and the water. The water is turbulent trials we go through and the light is my Savior who shines on me, and together, something beautiful is made. I've found I'm not so judgmental of other struggling mothers because so many times I've been in hard circumstances and judged. We go through a lot. So we might be a little crazy. Have compassion. We are getting through one day at a time. I hope we can all understand that everyone has trials. I know I am not alone. I know my trials aren't the hardest in the world; life is hard for everyone, but maybe by reading this, someone out there will feel that they can keep going, too. You can know God is there, despite the pain. Maybe you can discover that Jesus Christ loves all his children, no matter what they can or can't do; no matter what they did or didn't do.

17

The Dentist

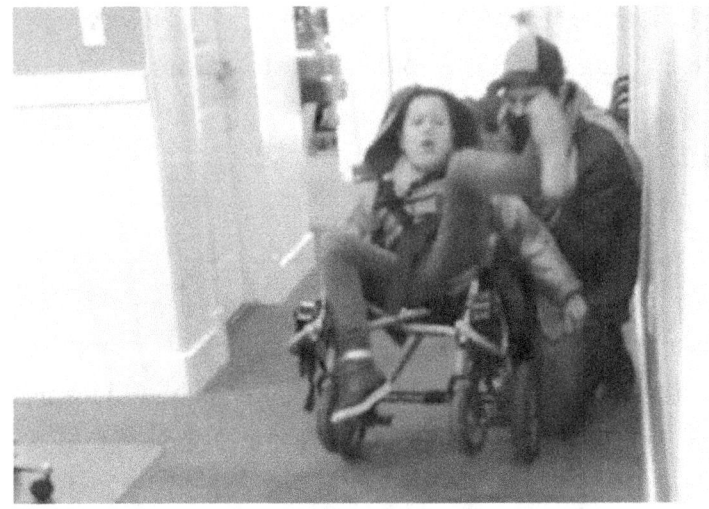

Isaac having a meltdown at the dentist office while Jeremy tries to help

"Cavities are meanies and meanies don't belong in your mouth."
−Storybots, "Brush Your Teeth"

A long with the doctor, dentists are also a nightmare with Isaac. When he was two, I started taking him alongside Amelia, so it's not like I didn't give him plenty of trial runs. No matter what we did, though, he screamed and cried. He tried anything and everything so the dentist could not even brush his teeth. We never even tried getting X-ray images. He never cared about a prize at the end, either. Amelia was always happy to get his toy, too, though. That was fine with me! One time we had to go in for an emergency appointment, because Isaac had a loose tooth that never came out and lodged back into his gums. The dentist ended up pulling it out right then and there, because we didn't want to have to put him under just for that. He freaked out at first, but as soon as the tooth was out, Isaac was a happy camper. Still, out of all our experiences prior, the last one was a time that changed things.

"Okay, Isaac," I said on our way to the dentist. "We are going to the dentist now. He is going to look at your teeth, okay?"

No response.

Five minutes later...

"Okay, Isaac," I repeated. "We are almost to the dentist. He is so nice and you will be so brave!"

No response...then we got close enough to see the dentist office building. Great cries and wails escaped Isaac and he moved about, kicking the back of my seat so my head bobbed and my voice got choppy as I said, "It's okay, Isaac. It will be quick. You'll be okay."

We parked in the parking lot and he started to flip. I took a deep breath and gave Jeremy a look of *here we go again* exasperation. We got his stroller out of the back of our minivan and pulled it up along the side where Isaac sat in his five-point harness seat.

"Okay, Isaac, we need to get out of your seat and sit in your stroller," I said. He just yelled and moaned back in response.

"Here, I'll get him out and you get the girls," Jeremy decided. He handled Isaac physically better than I could. Isaac pushed me around. I locked the wheels in place and Jeremy unbuckled him, but he was scratching and kicking. "Come on, Isaac," Jeremy prodded. "I'm going to tickle you!"

Before I knew it, Eliza tried to get out of the van and got her hair pulled by Isaac, so she started crying. "Oh shoot, sweetie, I'm sorry. Did he pull your hair? Oh, come here," I said as I hugged and consoled her. Shortly after that, our new dog, Luna, came out and wandered around (I don't know why she was there)!

"Luna! Get back in the van!" I got after Luna and put her back in the vehicle. At that point, I tried to comfort Eliza, keep the dog in the car, calm Evelyn down (she was mad to be stuck in her car seat), and all while Jeremy tickled and wrestled Isaac to get into his stroller.

Before I knew it, I looked and Isaac was only half on the seat of his stroller and kicked his legs so he was now halfway across the parking lot with Jeremy trying to get control.

"Whoa. Where ya goin', buddy?" I said, going over to help them. Of course people looked at us, wondering what was happening. We tried to laugh, because I didn't want them to think we were stealing him or hurting him, and it also helped to laugh instead of cry.

"Come on, bud. We gotta get in your seat," Jeremy and I kept bribing, prodding, and tickling and doing everything to get him in his chair before he ran out into the road or attacked one of his sisters. After several minutes of him scratching, arching his back, hitting, and pushing, we finally got him in the chair and wrestled him down to buckle him safely. Once in the chair, he tried to push back with his feet on the ground.

We were just barely through the doors of the dentist office and I already felt like I'd been in a rodeo when I heard, "Fowler family?" One of the dental assistants called out to signify our turn to go back. Of course, we couldn't get Isaac through the door to the next room. He yelled and fought and everyone stared.

"It's okay, Isaac. We just need to get through these doors. The dentist is nice and he will look at your mouth, then give you a prize," I said calmly. His response was to scream and push his feet into the floor and push so the handle of the stroller rammed into my stomach. I guess it was fitting that he was wearing a costume coat that made him look like Hulk. Exasperated, I looked at Jeremy.

"Here, Jer," I said, frustrated. "You take him and I'll take Evelyn." We got him through the door by turning him around and going through the door backward before he had a chance to grab the door frame to stop us. Then Jeremy and I took turns between wrestling Issac or holding Evelyn and helping the other two girls from the sidelines. Thankfully, Eliza did amazingly well and got X-rays for the very first time.

"Yay! Good job, Eliza!" I cheered while Evelyn clung relentlessly to me. Waiting made things worse. We continually tipped Isaac's chair back so he didn't ram into us, using his feet as leverage. At that point, Jeremy and I both had scratches and were at our wits end. While the two older girls got their teeth cleaned, Isaac sat, moaning and fighting in the background. Finally, it was time to have the dentist look in Isaac's mouth. The dentist brought his chair to Isaac, but he flipped out, kicking and screaming. There was me, Jeremy, the dentist, and three or four other nurses trying to keep his legs and arms under control so the dentist could do his job. It wasn't happening.

"It's okay, Isaac," I said soothingly. "It's going to be okay. The dentist is just going to look at your teeth. Can you open wide?" I tried to be calm and kind. I tried to be a good mom. Suddenly, he grabbed the flabby back part of my arm and dug his nails in as hard as he could.

"Isaac. Ouch, Isaac. Stop." I tried to remain calm and collected. It started to hurt and the embarrassment of it all piled on as a room full of strangers stared at us. All I could think is that I'm trying to help him feel safe, I'm being kind and nonthreatening, yet here is my own son, hurting me so much it's making me cry. Finally, Jeremy unleashed Isaac's grip and we continued. I saw a bruise and deep scratch marks on my arm, but we tried to move forward.

Suddenly out of nowhere, he bit my finger and I screamed out in pain and complete surprise. He'd never done that before. At that point, I am a mixture of fear, embarrassment, shock, and sadness. Thankfully, he let go of my finger and I walked away and said, "I'm done." I went in the corner and cried as I watched my son and a circle of adults try to calm him while he hurt others and screamed. It was an awful sight.

The dentist tried to look in his mouth and Isaac started to gag. He threw up a little and the chaos continued. Finally, Jeremy called out, "Stop! He's going to throw up everywhere. This isn't worth it." Everyone stopped and backed away. The dentist turned to me and Evelyn sitting on my lap. It was her turn.

I sat her, back down, on my lap so I could hold her arms and the dentist could look in her mouth. She fought and cried a little, but it was short and no one got hurt. The kids get their prizes. I tried to keep smiling and act like everything was fine. We left and there was no problem getting Isaac through the doors or back in the car, because he knows he gets to go home now. As we drove off, I started ugly crying. Through it all, I told Jeremy, "I'm never doing that again."

"I agree. He acts like we are trying to kill him. He goes into fight or flight mode and his strength triples."

We sat there without talking, just thinking. It wasn't silent by any means—Evelyn cried, Isaac made his noises, there was a movie playing, and I tried not to sob. Once home, I realized it was dinner time and I had to put on my big girl pants and feed my family. I decided to blast "Fight Song" and "Roar" while I fried ground beef for some easy spaghetti while I intermittently sang into the spatula. I ended it off with David Archuleta's "OK, All Right" song, and then... life went on as usual.

Later that night, Jeremy and I talked about the day. I was focused on how horrible and traumatic it was, but he brought something back to my attention. Before we left the office, the dentist came up and talked to Isaac. Not us. Isaac. I really should mention here that the pediatric dentist we go to really is amazing. We've been going to him since Isaac was two or three and he is nothing but kind. After all that had gone on, being spit upon, scratched, kicked, etc., he came up to Isaac and said, "Hey, it's okay, buddy. You did great." He had a tissue in his hand and wiped Isaac's mouth from the drool and boogers. He had no anger or frustration. It was just pure charity. It didn't matter what Isaac had done—he knew that wasn't really him. The dentist just talked to him and cleaned him up with love. I wish more people could be as loving and understanding as that dentist. If only we could all treat each other better.

However, I did have to face the reality of what had to come next because of this experience: sedation. The next day I coordinated with Isaac's doctors and dentist office to coordinate the necessary paperwork and get things moving forward. Isaac's doctors had wanted to draw several different labs for years, but were waiting for another reason for sedation. Well, this was it. We set up several labs to be drawn to check his thyroid, vitamin deficiencies, Celiac, and so forth. We knew he wouldn't sit still to get blood drawn or check his teeth for cavities, but these were things that needed to be done, so we went forward and scheduled his sedation at a nearby hospital. It took a month or two to get it all coordinated and underway, but I still wasn't ready when the big day came.

I woke up early in the morning, then woke up Isaac, and got us both ready. Jeremy stayed home with the girls because this was during the time of homeschool. It just so happened that it was April first, April Fool's Day. I should've known better! Isaac didn't know what he was in for; turns out, I didn't either. Isaac had been sedated one other time when he got stitches in his foot. We had to hold him down in the ER with a rag over his bleeding foot and it was awful. They ended up sedating him because they couldn't put the few stitches in his foot with him wriggling and screaming. I was right there with him. It was sad to watch him slowly stop moving and his eyes close. I cried because it was like looking at a dying child. I know it sounds dramatic, but it's true. At least I was by his side to make sure he was okay and be the last face he saw before falling asleep. This time would be different.

"Hi, is this Isaac?" A friendly woman at the front desk said, obviously expecting us.

"Yes. I'm his mom. We are here for a dental exam, but we also need to draw labs," I said.

"Oh yes, they told me there would be labs and we have everything ready to go. I just need you to look over the information and sign that everything is here and correct."

Surprisingly, Isaac was pretty calm and hadn't started freaking out yet. I looked over the paperwork and signed with no problem.

"Thank you," the woman said. "Cheryl will show you to your room where you will wait until we are ready for him."

"Okay, thank you," I said. Another woman brought us to an adjacent empty room where we sat and waited. Before she left, she asked, "Is he pretty good with doctors and shots or will we need some people to help out?"

"We will definitely need a few strong adults to help out," I replied. She nodded and smiled in understanding. Although Isaac was still doing well, I could tell he knew something was up. He was getting agitated and occasionally whined. There was a hospital gown I was supposed to be dressing him in, but he wasn't having it. They would just have to put him in it once he was out.

A short time later, the anesthesiologist came in with a few other men.

"We have a shot for Isaac that will be quick in his arm. Then he will calm down enough we should be able to get him on this hospital bed and get him sedated."

"Okay," I said. I was sad to put Isaac through this. After some sneaky moves and Isaac crying, a shot was given. We waited for a minute, but he did not calm down, so they gave him another one. He finally started zoning out and we hurried to get him out of his chair and onto the hospital bed. He was still crying and flailing his limbs. I began to pick up our jackets and get ready to follow them.

"Should I just leave our stuff here?" I asked innocently.

One of the men looked at me and replied, "You just need to stay here and wait in this room. You can keep all of the stuff here with you. We'll take good care of him."

I stood there in shock for a moment. I felt like a child, embarrassed that I expected to go and couldn't.

"Oh. Yeah. Okay," I stammered, trying to gain control of my emotions and rising panic.

"We'll keep him safe and comfortable and have him back to you," replied the man, an apologetic look on his face that made me feel even more stupid. I had just assumed I was going with him to comfort him as he went to sleep and make sure everything was okay. Instead, Isaac was still awake when they took him away. He didn't know what was going on and his mommy wasn't there. He was terrified, panicked, and crying. I felt so awful. After they closed the door to my room and took Isaac away, I just bawled. I wish they would have at least put him to sleep before taking him away. I wish I was better informed about the process before it happened, but at that point, there was nothing I could do.

I sat in my little hospital room alone. I did my grocery shopping on my phone to get my mind off things in order to stop crying and to try and lessen my burdens when I got home later. The nurses kept peeking in to make sure I was okay, but I just wanted to be left alone.

"Do you want any juice or a snack?" one nurse would ask. Then another would come in and say, "We have some really yummy crackers and Pepsi products, if you'd like." But I just stayed in my room, ate a few snacks I had in my bag, and waited and worried. Finally, after over an hour, the door opened and the dentist came in.

"Hey," he said, stepping inside. "He did great!"

I tried to smile and replied, "Oh good. He did all right?"

"Yeah, and guess what?" he said with a smile, "He doesn't have any cavities!"

I was surprised by this, seeing that Isaac's teeth rarely got brushed. I was happy, of course, but I also thought this whole thing was pointless if there weren't any issues with his teeth—at least now we knew that for sure.

"That's great news. Surprising, though," I laughed. He smiled.

"Yeah, he must have nice, strong teeth. He's pretty lucky," the dentist replied. I smiled and nodded my head in agreement. He continued, "Well, he is just waking up and it's taking a little longer than expected."

"Is everything okay, though?" I asked, worry coming into my voice.

"Yes, he will be out soon. Just be aware our kids that come out of this are often very irritable," he said. "You may see a little blood in his mouth as well, which is normal. I have a paper here with all the information you need, but my number is at the bottom if you have any questions."

I couldn't think of any questions at the moment and just wanted to see my boy. The dentist left me alone again and I waited some more. Finally, I heard Isaac's familiar moans and wails coming down the hospital corridor. They brought him in, and although he was still mostly out of it, he was awake enough to try and escape the bed.

"He needs to stay lying down or else he will probably throw up," said a nearby nurse that had come into the room with several others. They tried to offer him crackers and water, but he just shoved them away, moaning and crying. Again, I tried to be strong. I couldn't be a bawling mess; my kid needed me. I know they wanted us to stay longer, but Isaac would not stay in that bed and was freaking out, so I decided we just needed to get into the van ASAP.

"Would you like help getting to your car?" a nurse asked me.

"No, thanks," I replied with a slight smile. I just wanted to get Isaac out of the hospital and away from strangers so he would calm down. I also wanted my own anxiety to chill out. So there I was, alone in the parking lot, having wheeled him out and locked the stroller breaks by the side of the van. I opened the van door and got everything ready to make a smooth transition from stroller seat to car seat. What I had not anticipated was the complete dead weight of Isaac, since he was still a little sedated. Holy cow, I'm surprised

I didn't burst an eye vessel or pop out a hernia. *What was I thinking?* I wondered. I pleadingly looked in the windows of the rooms we just left, hoping to find someone watching me, though terrified they had seen me attempt a time or two with no success. There was no one and I was in the middle of the stroller and the car, so I said a prayer and did a heave ho! It wasn't the smoothest transition, but Isaac didn't complain and all my innards stayed inside me, so I say it was a success. Next time, I am definitely getting help, especially because he weighs much more now.

When we got home, Jeremy helped me. We had a caregiver there to sit with him the rest of the day and make sure he wasn't just sleeping. If I'm being honest, it was kind of nice to have him lethargic for a day. He was so chill. It was still sad to watch, though, and the poor little guy got a bloody nose. It was no small feat for him. The one positive thing I saw was with him being so laid back and tired, we didn't see any behavior problems whatsoever. He was calm and snuggly and he didn't bug his sisters once. If only we could get that good behavior without the lethargy.

18

Church & Religion

The Fowler family ready to go to church Easter morning

"I'm still standing!"
–Elton John

B ehavior is a huge issue I deal with as a parent of special needs children, and one any parent has to deal with, honestly. When Isaac was little, his behavior at church was the hardest to bear each week. Sunday was a day I dreaded. It is supposed to be a "day of rest," but for my family, it was the hardest, most hectic day of the week and I would get anxiety Saturday night just imagining the next morning. Even thinking about trying to button up a shirt for Isaac to wear gave me anxiety, so I bought polos instead and it saved me. I remember crying and asking God if He really wanted me and my family to attend church, why was this so difficult? I didn't understand. My life seemed to be a contradiction, because everything spiritual we wanted to do, Isaac seemed to fight against us.

Despite people saying our children were angels, Jeremy often thought aloud, wondering if this wasn't the case. We related so fully with a scripture in Mark: 24 of the King James version of the Bible where a father brings his writhing son to Jesus for healing, because he is constantly hurting himself and others. He states, "And ofttimes it hath cast him into the fire, and into the waters..." which we understand, because our children have no idea of the dangers as they run into the road, walk toward a bonfire, or nearly drown in a pool. I've always loved a talk Elder Jeffrey R. Holland gave in General Conference of April 2013, talking about this exact story:

This man is saying, in effect, "Our whole family is pleading. Our struggle never ceases. We are exhausted. Our son falls into the water. He falls into the fire. He is continually in danger, and we are continually afraid. We don't know where else to turn. Can you help us? We will be grateful for *anything*—a partial blessing, a glimmer of hope, some small lifting of the burden carried by this boy's mother every day of her life. If *thou* canst do *anything...* "

The scripture goes on to say, "And straightway the father of the child cried out, and said with tears, Lord, I believe; help thou mine unbelief." Jesus then heals this boy. To be completely honest, I have wished more than once for God to heal my boy—but it is not meant to be. Slowly I learn there are reasons behind this I do not fully understand, but know is for the best.

In the Church of Jesus Christ of Latter-day Saints, we have a special Sunday where new babies can be blessed by a worthy male member, usually their father. It came time to bless our Eliza and Jeremy was going to be the one to do it. A lot of our family from both sides were there to watch and support us, but no one could help us with Isaac that day. Before the meeting even began, he thrashed on the floor and wailed. He started to hurt himself on the metal folding chairs we were sitting on toward the back of the crowded room. Family and ward members watched and tried to help or ignored us and tried to give us privacy in a hard situation. Finally, Jeremy and I left Eliza with my mom while the meeting started and we both struggled to get Isaac to an empty room in the church. There we prayed. Isaac tried to give him a blessing while Isaac was banging his head on the hard floor and screaming. We truly hoped for a miracle, but the miracle we wanted didn't come. We knew it was almost time for Jeremy to bless Eliza in front of the congregation, but we couldn't bring Isaac back in there. We decided he had to go and I would have to miss this special and important moment in our lives. Just as he was about to leave, a young man who had worked with Isaac before came into the room and said, "Hey, they are about to do the baby blessing. I saw you guys leave and wondered if I could sit with Isaac so you can be in there." That was our miracle. I was able to go and watch this beautiful blessing because a young man followed the direction of the Spirit and came to serve our entire family in what may have seemed to some like a small, insignificant moment. Honestly, it was the most memorable and spiritual blessing Jeremy has ever done for our kids. Through this experience and others, I have slowly come to understand how important it is to have faith in my Savior, Jesus Christ, and not just on desired outcomes. I've learned to be faithful, even if things don't work out the way I want. I've learned to follow the example of Shadrach, Meshach, and Abed-nego in the Bible who believed God could save them from the fiery furnace, and yet said, "*But if not*...we will not serve thy Gods." God can heal me, my son, and my family, *but if not*, I still believe and worship God, the eternal father and His son, Jesus Christ. Over and over I have come to realize miracles happen all the time all around us, but sometimes we just have to realize they don't come in the time or way we want.

After that difficult but memorable Sunday experience, there have been a plethora of hard Sundays to follow. In fact, just trying to get ready for church on a regular Sunday each week felt like a joke. I'd come up to the church building with my hair disheveled, dirt on my clothes, and a few scratches on my arms before church even started. After church, I felt and probably looked just like Marv on *Home Alone 2* after Kevin chucked bricks at his head. "Harry? Harry? Harry...?" But it was during church that really took the life out of me. We tried so hard to listen to talks and partake of the Sacrament, but it is pretty much impossible when there is a child flailing on the floor and screaming. We made a permanent residence on the couch outside the chapel in the foyer area.

One time, Jeremy held one year-old Isaac during the main meeting as Isaac cried and had a meltdown. Suddenly, out of nowhere, Isaac's head slammed back into Jeremy's cheekbone. I heard the sound of impact ten feet away. For weeks, Jeremy had a huge bruise on his face, courtesy of Isaac's head. In fact, we all have multiple battle scars from Isaac over the years. It's no surprise we were worried about putting him in a Sunday School nursery class with a bunch of kids ages eighteen months to three years. Sometimes Isaac was happy jumping around, but his energy and lack of spatial recognition would cause harm to others; let alone the times he was actually angry and acted out.

First, we put door handle guards on the inside of the nursery so he would stop escaping and not run outside to the road, but that was a fire hazard, so they were required to remove them. In my opinion, it was far more likely that Isaac would run out and get hit by a car than a fire breaking out where an adult couldn't open the child-proof door handle, but we did our best. I knew we were in trouble, though, when I got pulled out of my church class to attend to Isaac. The woman had wide eyes and a panicked look as I quickly (yet reverently) booked it out of class, trying not to be embarrassed. I soon discovered the entire nursery had been evacuated out into the hall—all except Isaac. He was butt-naked because he had stripped off all his clothes, including a full, poopy diaper, the contents of which were on the carpet and spreading fast.

I took action and cleaned up Isaac and put on a clean diaper, all while he jumped up and down. I cleaned up what I could in the nursery, left the rest to the other women in the room with terrified eyes, then left the church with Isaac in nothing but a diaper and walked home in high heels. I don't think Isaac went back to nursery again after that. We ended up going home early, going on walks while waiting for our other family members to be done, or playing in the gym room. Once, I brought the red wagon for him to ride in on the gym floor while Jeremy taught his lesson in Sunday School, and then we switched so I could teach my lesson to the women's class afterward. I always felt like a three-ring circus. Thankfully, everyone at church was kind and still wanted us to be there, despite everything.

When Evelyn first went into nursery it was hit and miss. The year she turned three and was old enough to join the next group called Sunbeams, I had a lot of anxiety. The first day didn't go well and I had PTSD thinking this would be like Isaac all over again and she would never go to class. But one Sunday she tentatively did it with the help of kind teachers. Since then she literally can't wait until it is time to go to her class. I am so grateful for nursery and primary school teachers. I don't think they often get the credit they truly deserve. It's a tough job to be volunteering for, yet it has made a huge difference in my family's life. There were times when having my children in a church Sunday school class was the only respite I got during the week. They are truly angels to do what they do!

When Isaac got older, we obtained a Convaid Stroller. It was a way we could go to church with him more contained for everyone's safety, but even with the stroller, we had some mishaps. Isaac has the bad habit of sticking his hands out as we push him along the hallways and they are just at the perfect height to hit people's backsides or pull at women's skirts. One time, I thought he was going to expose a woman we passed. Sometimes I reassure people it wasn't me, it was an accident, we aren't being inappropriate, and we continue walking with red faces. Other times we just laugh about it, especially if the person knows our family and Isaac well. A well-intentioned woman came to bend down and say hello to Isaac one Sunday, but he wasn't in the best mood, so he grabbed her hair and pulled. I was mortified and worried he would hurt her, but she was incredibly gracious. I saw the same woman while walking home a little later that day after church and she made sure to approach me and say Isaac didn't hurt her, she loved us all, and everything was okay, to which I cried because I was relieved, embarrassed, and felt her unconditional love.

There are times Isaac stays for most of church while others we have to walk him home because his crying, whining, and screaming are too much for anyone to bear. No one can hear anyone talking over the speakers and I get so flustered trying to keep composure while he is kicking and yelling and scratching. There were many times Jeremy and I took turns having "church" with Isaac outside. We'd walk around the church and sing songs, look at nature, and wait for the others to come out of the building so we could all go home together.

Most of the time people are kind. Some have come up to me to talk about their own relation with autism or a disability. We get so much love from others for our entire family. In fact, there have been several people that have told us Isaac actually brings the Spirit more at church. It's at that point I feel loved and accepted instead of unwanted and disturbing to others. I really wish everyone could have such kind neighbors as I do right now. There's always someone making accommodations for Isaac to go to his classes, participate in activities, and feel welcomed, even though he shows no outward desire to go to class or appreciation toward them. I often get asked what others can do to help Isaac at church. I don't always know what to say, and oftentimes Isaac goes home early with our nanny now, but the fact that there are people concerned and trying is what matters. It makes it so we don't feel so outcast and alone.

We feel wanted and thought about. People pray for us on a daily basis and sometimes that's all we need; most of the time that's all anyone can do for us.

Still, we continue to struggle off and on. At one point, we met with our bishop, a leader in our church congregation, to talk about what to do. We felt it was better if Isaac stayed home, but at the time, we didn't have a caregiver to do that, so Jeremy and I had to miss church every other week. There was just so much stress, embarrassment, and scenes caused by us that it was becoming too much; however, our Bishop was concerned we wouldn't be getting the sacrament each week, assured us Isaac was welcome, and helped us to see the importance of continuing to push through and go as much as possible. Isaac has gotten much better at church as long as we follow certain routines. We have to walk him to church in his stroller from our house, rain or shine, or else he will not go. If we try to ride the surrey bike like we used to or ride in the car, the transition to his stroller is practically impossible and then he is a nightmare inside the building. Pretzels and water are essential to have as well. Sometimes we do the tablet on mute if we are desperate. I'm just grateful we get to attend church and now Diana is here to help when needed.

Between Sunday attendance during the week, we try to do family scripture study and prayers. Isaac runs away whenever we start! Prayer and scriptures study looks something like this: we sing a song "together." Usually it's just me, Millie, and Jeremy, and then one of us tries to share a scripture and spiritual insight. Evelyn sings and talks about her book she's trying to read, Eliza plays with dolls and sometimes participates when prodded, and Isaac bolts out of the room and comes back when we are all finished. I have to do fun activities and include Isaac in the details if I want him to stick around, but as time moves on, it's getting better. We are all learning and I am learning he doesn't need to be pushed so hard. We all do what we can and try to keep peace.

I take comfort in the promise made by Russell M. Nelson in 2018 concerning the new program in my church curriculum called, "Come, Follow Me." He said, "...as you diligently work to remodel your home into a center of gospel learning, over time your sabbath days will truly be a delight. Your children will be excited to learn and to live the Savior's teachings, and the influence of the adversary in your life and in your home will decrease. Changes in your family will be dramatic and sustaining." Believe it or not, I have seen these promises come to pass. The more effort we put into our family spirituality, the more blessed we are. I don't think Isaac would've stayed in our home due to his aggression and all the issues if it wasn't for our constant diligence in scripture study. That's not to say that if we do all we can everything will work out peachy, but I do know we will find peace through upheaval and joy when the tough times roll in. I know oftentimes I have felt alone in my daily struggles, but my Savior is there. I like what Elder David A. Bednar once said:

In a moment of weakness we may cry out, "No one knows what it is like. No one understands." But the Son of God perfectly knows and understands...He has perfect empathy...and can reach out, touch, succor, heal, and strengthen us to be more than we could ever be and help us to do that which we could never do relying upon our own power.

Everything seems worth the struggle when I hear each of my children say their prayers before going to bed at night. Isaac's prayer entails mostly gibberish with a few repeated phrases, but always ends with a big "Amen!" at the end with his arms up. When Eliza said her first prayer in front of my whole family, I was so proud. Hearing Evelyn try to say a prayer and always say "amen" at the end is precious. It shows me they *are* learning. I love to see Eliza play church with her dolls and talk about Jesus Christ and how He loves us in her own simple ways. It makes it all worth it. So even though pretzels get thrown on the floor, water dumped on dresses, screams are heard throughout the building, and sometimes the girls' hair isn't done, we still make the effort to go to church every week to worship, remember our Savior, renew promises with our Heavenly Father, and connect with our friends and neighbors.

The trials we face are what make us the people we are. This opposition and struggle is necessary for growth and becoming. Elder Bednar once told a story of a man and wife whose truck got stuck in the snowy mountains. Not knowing what else to do, they decided to do what they originally came up there to do: chop wood. They chopped and piled all the wood they could fit into the back of the truck. Then they decided to try once again to get out of the snowdrift, and with ease, the truck pulled out and back onto the road. Of this story he drew this conclusion:

"Sometimes we mistakenly may believe that happiness is the absence of a load. But bearing a load is a necessary and essential part of the plan of happiness...(and) our individual load needs to generate spiritual traction..." He then goes on to quote a scripture from the Book of Mormon, Mosiah 24:14-15, that says, "And I will ease the burdens which are put upon our shoulders, that even you cannot feel them upon your backs...And now it came to pass that the burdens which were laid upon (them) were made light."

I don't know how many times I have thought back on things I've gone through and thought the only way I got through that or did that is because of the blessings given to me by Heavenly Father, prayers from myself and others, and the atonement of Jesus Christ that strengthens me. I am also grateful for the many angels surrounding our family. Another helpful item I've come upon is a book called *The Accessible Church* by Kerri-Ann Hayes that can be shared with other members of faith and their leaders. There will still be hard days, though. Sometimes I look back at a hard Sunday and start rocking out to Elton John's song, "I'm still standing. Yeah, yeah, yeah." Thankfully, Isaac has become more tolerable to church these days.

My family and I keep standing through the difficult moments. Another one I remember is the year Isaac turned eight years old. In my church, eight is when children are typically baptized, so it's a big deal. I've heard of families going ahead with a regular baptism or choosing not to and instead having a special party to celebrate the child. We chose to do neither. His eighth birthday came and went. We realized a special event or party would only bring more anxiety to Isaac and wasn't something he desired. We also felt he didn't have an understanding sufficient enough to warrant being baptized and cleansed of wrongs for which he may not be accountable. We celebrated his birthday like we often do by getting him chips instead of cake and going as a family to a trampoline park. As different birthdays come in the future that mark certain milestones, such as driving and dating at sixteen, a two-year mission for our church at age eighteen, and so forth, I know it will cause a bit of pain for me and Jeremy as we reflect and mourn over what might have been; however, I know we will find comfort in the Lord and a way to celebrate our son and his accomplishments in a way that is best for him. After all, we aren't the typical family and so our celebrations, accomplishments, and happy moments may look different than others. Come to think of it, if Isaac ever gets out of diapers, *that* will be a moment worth celebrating! I'd definitely have a party for that!

19

Diapers & Potty Training

Isaac learning to go to the bathroom on his own

"I poop in the morning. I poop in the day. I poop when the feeling comes my way, and then bam! I'm full of jam!"
—"I Poop" by Auraganix Kids

Like I mentioned before, out of my four children, the youngest three are in diapers. Eliza is mostly in underwear now, but she still has plenty of accidents. All in all, that's a lot of poop. I've dealt with so much poop in my life that my family affectionately calls me the "Poop Queen." No joke. Over the years I have been given a poop emoji cup, bean bag, hat, pillow, balloon, and candy dispenser. My mom even has a poop emoji Halloween costume I wore. I've seriously thought about buying the poop emoji slippers. It's like Nacho Libre's stretchy pants—"it's for fun" (say that last part in his accent).

Too bad poop isn't fun. I'll tell you, though, I am the fastest poopy-diaper-changer this side of the Mississippi. I can clean up some of the nastiest diapers quickly and efficiently. I even change diapers with them standing up! In fact, Isaac used to jump constantly and I sometimes changed poop diapers while he stood there, jumping up and down (mostly just wet ones).

There are times I feel like a rodeo queen roping calves. I know that sounds crude talking about my kids, but if you saw how it goes down, you'd see how similar it is. My mom always felt the same way when changing Isaac's diaper. He was always the wildest, and literally bucks while he's on his back and you're trying to wipe him. Now Evelyn, being the youngest, gives me the hardest time as I try to wipe her and she squeezes her cute little cheeks and tries to kick or roll over. As much as I dislike changing diapers, I have grown quite used to it. Sometimes I line them all up with diapers and wipes and go through like a machine. I've joked that I feel like Oprah Winfrey giving out gifts to everyone, but instead I'm telling all my children, "You get a bum change! And you get a bum change! And you! You get a bum change, too!" as I line them all up.

Isaac often poops three times a day, and sometimes we have to change him ten times. We go through so many diapers with him alone. Another of my children has the opposite problem and we are trying new things to make sure they don't have hemorrhoids as a child, because it's just unnatural the way it comes out when it does. Throughout the years, I've seen it all, from yellow and green to the consistency of water and baseballs.

When Isaac started to get too big for the regular diapers I could buy at the grocery store, I started to panic a little, wondering what came next. Depends?

Thankfully, I talked to more experienced parents and professionals who told me about getting a prescription for diapers and wipes. We were blessed to have Medicaid for Isaac as he approached this point, so that was another plus. Nowadays there are options on Amazon and independent special needs sites. I was out of luck when it came to swim diapers, because those aren't covered under Medicaid and companies I go through don't carry them. Thankfully, I finally found some on Amazon that I buy regularly, paired with plastic liners that look like clear underwear, just in case things get real messy in the pool that day. Have you ever seen diarrhea floating through the water at the pool? Nobody wants to see that, trust me.

For some reason, Isaac's bowels have always been a mystery. No matter what he eats, he will poop *at least* three times a day. It probably doesn't help that sometimes he eats his own fecal matter...barf. He will often take off his diaper. For a while, he took a diaper off, pooped on the floor, and painted with it on a regular basis. We tried one-piece pajamas, special clothes with a zipper in the back, strong tape on his diapers, and everything we could think of, but somehow the poop still escaped and he often ran naked. Over the years we have done labs, stool samples, and other tests to find answers concerning Isaac's stool, but there seems to be no known reason for his loose bowels and, therefore, no sure treatment. But it sure makes for a lot of diaper changes, baking soda baths, nightmare clean-ups, and lots of extra laundry. Thankfully, we are usually with my kids at home when the Poop Menace strikes. If we're *not* at home, it is the worst! This is partly the reason why I practically bring my whole house in a giant diaper bag or backpack when I go anywhere with my kids.

The worst time to change a diaper is in a public restroom, and I'd rather change my kid in a car somehow than brave a porta-potty, if that's the only option. No parent wants to lay their child on that poop-infested fold-out piece of plastic, but you do it because you have to. You take whatever sanitary precautions necessary and get the job done. But when your child isn't a baby anymore and you still have to change him or her...then what? There's nowhere to go. I can't put my eight-year-old up on the baby changer—he would break it! The last time I attempted doing the diaper changing table in a public restroom was at Disneyland when Isaac was maybe four. It was a more sturdy one built into the wall and not just a flimsy fold-out one, but I still got some interesting looks and I was very self-conscious. If you thought I could change diapers fast before, you should have seen me that day!

It is essential for more public places to have a family restroom, otherwise you run into problems. For example, if I bring my eight, sixteen, or thirty-year-old disabled son into the women's restroom with me so I can somehow change his diaper in the handicap stall, there would be looks, complaints, and rude comments. And yet, what should I do? I obviously can't use the changing table anymore, a regular stall would be a nightmare to maneuver in, and I would never go into the men's bathroom. I can't send him into the men's bathroom by himself, either.

These are the kinds of things other people don't think about. These are the kinds of things special needs parents think about a lot and so much more. It's part of what makes being a special needs parent difficult. It's like our children weren't made to fit into this world. That's okay. It's the world that needs to start learning, changing, accepting, understanding; stop judging, staring, and wallowing in ignorance. One type of person that would be especially helpful in this area of learning is doctors and other specialists. I can't tell you how many times my other Carrier family members and I have been the ones to teach doctors what Fragile X is. It makes a world of difference when a professional knows something about FXS and/or is open to learning; some refuse to be educated in new and upcoming ideas.

I want to help everyone out of this situation by potty training. After all, Wayne Gretzky once said, "You miss 100-percent of the shots you don't take." That includes those made in the bathroom. If there was ever a time of desperation while parenting, it came during potty training. If you are reading this book in hopes I have some great all-knowing answer to how to potty train your special needs child...just put the book down now and call me when you get the answer, mmkay? I *am* here to make sure you know you aren't alone in the crazy, literal mess of potty training. Maybe you'll even be grateful once you read my stories.

When Isaac was still in preschool, we decided to try the potty training thing. When he was three, we had a behaviorist come in with a plan. That plan was to take Isaac to the potty every fifteen minutes. At the time, I was to take vigilant notes about his behavior issues and take care of my two other girls. At that time, Eliza was just a baby. Because I am not superhuman, I had our first-ever staff member take on the task, because I just couldn't do it. The trouble was, it takes at least five minutes to get Isaac to the bathroom. Then you sit for ten minutes, entertaining him with various things and before you know it, it's time to do it all over again. There was little success. But that staff worker, Jeremy, and I had *Green Eggs and Ham* memorized...at least the first two or three pages, since that's what kept Isaac sitting on the potty, but he never wanted to read the whole book. I love *Green Eggs and Ham*, but boy does it get on my nerves after reading the first few pages over and over and over and over. Dude, I know, your name is Sam-I-Am!

One good thing that came from all of this is that Isaac usually will go into the bathroom each morning and pee in the toilet. Sometimes he tries to run away and others he's already peed the Mississippi river in his room. If we can't get him in the bathroom in time, he pees through his diaper and pants to make a puddle to clean up on the floor, but we count our wins, however small they may seem. I'll take Isaac's morning potty break. It's a start.

Often he decides he doesn't want to go potty, but he also doesn't want to have a full diaper, so he disbands it wherever and starts to walk around nonchalantly butt-naked. If we don't catch him in time, he pees on the floor. A few times he peed on the floor and before I could do anything, Evelyn came by and slipped on it, hitting her head and getting soaked in Isaac's pee. It's a nasty thing to clean up.

More recently, I decided to give my best and my all to potty training Isaac who was eight-years-old. There are three in diapers right now and I feel like half of my day is spent changing nasty diapers. Not to mention I feel like I am filling up the entire landfill with crap. Guilty. So Jeremy and I talked, I read another book on potty training, Jeremy took a whole week off of work, we canceled all plans, and I was determined to have this kid potty trained by the end of the week, if not at least somewhat there to give me hope.

The book I read suggested having the child naked or at least with no pants or diaper on. That was easy, because Isaac goes around the house mostly naked most days anyway. Check. The book also said I needed to watch him like a hawk every second. Check, because Jeremy was watching the other three girls. When he started to pee, I picked him up and sat him on the toilet. Whoa. Stop right there. I can't pick him up. Okay, so I figured I could coerce him into the bathroom and say, "Stop! Hold it!" Well, that didn't work. All I ended up doing was cleaning up a line of pee from the living room to the toilet. By the time he got to the potty—*if* he got to the potty—he was pretty much done or just stood, confused, peeing by the toilet. Unfortunately, Isaac can no longer sit on those little baby toilets so I couldn't just set it a few inches away from him and make him sit when he started to pee.

After a day or two, I didn't see a whole lot of change or progress. If Isaac ever went on the potty, it was because I had him go every hour or so, but I felt like I was potty training myself. He still didn't understand that urge to go and that it meant to sit on the potty. He didn't care if he peed on himself or the floor, especially since he'd been doing that for years anyway. I was getting discouraged, but I decided by the end of the week and with so much repetition he'd start regularly going on the potty. I was determined. No more diapers!

Wednesday came along, the third day into our week of solid potty training. Jeremy decided to take the girls up to his parents' house to hang out and visit. That was okay with me, because it meant greater focus for me and no distractions for Isaac. Halfway through the day, Isaac had had several accidents and I felt defeated and frustrated, but no matter how angry I am, I have to mask it and pretend I'm okay, because otherwise he will push every button, cry or whine, and do anything in his power to make things more difficult. Unfortunately, I wasn't masking well and he could tell I was frustrated with him, so when I tried to get him to the potty, he rebelled. He whined and scratched me. I stopped cleaning the carpet, handed him a diaper, told him to put it on, and I left to go upstairs to take a break so I wouldn't snap.

I went to my room, said a prayer to help me be calm, laid down, took a few breaths, and told myself things would be okay. I didn't stay there longer than a minute or two, because I can't trust him on his own. We end up with a lot of messes, water damage, and expensive repairs if he isn't watched. I came out of my bedroom and heard him in the kitchen. I walked partly in to find him crouching on the hardwood floor, surrounded by pee, and playing in his poop like it was sidewalk chalk. The diaper I had given him, along with his t-shirt, was disbanded on the floor. When I saw this sight, I wanted to scream at him out of anger and bawl my eyes out in frustration, but I did neither, because I knew it wouldn't do any good.

If I yelled at him or tried to make him get in the shower, I would've ended up with poop on me and likely flung around the kitchen and everywhere else. Getting mad would only make my situation more awful. I was past crying. What would be the point? The mess had to be cleaned and I was the only one to do it. Isaac needed to be brought to the shower downstairs so I could spray him down with the removable shower head. I waited for him to finish "painting" and calmly asked if he could come down to the shower. When he was ready, I held onto his arm and led him down the stairs and into the bathroom. He left footprints of pee and poop the entire way down.

I put him in the shower, cleaned and scrubbed him head to toe, then went upstairs to clean my kitchen. He likes to stand in the shower, which is lucky for me, because he would've just come upstairs and played in the filth again. I grabbed all our pee-cleaning rags and towels and some cleaner. I soaked up some pee with the rest of his shirt that was wet anyway. I threw away the diaper and began from one end of the kitchen to the other soaking up pee, spraying cleaner, and moving slowly along. At least the poop wasn't dry and crusted on the floor like other poop I've cleaned from his art tactics. I'll save you the other details and just say I wiped the whole floor down two or three times and made sure everything was clean, dry, and disinfected. After that, I was done. Not just done cleaning the kitchen floor, but with trying to potty train Isaac. Like everything else, when he decides he wants to do something, he will. He is fully capable in my eyes, but the desire is not there.

Even though we laugh and joke about all the poop and potty jokes at my house, it has truly been a difficult and often traumatic thing for everyone. I have many more stories, but one more I want to tell is a time when Jeremy wasn't home and everything went wrong. Something always happens when my husband is gone on a work trip or otherwise out of town.

"Mom! Mom!" I heard Millie yelling from downstairs as I finished up draining the spaghetti noodles I was cooking for dinner. It's one thing five out of six in my family will eat. That's a definite win.

"Yeah?" I called back down to her, a bit annoyed. I was frazzled from an entire day alone with the kids.

"Poop fiasco! Isaac pooped!" Millie hollered back. My eyes got worried and my stomach sank. *Oh no*, I thought. *Not again*. I turned off the stove so nothing would burn (I don't always remember) and rushed down the stairs. What I saw was a nightmare of brown. Isaac was covered, the carpet was covered, the two younger girls had gotten some on them somehow. I looked around and assessed the situation. I told Isaac to get into the shower, but he wouldn't. I washed off the two young girls and told Millie to take them upstairs and not come down until I said so.

While Millie tried to entertain the girls upstairs, I coaxed and physically moved Isaac into the shower. Poopy footprints led the way. Did I mention there was cream-colored carpet all throughout the downstairs including *in the bathroom?* As a side note, carpet in a bathroom is the downfall of society, mostly reflecting on the 70s era. Come on, people, it's just not sanitary. We don't need to be *that* cozy in our bathroom, mmkay? Okay, back to the poop.

I turned on the shower and planned on letting him stay in that clean, safe spot for as long as it took to clean up. Well, it took well over an hour, if not two. There was one point where I wanted to get a kitchen knife and start slicing at the carpet and ripping it up, but I knew I didn't have the energy and strength at that time to do so and I had no idea what I would be getting myself into. I just scrubbed and scrubbed and scrubbed. I got the poop chunks into the trash, used rags and cleaner, then got out my carpet cleaner, which, by the way, is a must with these kids. During most of this time, the girls were all crying upstairs, including Millie, because she didn't know what to do anymore and it was too much responsibility for her little self—not to mention she was hungry and it was way past dinner. By the time I got it all cleaned up, it was past the kids' bedtime and everyone was hungry. It was the longest night ever and when it finally came time, I went to bed crying.

We've tried and tried with Isaac and wonder if he will be thirty by the time he decides he's ready or if he will ever be ready; I'll be in my sixties changing his diaper. It's no wonder that I didn't even try to potty train my next youngest after Isaac until more recently. At first, I only put half my heart into it with little success, though I know she can. Our big motivation came when I found out she was capable of going to typical Kindergarten with only speech therapy. This was huge! I've since brought in occupational therapy, but I never thought my kids would be able to go to regular classrooms; however, she couldn't go to regular Kindergarten unless she got fully potty trained. So, of course, I took a few days and went full boar! We saw a lot of hope in those days and decided not to put her in a Pull-Up again, except at nighttime.

Since that time, about nine months ago, she still has had accidents every day. She typically has one accident a month at school and I have to go pick her up, which can be a challenge with Evelyn. Sometimes the thought of picking Eliza up causes me anxiety as a Carrier.

"Hello?" I answered my phone, hesitant. I didn't want to know what I would hear on the other line as I saw the name of Eliza's elementary school scroll across the phone's face.

"Hi, is this Mrs. Fowler?" a kind voice asked.

"Yes, it is." I waited.

"I have Eliza here in the office. She's had an accident and needs some new clothes."

"Okay, I'll gather that and come over," I replied.

"Thank you, bye."

After hanging up, the anxiety set in. I had a full on panic attack and couldn't go get my child in her time of need. Jeremy worked at home that day, but had many meetings and was a stranger to panic attacks. He didn't understand that I might as well have been dying at the time, because I wasn't going anywhere. I called my mom.

"Mom, are you by my house today?" I asked when she picked up. She often goes to stores in my area.

"No, but I can be. What's wrong?" she asked.

"I don't know. I need to pick up Eliza, but I can't leave my bed. I don't know what to do. I'm the worst mom ever. What am I going to do?" I cried as the panic continued to rise out of control.

"It's okay. I can come get her," she offered.

"That means she has to wait over fifteen minutes in the office in her pee," I said. "Let me see if Diana is around to go get her."

"Okay, but call me back if she can't. I can go get her," my mom said, worried. "It's going to be okay. You're a great mom. It will be all right."

"K, love you, bye," I said through tears. Then I called Diana.

"Hello?" she answered.

"Hey, are you home?"

"Yes, what's wrong?"

"I just. It's so stupid. I...I need to pick up Eliza. She had an accident at school, but I think I'm having a panic attack. I just can't do it. She needs me, though. She needs me," I said, crying.

"It's okay, I'll leave right now and be there in a few minutes, okay? I got this. Don't worry," Diana reassured me.

"Okay. Thank you. Thank you so much," I replied and hung up. Shortly after, I got another call from the school. I put on my brave mask and told them, "Hi, yes, I'm having my nanny come pick her up. I apologize for the wait. Tell her Diana is coming." After I hung up, I cried on my pillow. I questioned how Carriers are supposed to handle life, let alone taking care of special needs children. I was so disappointed in myself as a mother, but I had to forgive myself and know things would be okay. It's days like that I wonder what I was thinking, having children at all, and I'm sure so many people out there wonder the same thing when they see me out in public with my kids. My faith in Christ and prayer and the decisions we've made help keep me going. I just have to know God has a plan for me and I am doing my best.

Since then, there have been many unexpected pick-ups at school. The teacher requested she be put in a Pull-Up at school. I was so reluctant to do this, fearing we'd lose all our progress. Sure enough, after some time, she stopped going potty and began pooping in her Pull-Up at school, so then I was still picking her up from school but with less hope for her future. It's something I am currently working through and I wonder how to make it work. She is intelligent and capable of being in a regular class, but if she cannot learn to go potty, she won't have that opportunity. In fact, she will miss out on many opportunities, no matter how smart and capable she is in other areas.

Here at home she struggles with accidents, too. Like many other kids, Eliza struggles the most pooping in the potty instead of her pants. I hoped a potty watch would work, but it wasn't the magical item I hoped. We've tried various charts, different kinds of rewards, encouraging words, and suggestions of numerous books and parents with little progress. Sometimes I think changing the diaper was way easier and required less laundry. It's so taxing, but I just can't give up, especially because she will be going to a regular first grade class next year. I don't even want to think about Evelyn's potty training right now. Her anxiety is so high and I already have two kids peeing everywhere and being taken to the potty at certain times, so I don't want to try and juggle three.

However, I am discovering there is *never* a good time to start potty training, so it is pointless to wait for the "best time." Also, I don't suggest potty training more than one at a time. I tried to potty train Isaac and Eliza at the same time...I know, I know—it was stupid and unrealistic. But man did I feel powerful that day (until the end). Now I just do one at a time and devote everything to that one child until they get the concept, but it's still a struggle. We have seen many successes, but still a lot of accidents. Now, instead of changing three kids' diapers every day, I only have two...and one with dirty underwear. Isaac only goes a few times a day. Soon it will be Evelyn's turn, but I have high hopes. She has often watched Eliza during the training process and sometimes wants to sit on the potty, so we let her. Hopefully one day we won't have any kids in diapers. Cross your fingers.

20

Hygiene & Grooming

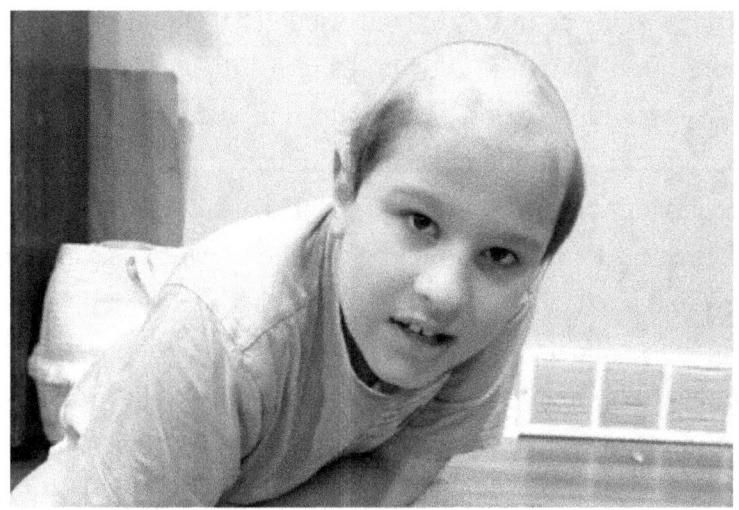

Isaac taking a break in the middle of a hair cut

"You're never fully dressed without a smile."
–Annie

I t's hard enough to keep a typical child clean and groomed, but when they have a multitude of other challenges to deal with, it gets quite tricky—if not impossible. You would think Isaac has a great immune system because he touches and licks just about everything in sight. There's a reason I homeschooled during 2020 COVID. Besides trying to keep my kids, particularly Isaac, sanitary with hands washed and regular showers/baths, there are four especially difficult things: getting dressed, cutting nails, cutting hair, and brushing teeth.

Clothing

I can't read that line without singing it in my head, but I have to wonder if just wearing a smile counts as fully dressed? That would be nice for Isaac's sake. More often than not, Isaac chills in his diaper. He's nine years old and weighs over 100 pounds, so his cute rolls and cottage cheese legs are the highest fashion around our home. Throughout the day, we discover him crouched in a corner watching his tablet stark naked—but he's got a smile! It's like an Easter egg hunt to try to find where he discarded his diaper. Okay, it really isn't that fun. Usually I find a pee spot I have to clean up around there, too. Then there's the dreaded poop. You know about that by now.

I am proud to say that he at least wears clothes in public...most of the time. Heck, I'm just happy when my kids wear clothes at all. I can't count how many times Isaac has gone streaking at a family party or the school playground. Thankfully, he now puts his clothes on by himself, even if they are inside out and backwards most of the time. He's getting pickier about the feel of his clothes, like most autistic children, but I'm still trying to figure out why he likes the tag in the front on his shirts, or the back pockets of his shorts in front while the drawstring dangles in the back like a tail. He puts them on like that almost every time, no matter how I lay it out or what I say. Shoes, on the other hand, can be even harder to keep on than his clothes.

I'll never forget how difficult it was when he was a toddler to get his shoes on! I felt like I was wrestling an octopus. His four appendages doubled and his strength did, too. Sometimes I didn't even know how I got kicked in the head or gut. I had to plan an extra ten to twenty minutes to make sure I got to my destination on time, because those minutes were spent wrestling him to get his shoes on, change his diaper, and/or convince him going into the van would be fun. Unfortunately, unless we were going to Grandma Judy's house, it wasn't going to be fun to him and he screamed bloody murder once he realized we weren't going there after all.

It wasn't just fighting him to get his clothes on, but to keep them in his drawers. Eventually I put on drawer locks, but he stuck his little fingers between the cracks and pulled out almost every piece of clothing when I wasn't looking and often peed on them so it made even more laundry. *So much laundry*. He soils so many clothes I have to buy him twice the amount and then I do twice as much laundry, especially because he soaks his bed almost every morning. I've learned to keep his clothes in a closet under a hook lock so only I and Jeremy can access them, and I leave a few items for him to pick through when he decides he doesn't want to wear his current outfit. He also likes to take everything out of my dryer and put it on the floor to find something-usually his swim shorts. He's obsessed with swimsuits and even carries his sister's around the house and to school.

If there's anything I've learned about my kids and their clothing, though, it's to let them wear what they want. Of course, I don't want my children to be seen in clothes that are too small, dirty, ripped, or twenty years old; although, I'm sure people have seen my children in all of the above for one reason or another. I try to provide clothes that fit in with my tolerance and their comfort. They rarely wear jeans, and if Isaac does, they are the pretend ones with an elastic or drawstring waist. Let's be honest, *I* don't even like to wear jeans!

The truth is, I let go of the perfect baby look years ago. It's too stressful for me and often torture for my kids. Let people judge. Maybe there are those with special needs that can tolerate the cute clothes, especially all those Down syndrome models emerging now (yay!), but sometimes I'm just happy my kid is wearing clothes at all. If my daughter with a disability picks out her own outfit and puts it on by herself, I consider it a miracle. Other children have fewer choices than that. We try our best as special needs parents to help our children look and be their best, but I've learned to pick my battles. The clothes my kids wear just aren't that important to me compared to, say, getting them to eat with a spoon instead of their hands. This is especially important if their hands aren't the cleanest things in the world. Sometimes I feel there's no keeping things clean under Isaac's fingernails.

Cutting Nails

Cutting Isaac's fingernails is a joke, but cutting his toenails is a WWF match. He loves to be held and touched, but once the fingernail clippers come out, it is another matter entirely. He was about five years old when I finally figured out how to cut his fingernails in a more acceptable way for both of us.

I sat by him while he watched his tablet or a movie on the TV. I'd tell him, "Okay, Isaac. It's time to cut your nails." Then I'd pause. "Okay Isaac, let me see your hand." I'd slowly and gently hold his hand and lock my eyes on the first fingernail victim. He wouldn't let me hold it long, so once I had it, I clipped fast. Then his hand shot back to his side. I'd praise him and say, "Good job!" I'd have to wait until he was ready to give me his hand again and I'd clip another one. Oftentimes each nail required two of these hasty cuts. It. Took. For. Ever. And. So. Much. PATIENCE. But it was worth it, because he was a scratcher.

One of his behavior issues was scratching others when he didn't get his way or was mad. Although newly cut nails may be sharp, long, uncut, jagged nails are worse—trust me. Most of my family have at least one scar from his scratching, not to mention teachers, teacher aids, classmates, and others. When Isaac was just a baby, he started self-harming and has a scar on his cheek from scratching himself. One of his behaviorists even bought these special black arm guards for us and others to use so we would have some protection while working with him day to day. They didn't get used much, though, because he was unpredictable. If I'm being honest, it was weird walking around all day with pieces of body armor on to protect against my son; I felt like an angsty gothic teenager from my junior high days.

It's no surprise that clipping Isaac's nails is a necessary evil in our household. Sometimes to get the job done, I had to sit on him or have Jeremy help me hold his arms so I could get his fingernails cut. I'm sure we looked like a circus on the floor trying to do what is usually a simple task, but who am I kidding? My family is always a circus. We all take turns being the ringleader. We learn to laugh whenever we can. We have a saying that you can either laugh or cry, so we choose to laugh as much as possible. A lot of times the laughter only comes after a stressful event, but we are learning to laugh through the pain and the stress. It makes life a lot more tolerable each day and more joyful overall. There's just something about laughter that chases away anger or despair. But it's okay to cry, too. Even clowns cry...but those are usually the creepiest ones, so that's just another reason to smile and laugh instead.

Hair Care

Another fun circus act in the Fowler home is cutting Isaac's hair. I've always used barber clippers to give him a buzz cut so it will be a while before I have to cut it again. It also means I don't have to style it. I tried that a few times and he looked so handsome, but he messed it up after a minute and then it looked worse than before.

I've tried many different methods to cut his hair. The best one yet was putting him in a restrained seat, such as a high chair, but he soon got too old for that. I had a large booster seat for toddlers to sit at the kitchen table and that worked even when he got a bit older. I usually tried to entertain him with my phone or his tablet. Even the special tablet or my phone backfired, because he expected to get it when he sat on the special chair. When he got even bigger, I put him on a high stool in hopes he wouldn't walk away as easily, but it usually ended with us both on the ground with me wrestling his head with his arms flailing and legs kicking. It often takes a few days to a week to get all his hair trimmed. Sometimes he has to go to school with crazy hair. The funniest haircut was when I just decided to go for the top first. I got all the hair buzzed off on the top of his head, but then he put up a fight. He looked like Friar Tuck. Millie and I couldn't stop laughing! I wish I'd taken a picture. He would've gotten a good laugh, too, if he'd only seen it. He has a great sense of humor.

Once I had a helper come while I cut his hair. I thought it would be a great idea to give him a popsicle while I buzzed away. Turns out popsicles and haircuts don't go well together. It became more of a furry popsicle and he got so frustrated with the hair in his mouth I had to call it quits and give him a new treat.

I finally reached a point where I gave in and let him watch my phone just so I could get the job done. He has a tablet he's addicted to, but he likes my phone the best, especially because it has YouTube; however, there were many unwanted consequences to this brilliant idea that only half-worked. My phone got covered in hair clippings, I had to fight to cut his hair, especially around his ears, and he wouldn't give my phone back when I was finished. This caused a major meltdown. But the worst part of this, and also the funniest, is for days afterward Isaac kept bringing out the chair and sitting on it. If I had cut his hair outside, he'd bring stools outside. That was quite the feat. Banged up walls and chipped paint were luckily the only things getting hurt. If I had last cut his hair in a certain area of the kitchen, I found him sitting there. He learned very quickly that to get mom's phone, he just had to sit on a chair where we last cut his hair.

Unfortunately, that isn't quite how it worked and I tried to explain to him that we already cut his hair and he couldn't have Mommy's phone. I tried to give him alternatives, but it always ended in a huge meltdown. After a long time, this behavior faded and I'd give him another haircut with no other option to keep him somewhat still but to give him my phone. I talked to a therapist who said to slowly take away the phone privilege by only giving the phone once in a while. He wouldn't expect it every time and therefore wouldn't have a meltdown. It would be hard at first, because he would obviously rebel; unfortunately, I wasn't in a place at that time to even think about trying and dealing with the repercussions. I did, however, find some cutting tools especially for kids with autism on Amazon.

This was a special set that used scissors instead of a loud buzzer, but still had the different numbered attachments. So basically, instead of a motorized buzzer to hook the hair guides to, it is a special set of scissors. This was mainly to offset the loud noise the buzzer makes that autistic children tend not to like. I didn't think the noise was a huge issue for Isaac, but I thought maybe he would be more willing to let me cut his hair with these quiet tools instead of the usual barber clippers.

I started with a few cuts in the back. He didn't really like it, but he wasn't freaking out. Jeremy followed me around with a vacuum so I could follow Isaac as he walked away and cut his hair en route. He eventually went into the kitchen, which I was happy about, because wood floors are easy to sweep. Jeremy decided to go vacuum downstairs at this point, since it didn't look like I needed him following me anymore.

I remember telling Jeremy as I first started that maybe this scissors thing wasn't such a good idea, because Isaac doesn't like his head to be touched unless he knows you are playing and rubbing his head for fun. Eventually, though, I cut his hair and asked if he wanted to help me so he could be included in the event and maybe not be so adverse to it. I put his fingers with mine and started cutting. It was going really well and I was quite happy about the whole thing. I thought, *Huh, maybe this will work after all! Yes!*

Suddenly, Isaac's hand shot away from his head and down to his chest. He looked at me. This is what he does when I cut his nails sometimes, even if there's nothing wrong, so I didn't think much of it at first. I said, "Uh oh, what happened?" He didn't say anything. Then I thought for a moment and said, "Oh, did you get pinched with the scissors or something?" And then I saw the blood.

Somehow his finger had gotten in the path of the scissors and been cut. I didn't know how bad. All I saw was blood everywhere. He doesn't know how to handle situations like this, so he wiped it all over his body. I should mention at this time he was just wearing his diaper. He also kept flapping his hands like usual, spattering blood on the floor, the kitchen walls, and the windows.

I couldn't bring myself to look at the injury. If I was alone, I would've put on my big girl pants, but I wasn't, so instead I yelled for Jeremy. He was still vacuuming and couldn't hear me. The vacuum was plugged in upstairs, so I ran and unplugged it, then yelled again. He came up and I told him what had happened, but I didn't know how bad. He rushed over, but it was difficult to see through the blood and Isaac wouldn't stay still. I asked Jeremy if we needed to go to the hospital, but he didn't think so. Something was cut on his thumb, but we needed to get a better look. We quickly picked up all his 100 pounds and rushed him to the bathroom. Blood got all over Jeremy, his clothes, and some on the floor as we carried him.

All this time Isaac didn't seem super aware of what was going on or why. He was happy once we got him in the shower. Jeremy then saw the cut was bad, but we didn't need to go to the hospital. We formed a plan so we could get him out of the shower and get him bandaged up. We weren't sure how this would work, because he doesn't like being held and he won't wear Band-Aids—he won't keep anything like a bandage on.

Suddenly our whole night was getting Isaac's wound to stop bleeding and keep some kind of bandage on. I ran to get all the beneficial supplies I could think of: Neosporin, two large Band-Aids, squares of gauze, bandage tape, packing tape (I couldn't find trusty duct tape and I had to bring it just in case the bandage tape didn't work). I grabbed a hand towel and Jeremy brought Isaac out of the shower, holding his hand in the towel. Isaac did not like that and fought back. I hurried and slipped a diaper on him and then we led him to the family room to watch a show. We wrapped his favorite blanket around him and talked to him softly, trying to help him understand.

After Isaac had calmed a bit, I could tell he was in pain. Every time he happened to get a glimpse of the wound, he dry-heaved. He's his mama's boy. We held him tight and wrapped his thumb in gauze and tape. He tried to take it off immediately, but we distracted him with the movie and talked about it. Soon we were into the movie, just sitting there, and I looked down and his bandage was off and blood was dripping again. Jeremy had stepped out of the room, so I did what I could. I grabbed one of the big Band-Aids and quickly and sloppily put it around his finger. By this time, he understood his finger was hurt and we were trying to help. This alone is huge. That he understood we were trying to help him because he was hurt and allowed us to help was a first. I was so proud of him. I knew he was growing up and his understanding was improving.

Miraculously, he kept the Band-Aid on for an hour or two and took it off at bedtime; however, the bleeding had pretty much stopped and I put another one on before he went to bed. I believe he kept that one on most of that night. Boy was I grateful. Later, we saw that somehow I had cut the corner of his thumbnail and some skin, so it was a slow healing process. Eventually his body did its magic and by the next day he was fine and it didn't bother him again. I was so grateful. The downside? He had some choppy hair in the back and long crazy hair everywhere else, but I wasn't going to try cutting again any time soon.

When I did finally get my gumption again, my husband got his cordless trimmers and we followed Isaac around inside and outside, cutting his hair as he walked. We first tried to just go for it, which made Isaac fall to the ground and bang his head with an audible thunk on the cement two times, even though we tried to protect him. It was awful. We slowed it down. I talked to him and let him know he could trust me. I spoke softly, asked him to help, and told him to breathe. I even touched the buzzer to his body and hands and top of his head to feel it and know it was safe. It was a slow and difficult process and I still didn't get by his ears well, but we did it and we were all proud and cheered Isaac on. It was one of the better experiences cutting his hair. Anything beats the scissors incident!

We have finally gotten to a point where we use cordless trimmers to follow him around wherever he goes. We have a vacuum to pick up after him as well. It helps to have him feel the trimmers as long as he doesn't chuck them across the room (which he often does). I say "buzz buzz" and he copies me. He lets me get the top of his head, but not around his ears, so we just tell him what is coming, then pin him down the best we can while I buzz around his head with the trimmers at super speed so it is over as soon as possible. He cries and it makes me sad, but I have to cut his hair; otherwise he looks unkempt and uncared for. That's the last thing he needs! I try to talk him through it and make jokes. Through his tears, he copies what I say, like, "Happy Halloween!" and "Dinosaur!" After it's all done, we slowly convince him to get into the shower and let him have his tablet afterward. I hope someday he will sit and let us do his hair without a huge struggle and crocodile tears.

Thankfully, the girls allow me to trim their hair. The difficult part is brushing through it! Every time I attempt to style their hair it sounds like I'm torturing them as they scream and wail. I've learned to use lots of conditioner, detangler, and special brushes. There are times I've had to send them to school in a sad pony tail. Maybe they just need short pixie cuts to make it easier on everyone.

The moral of this story? Don't judge if you see my son or any special needs child with some crazy hair. Too often people think we don't care or don't take care of them at all. Having a clean face all the time comes secondary to surviving each day. Also, don't roll your eyes when you see a person at a hair salon has taken the extra time and attention to give a haircut to a child with special needs. Yes, they do deserve to be in the newspaper and on your Facebook feed. It really is that big of a big deal. In fact, anyone in their chosen profession who goes out of their way to help a child with special needs is a hero. Not just to the child, but to their parent(s) as well. If you love our child(ren) sincerely, you hold a special place in our heart. My children's dentist, Dr. Ryan Blankenship, is one of those people. He actually tries to brush Isaac's teeth. Now that's a feat.

Brushing Teeth

How many toothbrushes does it take to brush my son's teeth? I don't know, but it's a lot. He practically eats them. If the toothbrush isn't mashed and mangled or completely broken from biting too hard, it is likely his teeth aren't getting brushed at all. I've bought *so many* toothbrushes. In fact, I even tried to buy fancy ones, thinking it would help motivate him. Nope. Fail. That was just more money down the drain, which happens a lot in the special needs world. You try all different kinds of toys, therapies, clothes, blankets, swings, furniture, etc. that are extra expensive because they are for special needs children, and then you turn around to find that your kid doesn't even like it. Well, the toothbrushes I bought were no different. Surprise! At least they were cheap compared to some of the other things we've purchased.

For Isaac, the light-up toothbrush was cool, but it was a smaller one for toddlers and he bit down and busted it in the first week. The three-sided toothbrushes were good, because they brushed more area, but they were more expensive and didn't seem to last long. I bought a cute purple princessy toothbrush for Evelyn with different modes—even a massage mode—but she couldn't handle the feel of any vibration in her mouth. We stick with the cheap toddler toothbrushes you can buy at the Dollar Store or Walmart, and we use the ones from the dentist as long as they last. I say "as long as they last" because she often walks around sucking and biting on hers all day. I figure that counts as some brushing, right? If I don't watch her, though, the dog ends up brushing its teeth or gets dog hair in it. Evelyn will even use it as a tool for various projects, like brushing her dolls hair or cleaning the floor. Needless to say, we have a lot of backup toothbrushes.

In the early years, I was paranoid about brushing Isaac's teeth, and he tried everything not to let that toothbrush in his mouth. I even learned this great ninja move from my sister where I kneel over him with his arms in my knee pits so he can't reach the toothbrush. After a while, though, it didn't seem worth the fight and I decided it would be better to approach it in a more patient way, like the nail clipping. I invited him to help me. He held the toothbrush and did what he felt safe doing while I tried to stay calm and natural, gently guiding his hand to reach to another spot besides his two front teeth. It was a lot better and less traumatic for everyone. I wouldn't say it is super effective for cleaning, because he only tolerates it for a short time and half of that time he is biting it, but it seems to be the best option. I have the most success with this approach when I get all my kids in the bathroom to brush together. Both Evelyn and Isaac like brushing their teeth with their siblings. It makes it fun and they have others to follow. I am very grateful for a typical daughter, our oldest, to be an example for the other three. She is truly an angel.

Having a proper example to follow is very important for these special needs kids. Nobody wants to be forced to do things and kids with special needs are no different. They want to be independent; it's just a greater challenge. My son also has anxiety and Oppositional Defiant Disorder (ODD), making it especially difficult to get him to do anything that wasn't his idea first. I try my best to encourage, demonstrate, and use lots of repetition so he feels comfortable doing things on his own. Unless I absolutely have to, such as emergencies or doctor visits, I do not force; that only makes the situation worse by a hundred times, although I won't deny I have bribed a time or two. What parent doesn't get into bargaining when desperation arises? I know with each of them I'd try all kinds of tactics to get my kids to eat healthy food.

Eating

It started with Millie. I gave her some baby food, like bananas, because that's what she liked, but every other bite I'd switch it for some vegetable, like green beans. The old bait and switch, as they say. It didn't work as well for Isaac. The older he got, the more picky he became. When he was one or two, he ate fresh avocado, oatmeal, and various other foods he would never eat now. He occasionally eats spaghetti, pizza, and rice, but they have to be served a certain way and the pizza has to be Little Caesar's. His diet mainly consists of pretzels, bread with butter and garlic salt, goldfish, saltines, cheddar cheese, and sometimes the occasional treat, such as Fruit Loops that turn his poop a green color. Once in a while he will surprise us. He likes to try things and branch out on some really random things we would never think to have him try.

"Hon, where did that last Crumbl Cookie go? Did you eat it?" I asked one day as I peered into the pink rectangular box from one of our favorite cookie franchises. We usually cut the big cookies into at least fourths, so it seemed odd there was a whole cookie missing when I'd just seen it not too long ago.

"No, I haven't eaten any of it. Is it gone?" Jeremy said, surprised.

"Yeah, it just disappeared. I know Evelyn didn't sneak off with it, because I put it out of her reach," I replied. I looked around, wondering how a giant cookie could just disappear. I wandered into the living room and saw Isaac on his tablet, sitting in his usual crouched position. But instead of occupying his hands with flapping, he was intent on finishing up the last of the cookie with crumbs all around him. I laughed.

"Isaac, did you eat that entire cookie?" I asked in disbelief. He looked up at me with a mouth full of evidence. I couldn't believe it. He had eaten a cookie on his own accord. A *huge* cookie! He's eaten chocolate chip cookies occasionally in the past, but the most surprising thing about this cookie was that it was cranberry white chocolate chip. For someone with such a minuscule palate, it wasn't expected. There have been times when he will take something out of my hands when I'm offering it to the girls, such as a caramel rice cake, and eat the entire thing. I just let it happen, because I get really excited when he eats something new.

I've gone through many vacuums trying to clean up after my kids and their smashed gold fish and other snacks. One thing people get a kick out of is that Isaac loves wheat bread with butter and lots of garlic salt. Whenever I go to pick up my groceries the person loading it in the back always comments on how much bread I bought saying something profound like, "Whoa. That's a lot of bread!" Sometimes I explain and other times I just let them guess.

Eliza is more typical in what she eats for a girl her age, but still picky. I have to laugh, though, because we've discovered she *loves* Lindor chocolate truffles—just like her mama. Now I have to hide my stash of good chocolate (don't worry, I share!) She also likes boiled eggs with lots of salt and pepper, baked potatoes with sour cream and salt and pepper, and other foods like peppers that little kids don't typically enjoy. She keeps us on our toes. One thing I know both Eliza and Evelyn love is milk with Nesquik; sometimes that's the only substantial thing Evelyn will eat.

When Evelyn was about a year old until she was about three, she ate cooked oatmeal with Nesquik chocolate powder mixed in every single morning. It had to have just the right amount of chocolate and be just the right consistency. It couldn't be too hot or too cold. On top of that, if you looked at her at all, her anxiety would rear its ugly head and she wouldn't eat anything. Instead, we'd spend half an hour getting her to calm down and eat something. She has developed a sweet tooth like I've never known. She would eat sprinkles, brown sugar, and candy all day if I let her. I admit there are days I want her to eat something, *anything*, and I let her just eat sugar. I never thought I would do something like that, since I am not a fan of too much sugar, but you get desperate for kids to eat anything to stay alive and gain weight.

I know Rachael's kids have their favorite foods as well. Brighton eats tons and tons of green apples and covers just about anything in Montreal Steak seasoning. At one point, to get Avery to gain weight, she was allowed to eat ice cream and Hostess Ding Dongs whenever she wanted. Joslin, Rachael's youngest, mostly has PediaSure drinks with fiber. Isaac used to drink PediaSure every day to get nutrition and we had a prescription from his doctor for a monthly supply—this was helpful financially, but even the regular kind gave him worse diarrhea, which was the last thing we needed.

Even though Isaac is currently nine, he still won't eat with a utensil. He mostly eats finger foods, but when he eats rice or spaghetti, it gets *everywhere*. I've gotten used to it and have figured out that you should let rice dry out on the floor before sweeping it up, because it gets hard and is easier to clean up. Thankfully, he is better at letting me clean his hands and face after a spaghetti feast, but it always get on his clothes. He often walks around in just a diaper, so thankfully he doesn't ruin many clothes that way.

I usually only cook dinner for three: me, Jeremy, and Millie. The other kids just snack and eat whatever; rarely do they eat what I make. Family dinners around the table are few and far between, but we are happy and fed! I'm pretty sure I used to be a mom who judged others for what they allowed their children to eat. Millie grew up on green smoothies, rare sweets, and homemade food—now here I am, feeding sprinkles to my three-year-old just to stay sane. Some days I have to survive and make sure my kids do as well. Thankfully, Evelyn also enjoys toast, frozen wild blueberries, raspberries, and strawberries. Other parents might not realize what it's like to have children who refuse to eat and yet cry and become ornery because they are starving. Even other moms with special needs children have their own opinions, but all I know is that each child is different. I can't judge and I care less and less how others judge me on the matter. Take a walk in my shoes for a day and we'll see. Plus, when you are as stressed and sleep-deprived as a mother, it is hard to do anything more than make through the day sometimes.

21

Sleep...or Lack Thereof

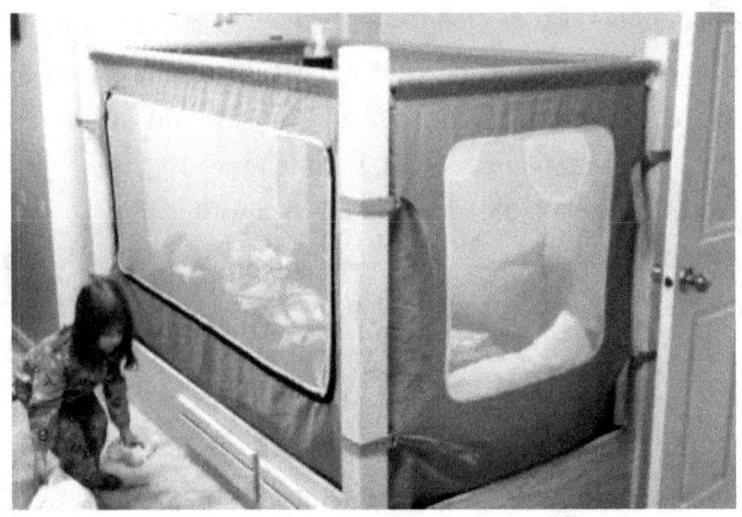

Specialized bed made by Isaac's parents and Grandma Fowler

"I wish I may, I wish I might, get more than an hour of sleep tonight."
–Unknown

One thing people don't often realize is that those with Fragile X have a hard time sleeping. When I say a hard time, I mean they don't sleep. Having no sleep on top of the stress of life made us feel like we were living in a nightmare. It's hard enough to do life in general, but it's twice as hard when you don't get your sleep. I did try giving Isaac melatonin at night when I was trying different natural methods and oils, but that didn't do much, nor have I seen a huge difference in either of my FX daughters' sleep patterns. I'll never forget those sleepless nights with Isaac.

"Okay, hon, it's your turn. I need a break. My arms are going to fall off," I said to Jeremy in the middle of the night. I had been rocking and bouncing Isaac for what seemed like hours.

"All right," Jeremy replied. "I'm wide awake anyway."

"Thanks," I said, relieved. I sighed. "Why won't he sleep?" I asked, exasperated.

"I don't know, but we need to do something," Jeremy said, frustrated. "I have work in the morning and we can't function."

"I know, but he's only a year old and we've tried melatonin and the cry-it-out method. I think he would've turned blue before he fell asleep. I just don't know what to do. He's too young for medication."

"I wish he would at least take his binky," Jeremy thought aloud. "It's like he can't physically keep it in his mouth, even though it helps soothe him."

We took turns half a dozen times that night and both of us were to our breaking point. I couldn't do any more lunges with Isaac in tow and Jeremy couldn't do anymore high-low bouncing, but it soon became my turn again. I sneakily tried to put Isaac down in the pack 'n play, but that didn't work. He fussed immediately. I quickly bounced and lunged or whatever would help him quiet down. I should've lost five pounds that night, but I've learned the rule of motherhood: you don't gain muscle or lose weight doing the crazy hard things kids require. Fact of life. Otherwise, everyone would be lining up to be a mother as some crazy diet fad. Eventually I sat on the edge of the bed and bounced there so I could at least sit down. I was drained of all energy, but I knew I had no choice but to hold Isaac to keep the peace. Jeremy already had his round, so there was no one else to turn to. Just me. No one else. Suddenly I realized there was someone else. With tears forming in my tired eyes, I closed them and let the wet drops fall down my cheeks as I prayed.

"Heavenly Father," I said silently in my mind. "Help me. I don't know what to do. There's no one else to hold Isaac right now and we all need sleep. Please, God, give me strength. Send angels to soothe your little one." I continued bouncing Isaac up and down for many more minutes while a special peace surrounded me. Not long after, I was able to put Isaac down and we all slept. I don't remember how long, but we slept and I was grateful. It was a good lesson for me to learn that Heavenly Father and my Savior are always there, since having a special needs child can often feel lonely. The lessons were just beginning, however; there would be many more nights of little sleep.

As Isaac got older, he finally learned to self-soothe sitting up in his pack 'n play and rocking against the mesh side. Unfortunately, one day while Jeremy played hide-and-seek with the kids, he decided to hop into Isaac's bed to hide. It broke the bottom. We didn't have a lot of money to go out and buy a new one and we still had a crib from Millie, so we decided to try that. Isaac didn't sleep well in it, though, because he couldn't rock against the hard wooden bars. Being an aspiring engineer, Jeremy made custom wooden rockers to put on the base of the crib to fit over the wheels. It was an idea I discovered online and Jeremy had the scraps and tools to make happen. Isaac didn't approve. It took more momentum than he was willing to give while going to sleep in order to make the crib rock. All that work and time for nothing. We went back to the regular crib.

We thought eventually Isaac would figure something else out, but he wasn't sleeping well. At one point, just because, I decided to turn the crib into a daybed. After all, Millie moved to a toddler bed at sixteen months and he was past that age! I quickly realized my mistake. He fell out and onto the floor several nights in a row. No harm done, but it was sad. It's just one of those things you do as a mom and look back on and laugh because you were so naive. It's like when a new mom freaks out over their first child eating dirt and the experienced mom with four kids laughs as her kid "gets more iron and protein."

On the flip side, there is also the determined mom. That's who I was when my baby wasn't getting sleep. The crib wasn't working well and we eventually went back to the broken pack 'n play and improvised with the base. We knew we had to get him a new bed, but he was growing up and we wanted to go big or go home. I did my handy work searching far and wide for the perfect bed for Isaac. I found one I thought would be pretty great, but it was thousands of dollars. We decided to make our own. It just so happened that we had bought our daughter a loft bed recently. It came with a separate twin bed with drawers that sat unattached underneath. We took that base and added four 4x4 posts to the corners. We went to work finding the best materials in our price range. We bought yards of mesh and gray canvas. My mother-in-law is an expert seamstress, and with our design, put together a masterpiece! It was a five-sided open box that, when attached with ties to the four posts, resembled a giant pack 'n play. Each side had mesh in the middle and canvas surrounding it. There was a zipper all around the mesh in the front for access in and out. The mattress sat on top of the bottom piece of canvas. It was truly a special needs parent engineering feat! And Isaac loved it. He rocked, he didn't fall out, and it was big enough for him. It also kept him contained, which was essential for everyone, especially since Isaac's room didn't have a door. We finally had the bed that could last him the rest of his life! Or so we thought...

We soon found out the masterpiece of a bed was masterfully hard to clean. Isaac had blowouts in the morning on a regular basis. He sat at the side of his bed between the mattress and canvas to make a poop smear that went all down his sheet to his mattress and the base of the canvas bed piece. The mesh often got coated with poop and looked like you could blow diarrhea bubbles through the holes. It was a mess. We began to only take the contraption down to wash if we couldn't get a good clean with water, rags, and cleaner. It took a beating in our washer and the D-rings on the ties beat up our washer as well.

It all had to be washed and dried in the same day to be used that night or else no one was going to sleep. Still, overall it was the best we had, so we kept using it.

Later, we noticed points where the mesh was ripping away from the canvas. Where it was sewn it was still attached, but just below in a weaker point, it was coming apart. We realized this was mostly caused by Isaac's constant rocking in the same place each night. Even with all we had done, there came a point I thought for sure he was not sleeping more than three hours. Sometimes he was up all night. Although it may sound mean, we were glad he was at least safely constrained in his special bed so the rest of us could sleep. Sometimes he wasn't happy hanging out and bouncing by himself and whined and cried. Nothing we did got him to go to sleep. I finally did what I swore I would never do—I put a TV in his room and popped in an old VHS movie (he couldn't destroy these like he did DVDs). I turned the TV to face his bed and left. It allowed Jeremy and I at least an hour of sleep if he liked the movie enough. We lived that way for a while. I knew it wasn't the best thing, but I didn't know what else to do and I needed to rest! We eventually turned to medication which was a trial in itself, but it did give us rest.

Meanwhile, we fixed the tears in the bed regularly, but eventually it got away from us and there was no hope of getting back together. It was time to move to a different option. We decided a cheap little pleather couch purchased off KSL (online classifieds) would do the trick. It was durable and easy to clean. At this time, I had just had my third child, Eliza, and it was time to move to another house. Here, Isaac would have his own room with a door to close, but, unfortunately, the room had carpet. Because Isaac was now free to move around, there was constantly poop to be cleaned up...everywhere. Once the baby got a little older and I couldn't stand cleaning up poop off the carpet anymore, we moved Isaac upstairs to a wood floor bedroom. The baby was put next to us in Isaac's old carpeted room, but our troubles weren't over yet.

Isaac was still up often through the night and early in the morning. He *loves* to jump and bounce on his bum. He also loves to laugh and squeal, and all of this was right above the baby in our small, echoey home. Eliza was a good sleeper, but she didn't get much sleep with Isaac right above her. We stayed in that house for two years—the least amount of time so we didn't have to pay capital gains. Divine intervention came into play and we found a house in the same neighborhood that met our needs. Isaac is now on the bottom floor with easy-clean rubber flooring in a room away from all other bedrooms in the house. There is even a fart fan in there, since it was going to be the original owner's hot tub room. A definite plus! But don't worry, we can hear him if he cries and we keep video surveillance on him. He is below our kitchen floor and I always hear him "singing" in his room when I'm doing dishes.

He has been through several pleather couches as beds through the years. Some were easier to clean than others. Each one had to go to the dump because of the horrible stink. He eventually graduated to a regular twin bed, but he broke several bed frames with his jumping. At one point, he slept on a pleather rocking chair. This got worse as the medication he was on made him gain weight. He also destroyed everything we put in his room, from books and clothes, lava lamps and fake fish tanks, dressers, and other things we thought would help him. Now he just sleeps on a mattress on the floor with a protective mattress pad and a protective sheet. Sometimes he still gets human matter on the mattress. I think he's had three.

Finally, when Isaac was about six and a half years old, we found a few helpful doctors and psychiatrists to help Isaac sleep at night, calm his aggression, and give our whole family the hope, sleep, and peace we needed—or at least enough to feel normal-ish again. I am forever grateful to all the doctors who helped get Isaac to his best self and continue to work with him. Although Isaac sleeps better, he still does not sleep quite as well as a typical child through the night and often wakes up too early. In order for there not to be poop and pee all over the house at five o'clock in the morning each day, we put a safety handle on the inside of his room so he could only get out when we opened the door. This at least contains the mess, but if we ever travel anywhere, it gets tricky. Thankfully, I found the pop-up bed tent off Amazon. Total game-changer. Now, wherever we go, we have a portable bed tent that can be enclosed with zippers. It is his safe spot and I don't have to worry about him getting out at someone's house or at a hotel to terrorize the rest of the family or smear poop everywhere. He likes it, because no matter where we go, it is familiar. He knows that's his bed and it's time to sleep. It even folds up nicely into a flat round bag for easy storage. I highly recommend this, even for home if need be. Finding the best accommodations for my children to make sure they feel safe, secure, and unthreatened is a much more pleasant way to live for everyone.

Eliza, on the other hand, has always been a pretty typical child. We've been trying melatonin and other medications, however, to help her sleep be more solid. Sometimes she will randomly get up at two a.m. and come into our room, ready for the day. A few years ago, a miracle happened: Eliza and Evelyn got bunk beds and shared a room. I was mostly worried about Evelyn at this point, but she ended up sleeping better, or at least being quiet, through the night from then on. It all started because we wanted to give Jeremy an office during his years of at home work due to COVID-19. Evelyn got up every night like a newborn and we were exhausted. She was ornery without enough sleep.

"It's your turn," I turned to Jeremy at one o' clock in the morning. "I've been up with her since midnight and she won't stay down."

Jeremy sighed. "Okay," he said groggily as he rolled out of the warmth of our covers. I tried to go back to sleep, but hearing her cry in the next room prevented that. Soon she quieted down, however, and I began to doze when I heard Jeremy quietly shut her door. You have to twist and hold the handle, then release slowly so she won't hear a loud click or thud as the door shuts.

"Thanks, hon. You must have the magic touch," I said as he snuggled in close to me under the covers again.

"I think you did the hard work," he replied. "It's like pickle jars. You do all the work and I get all the credit." Despite his tired voice, I detect a smile and I give a tired chuckle.

"Yeah, that must be it."

Night after night of this on and off had us questioning whether or not Evelyn should be in Eliza's room. We thought it might be a nightmare of them waking each other up. Although it does occasionally happen, for the most part, they do great together. They have become the cutest little buddies. I love when they come up (not too early) together in the morning to say hello. On the nights Evelyn wakes up because of a soggy diaper or because she threw the blankets off and is cold, Jeremy and I take turns when necessary. Sometimes Millie, across from the girls' room, will go in there at night because she hears crying and helps them by singing a church song, such as "I Am a Child of God." It is a well-known song in my church written by a talented woman named Janice Kapp Perry. Next to "Book of Mormon Stories" and "Jesus Wants Me for a Sunbeam," it's a favorite for my kids.

Evelyn still struggles to sleep through the whole night, but she doesn't cry out. She simply goes to her rocking chair and moves back and forth, often scooting all the way to the wall so that we hear a bonk, bonk, bonk of the chair throughout the middle of the night. We would like to get her on some mediation soon so that she can have a more restful sleep and be happier during the day as well, but I'm not looking forward to the trial and error of finding the right medication and dose.

I am just so grateful I get more sleep now than I have in years. Sleep is so essential and it is nearly impossible when it just doesn't come naturally to your child. I've noticed some of the most basic human concepts (sleeping, eating, going to the bathroom) are very hard for my children and it takes a lot of patience, understanding, compassion, and prayers. Overall, it is a rollercoaster at my house in all aspects. We go through highs and lows on a regular basis—even hourly. The one constant thing in all of it is the love we share for each other, no matter what.

22

Parenting Tips

Jeremy and Isaac playing in the backyard of Great Grandpa Fowler's house

"Think of the last time you felt humiliated or treated unfairly. Did you feel like cooperating or doing better?"
–Jane Nelsen

Jane Nelsen is one of my favorite child development researchers. She focuses on love and kindness in disciplining children. After all I've learned about child development, the one thing I've taken away is that children need to feel loved. It is the most important thing; everything else is secondary. I wish I could say all special needs children get the love they need.

"I can tell you really love him," Isaac's school teacher once said to me in an IEP. "Not every child in my class is loved and you can tell that yours is," she said through tears. Of course, I teared up, too, because I was grateful she saw my love for my son, but I was sad for the others she's seen that deserve more. I don't judge those parents. I get it. A special needs child changes your life and everything forever. So often, parents of a special needs child, whether they realize it or not, resent their child, leading to the child feeling unwanted and unloved. This doesn't help either party.

One thing that helped me through my admitted resentment toward Isaac is therapy. Finding the right therapist for me that I trust and I feel helps me has been one of the best decisions I've made. Through therapy, I recognized and came to grips with my feelings, and now I am more capable of freely loving without strings attached. I've always loved my son, but it's hard not to have resentment toward someone who has brought much difficulty, sadness, and heartache to your life. From the time Isaac was born, it was physical pain, frustration, and tears. After Isaac was born, my stress level went up and I had to be on anxiety and depression medication. My physical health started to dwindle and I developed autoimmune issues. It's a difficult thing to talk about. No parent wants to admit that they feel this way about their child, but I think it happens more often than not. Fragile X is an especially difficult disability to handle, because aggression, behavior challenges, and low cognitive functioning can make for a laborious life to live each day. So many times Jeremy and I haven't been able to go out with friends, be with family, go to fun get-togethers, or go on vacations. Besides therapy, it has helped me to remember it's not just about me.

My support coordinator often said, "I just feel bad for the little guy. He just doesn't know how to express himself. It must be so frustrating to have a body that doesn't work the way you want it to." Taking on that perspective, I stepped out of my own shoes and into Isaac's. Compassion then came much more readily. If I were in his shoes, I would want people to be accepting, understanding, and helpful. I would be angry most of the time, whereas Isaac often seems so free and happy, despite his challenges.

I feel I often contribute to the chaos in the home. Isaac doesn't always know better or understand, but I do. I know I shouldn't yell or hurt him or any of my children in any way—and yet I have. My uncontrolled anger allows regrets to come into our life. I've seen my husband try to force or yell to make them do something; in very few instances is such behavior necessary or helpful, but as parents, we get so defeated and frustrated that it is the go-to, like it is actually going to help. In my experience, yelling only makes things worse. If they are crying, they will only cry louder and longer. If they are hitting, they will only hit harder. If anything, yelling teaches them they should yell to get what they want. Example is a huge part of parenting, especially with special needs kids who watch and do so much of what you do.

Kindness and persuasion is the way to go unless the child is in immediate danger. When Isaac runs out into the road and a car is coming, I am going to yell for him to come here and run to grab him back to safety. There's no kindly waiting for him to comply there. Sometimes these things need to be done, but they should be few and far between in rare and extreme circumstances. I've gained insight by reading parenting books, like Jane Nelsen's *Positive Discipline for Children with Special Needs*, and praying for guidance on how to handle things, even if it's just to keep my temper.

Special needs children need boundaries and rules according to their abilities and needs just like typical children. True love is having boundaries and teaching them. Letting children do whatever they want is not the way to go. There is a balance to keep. I admit I let Isaac get away with so much more than Millie, and part of that is wanting peace and not war. It's choosing the more important battles. I won't fight him to wear a button-up shirt to church, but I will be stern when it comes to being kind to his sisters. There is some unacceptable behavior, however, whether you have special needs or not.

Naming their feelings and showing or sharing good examples of what to do is best, rather than yelling at them and saying what *not* to do. For example, if my kid is yelling at another to "Give me that! Mine! Miiiine!" I come and say something like, "It looks like you are frustrated. Let's take a deep breath." Sometimes they just yell at me when I ask that, but it's good to teach. "How about we take turns? Ask her nicely if you can have a turn. Say, 'Eliza, can I play with that toy, please?'"

One of the most helpful tools I have used over the years is redirection. If you haven't heard this word already as a parent of FX kids, you will. It basically means that when your child is doing an undesired behavior, you change their attention to something totally different. For example, if a child is crying at the park, direct their attention to the cute puppy dog coming by and say, "Oh, look! That is such a cute puppy! What do you think his name is? I would name him Clifford. Remember Clifford the big red dog? He's so fun. How about we look for a big red slide to ride down?" Mentally take them away from what's bothering them at the time. Obviously it is more difficult to do in times of high stress and high stakes, but the more you do it, the better you get.

Fragile X kids won't always be so easily distracted, however. They often get very stuck on one thing. With time, I have found something that helps each of my children calm down if redirection doesn't work. For Isaac, he needs a break alone to restart. For Evelyn, I rock with her and read a story quietly and sing a quiet song. Sometimes it takes a long time for the calm down to happen, but keeping cool and compassionate is key. I always say that, no matter what, if you are about to lose your cool, be sure your child is safe and remove yourself from the situation to cool off. It's better than hurting your child in any way. Maybe it even means giving them the iPad for a minute so you can breathe. It's okay. I can't count how many times my kids have watched TV for too long, because I just needed a break and no one else was there to help me.

Many times at the end of the day I think back and say, "Okay, I fed the kids, they wore clothes most of the time, I changed their diapers, and they are alive. That's good enough." Forget about all the things you didn't do and let the guilt melt away, because you are enough. You are doing better than you think. Not everyone can do what you are doing and it's okay to allow yourself a break, some slack, and some understanding. Just think of what those closest to you and who love you would say of you as a parent of a special needs child. They would say you're amazing! Allow for mistakes and begin again. You aren't a failure and the last thing that helps is putting yourself down. There is no denying raising a child with Fragile X is hard, but you don't need to make things harder by being your worst enemy.

I like to look at parenting as any other job where you have a physical or metaphorical toolbox. Here are some things I have in my own parenting toolbox that I keep handy when things fall apart:

1. Instead of telling children what NOT to do, give them options of what to do instead. For example, if my child is yelling, instead of telling them in a loud voice to "STOP YELLING!" I can first be an example by being calm myself and saying something as simple as, "Oh, let's talk a bit quieter in the house and use our inside voices, okay?" Sometimes it takes a few tries and changing of words, but it's a much better approach overall.

2. Have business cards with information about Fragile X Syndrome so when you are out in public, you can just hand a questioning or complaining onlooker the card instead of explaining for the hundredth time what is really going on. I really wish I would've had these early on. I'll never forget when a woman at the store snobbishly said, "Oh, well, it looks like *somebody* needs a nap!" to Isaac when he was having a meltdown at the store.

3. Join support groups of various kinds, such as on Facebook or your local Fragile X Association or local chapter. This can connect you to other parents, caregivers, and children going through similar experiences. It

helps so we don't feel so alone in the journey. It helps to see others and realize your kid isn't the only one doing that. Sometimes it even brings some needed laughter.

4. You can't push too much, but you have to push a little. The anxiety that comes with FX can be so overwhelming; yet, these kids often want to be social and do things out in the world. It takes a fine balance of knowing how much to push them and when to back off. For example, encouraging my daughter to come out of her room to be with close family may be needed, but I do not expect her to go on stage in a crowd by herself and perform just yet.

5. Patience. So much patience. There are times you just have to wait. For example, I know it takes a minimum of ten minutes for Isaac to get out the door and into his stroller to be rolled onto the bus each morning. I plan accordingly. Sometimes we are in high-stakes situations where we need to go and I do a bit more pushing, but it always seems to backfire in the end anyway. We wait a lot around here. Sometimes it is so frustrating and I feel completely powerless, but I just think positive and tell myself this will pass.

6. Love. I keep a copy of Jane Nelsen's "Mistaken Goal Chart" on my fridge or somewhere I can always see it. It helps me to sort out my children's undesirable behavior and figure out what I am doing that contributes to it and what I can do to help in a loving way. No matter what my kids do or don't do, I love them unconditionally. The love is always there.

7. Be open with neighbors and friends. There is a fear that if we tell people our child has special needs, they will be treated differently. Although this is true, most often it is for the good of all. My children *are* different from other children, so I expect them to be treated a little differently—with a bit more understanding and patience. If I saw a nine-year-old boy walking down the road by himself in the neighborhood, I might not think much of it, but when my neighbors see Isaac, they know to take immediate action

to contact me and make sure he is safe. I once had a neighbor sit with him on the corner, despite Isaac not liking it at all, so that he didn't walk into oncoming traffic when he escaped from the house on a hectic day. I understand people may not give a child a chance to grow or be respected in some cases. Eliza, for example, is more high functioning, so I don't talk quite as openly about her disability as I do Isaac, because he needs a lot of explaining. Sometimes people don't know what to do or how to act if they can see something is off. Sometimes they do better knowing what to expect. It's a balance that each parent must consider for each child.

8. Get signs in your neighborhood to warn cars, especially those out of the area, that there is a special needs child and to slow down. These signs can be acquired through the city or even simple ones can be found on Amazon.

9. Fence the yard. We cannot live without a fenced-in yard. It's not safe for our kids. With a fenced yard, Isaac roams in and out of the backyard freely without me worrying he is going to run away or get hurt.

10. One-on-one time with each of your children is important. Sometimes Jeremy and I take Millie and Eliza out to do things we cannot do with Evelyn and Isaac. It breaks my heart not to have our family together doing fun things, but I also want to give them opportunities other kids have on a regular basis. Besides, I know Isaac and Evelyn won't enjoy going out and would rather be at home anyway. Each of them should get one-on-one attention doing things they like, even if all we do is take Isaac for a walk around the block or go swing at an empty park. Spend time with each child and find joy being with them and getting to know them as individuals.

11. Get a will. Unlike other parents, we must think about how our children will continue after we are gone. The last thing I want is for tragedy to strike and not have a plan to execute for my children's greatest benefit.

12. Get in contact with local police. As mentioned before with Melina's case, giving the police a picture and explanation of your child and how to

handle him/her can make a huge difference if a future encounter is made, whether serious or not.

13. Set up a trust fund and get finances in order, whether it is through Medicaid, SSI, or other means. Plan for the future of your children financially.

14. Therapy. As mentioned before, couples therapy and personal therapy has given me other tools, such as mindfulness, to help me and my family continue.

15. Redirection. This is my go-to when my kids need to get out of a funk. You simply distract them by talking about or doing something else.

16. Scaffolding children is important. This means leading them along to meet their goals and find success without huge, unrealistic jumps. I think of it as a ladder where my child is at point A, and to get them to point B, I set up multiple achievable goals. For example, expecting Isaac to walk on his own was not realistic. Instead, we used several different walkers, exercises, and different techniques to get him in the standing position in order to achieve the end goal of walking. Along with this is giving your child simple step by step instructions. I know that Eliza gets frustrated if I tell her to clean her room, but when I tell her a few steps at a time and break it down she does things easily. Sometimes this means making a to do list. Sometimes it means doing pictures to follow. She also likes having a poster with TO DO items on one side, then moving them to the DONE side when she is finished.

17. Parenting is different for each child. This means a neighbor who raised seven typical kids, despite all their good advice, may not actually know what is best for my special needs child. These kids seem to be wired differently and what usually works with typical children won't necessarily help with my FX child. I've found I should not be afraid to try new things or do things differently, despite what others may think, as long as it is what is best for my child and my family. Finding my own groove of

parenting, praying for direction, doing the research, and knowing my child individually is all key.

18. Do more online shopping. I know my sister got creative with backpacks and contraptions before online shopping was big, but I've learned to simply do what causes less stress. After my last trip trying to take all the kids to Costco and not even getting in the doors, I decided it was okay to get a few old pieces of fruit from the delivery guy if it meant peace and happiness with my kids at home.

19. Don't talk to your child like a baby unless they are one. Just talk with them and listen even if they don't say much back to you.Spend time with each child. Find joy being with them and getting to know them as individuals.

20. Start as early as possible to get your child in Early Intervention, speech therapy, physical, therapy, etc. And the earlier you get on a waiting list for medical aid and respite, the sooner you will get in. It can take years, so start now!

I'm sure I could go on, but each parent will need to find a flow and fit for their family and their own "parenting toolbox." I'm not perfect and I don't know everything; I am just another mom trying to get through. It takes a lot of work to raise children with such varied disabilities, but somehow I've made it this far and I'm still alive and finding joy.

23

A Day in the Life of Fragile X

Isaac being pushed in the baby swing

"I just live one day at a time."
–Rick James

I don't often talk about my day-to-day life with other people. There's a few reasons for that. For one, it makes me realize how horrible my life sounds. Two, they just feel sorry for me and give that horrible look of pity. Lastly, this is just my normal, so I roll with it and don't make a huge deal. There are some days, though, I look up at the sky and yell, "Seriously?" But just so others won't feel alone, may get a chuckle, or just come to better understanding, here are a few examples of my day to day life:

"Good morning, beautiful," my husband said as he snuggled in close. He was fully ready for the day and I was just waking up.

"Good morning," I said groggily, then gave him a morning breath kiss. I grabbed my phone to look at the time. Just then my alarm song played and I immediately pushed the stop button.

"Did the words over your alarm say 'You won't regret waking up?'" my husband asked, chuckling.

"Yes," I laughed sheepishly.

"I didn't know you could customize that."

"It's my motivation," I said with a smile. "It doesn't always work." Right then my phone started to buzz and I saw Diana calling.

"Hello?" I answered, still sounding like there was a frog living in my throat.

"Hey, I'm not coming this morning," she said over the phone. "I have diarrhea," she laughed. "It's from your kid!"

"Oh no!" I said. "I'm sorry! I didn't think he was that bad. Besides, his poop consistency is always all over the place, so I never know when he's sick or not."

"Well, I'm hoping this Imodium kicks in and then I can still go to school with him," said Diana.

"I don't know if I'll send him to school if he has bad diarrhea. I noticed his nose running, too," I said sadly.

"Yeah, and he won't wear a mask, so it might be a good idea. Just let me know. If I feel better soon, I'll just come over to the house if he doesn't go to school," she replied.

"Okay, sounds good. I'll see you later. Bye," I said, then hung up.

"No Diana?" Jeremy asked, concerned.

"No," I said. "But I think I'll be okay. I'm glad you're working from home today, though."

"I have a meeting this morning, so hopefully things go okay," he said. We said our morning prayers and he went to his office across the hall while I got all the kids ready for school. Usually Eliza and Evelyn come up early in the morning and wake me up before I can get down to them. Not today! I got dressed and wandered downstairs. First, I went to Isaac's room, hoping to prevent a poop fiasco in his room. When I opened the door, I was relieved to find no poop, though his clothes and bedding were pee-soaked.

"Okay, bud. Let's go sit on the potty and get dressed." I wasn't sure if he would get in the shower, but I figured I'd start with the potty first. As he slowly got out of bed and waddled to the bathroom with a saggy diaper, I opened the room for the little girls and saw they were awake but still in bed. They smiled with their puffy little eyes and fuzzy hair. Evelyn somehow manages to have dreadlocks on the back of her head every morning, and when you brush it out, it becomes a flowy, frizzy, poofball off the backside.

"Good morning, cuties!" I said with a smile.

"Morning, Mommy," Eliza said and Evelyn then repeated, "Morning, Mom." So cute!

"Come on, sleepy heads, it's time to get up and go to school!" They got out of bed and I picked out clothes for them to wear. I started to get Evelyn dressed when I heard Isaac say something.

"Is the water too hot, bud?" I called. He was standing in front of the bathroom sink across the hall. "Remember, you have to turn it to the other side." All I heard was some sad little *ohs*. I stepped away from the girls and went into the bathroom to find Isaac had the hot water running, but there was more than that. A big pile of diarrhea was on the floor underneath him and a small puddle of pee as well. The smell, as usual, was horrific and permeated everywhere.

"Dude! What in the world?" I asked, exasperated. "Okay, go get in the shower please." He didn't get in at first and I kept repeating myself, as usual, to get him to process and comply. Meanwhile, I tried to keep Evelyn from stepping into the mess. Once he was in the shower and Millie had Evelyn occupied, I grabbed the cleaner (we always have cleaner in every room unless it gets taken to another room), rags (we have two designated spots for rag piles to clean up such messes), wipes (these are great because you don't have to wash out the poop), and went to work.

"Eliza, I've laid out your clothes. Please get dressed," I called. I hoped she could do it. She's capable, but sometimes gets both legs in one panty hole or tries to put her hips through the leg hole. Meanwhile, using the wipes to pick up most of the poop sludge, I grabbed it and put it in the trash, then wiped away the residual. I then soaked up the pee with one rag and used the other to disinfect with the OdoBan spray. I looked over at Eliza and saw, thankfully, that she had gotten dressed just fine.

"Good job, sweetie!" I praised her. "Go get some breakfast. Your chocolate milk is upstairs." I turned to Isaac, still sitting in the shower, threatening to come out with poop on his body.

"K, stay in the shower," I said, warning him with my eyes to not put a poopy footstep out of that tub. After cleaning up the nasty mess, I went to the shower and saw he had pooped once or twice in there as well. More diarrhea. Thank goodness for the detachable sprayer in the shower. I can't live without it! I unhooked the spray head and turned on the water. I sprayed the poop down the drain and sprayed Isaac down to get off the remaining. I then lathered up the soap and covered him and the tub with cleansing bubbles. Rinse and repeat. Done!

"Okay, bud. Hop out and let's get you dry," I said as I grabbed a towel. I dried him head-to-toe once he stepped out of the shower and immediately pulled his diaper up over his still-damp body that acted like a velcro mat against the diaper. Getting dressed right after a shower is a pain. I then slipped his shirt over his head.

"Ew! What's that?" Millie asked as she came out of her room. Her wide eyes stared at a big streak of green, nasty boogers. My eyes grew big and I looked at Isaac's nose.

"That would be his boogers," I said matter-of-factly. Then I sighed. *Okay, this kid is staying home today.*

"Evelyn's bus is here," Jeremy said. He had come out of his office and snuck up behind me.

"What!" I exclaimed.

"Yeah, there's a bus out there. I'm pretty sure it's Evelyn's," he said.

"They aren't supposed to be here for another twenty-five minutes! What the heck?"

"What do you want me to do?" Jeremy asked.

"Put your head out there and tell them to hold on a minute," I said. I rushed to grab a bow for her frizzy head and ran in the kitchen, skidding across the wood floor in my socked feet, to grab her backpack and sandals. In the meantime, Jeremy got her morning chocolate milk in a sippy cup. I heard the bus honk.

"Okay, gooey," I said, picking her up. She started screaming.

"Bag! Bag!" she screamed. Apparently she had to have her little bag of necklaces and treasures. Not sure how that would work on the bus or school, I wasn't going to fight her now. I grabbed the bag and added it to her comfort blankie she already clutched in her arms, then rushed down the stairs.

"Okay, it's time to get on the bus!" I tried to sound happy and calm so she didn't freak out more than usual. I ran out in my socks only to see the sprinklers had come on that morning. I ripped off my socks before running through the grass. I realized I couldn't put her on the bus in bare feet and the bus helper was on the phone with a parent. The bus driver had to come get her and she only fussed a small bit.

"Thanks!" I said, apologetically. "Will you be here at this time from now on?" I asked, a bit out of breath.

"Yes," the bus driver replied. "Give or take five minutes." *Okay*, I thought. *Good to know.* The bus schedules were so weird at the start of the school year. I waved goodbye to Evelyn and, thankfully, she smiled and went on her way to preschool. I came back in the house and texted Diana: *Isaac is going to stay home.* She replied: *I'll be over in a bit.* At that point, I realized I had a meeting with his teacher later that morning, so I was grateful Diana would be there. I proceeded to take my morning medication and get Isaac's into syringes for dispensing. He takes his medicine really well, thank goodness! I went downstairs and did Eliza's hair for the day while she watched ellieV on YouTube. She only screamed a few times as I did a simple half-updo. Brushing the girls' hair is never a pleasant activity. Afterward, I sighed in relief, knowing Evelyn was on the bus, the other girls were ready to go and looking cute, and Isaac was staying home with Diana here to help.

I went upstairs and peeked in Jeremy's office.

"That was a bit crazy," I said.

"Yeah," he agreed.

"I wish they would've told me when they would be here," I said, annoyed, but laughing.

"Yeah, no kidding," Jeremy replied. I looked over at the cat tower in the corner of his office and saw there was no food on the plate where he feeds our cat, Snowflake.

"Has the cat eaten yet?" I asked.

"No, I didn't have a chance this morning."

"Oh. Well, I can do it," I offered.

"K, the rest of her food is in the fridge. Just mix some with the dry food we need to get rid of."

"Deal," I said as I turned and went into the kitchen. I mixed up the cat's food and she appeared out of nowhere to follow me back into the office to perch on her tower.

"She's such a princess," Jeremy said. I laughed and let our dog, Luna, lick the utensil I used to mix the cat food.

"I know," I replied and we both laughed. Then Isaac came up to me and said, "Bum?" which means he needs a bum change. He pooped again and I changed his stinky tush, then washed my hands and said to no one, "Well, I guess I better get the girls off to the bus." I walked downstairs and was about to tell the girls to go when I saw a yellow puddle behind Eliza, crouching down on the ground playing with Duplos and still watching TV.

"Eliza?" I said, walking closer to inspect. "You peed!" I said in surprise. "How come you didn't put it in the potty?"

At this point, they were supposed to be walking out the door to catch the bus. I hurried to grab the cleaner again and another rag. I grabbed the first decent outfit I could find that didn't have button-up pants. I counted my lucky stars that she was crouching and didn't pee into her socks and shoes. Those were still salvageable. Her long shirt and stretchy pants, on the other hand, were soaked. I peeled off the wet clothes and wiped her down with cold cleansing wipes. I didn't care that she was uncomfortable and hoped it would be a consequence she would learn from. I soaked up the pee, sanitized everything, and rushed to get her in her new outfit. Her shoes are so hard to get on, despite thinking they would be easy slide-on shoes when I bought them.

Suddenly Luna was right in my face. Feeling my anxiety and frustration, she tried to make things better, but was only in the way and adding to the frustration with her cute, furry, annoying face. Finally, I got Eliza's shoes on, stuck a mask on her, adjusted it to match her little face, and sent them out the door.

"Okay, hurry, hurry!" I pushed them out the door with side hugs, but Eliza wouldn't have it. She felt the rush and anxiety and started to melt down. Millie and I quickly made it into a game and I grabbed Eliza's hand to go follow Millie. They were off! I prayed they would make it to the bus, then shut the door and sighed a long, annoyed, exasperated sigh. I went in and laid on my bed, reliving the crazy morning. Then I heard something. Part of me thought it was Eliza crying, but I thought, *Nah,* and didn't move. I heard it louder and there was someone at the door. I hurried down the stairs to see Jeremy going out the door, telling Amelia to "Go!" Eliza was crying in the driveway.

Jeremy and I were out there in our socks, Millie was running to the bus she had likely missed, and Eliza was dirty from sitting on the concrete. Jeremy dusted her off, hugged her, then walked in his socks to the bus stop a few blocks away while I stayed home with Isaac, wondering what in the world just happened. Millie and Eliza got on the bus together when it came back around (luckily it came by twice). They missed the first time around and, even though it's not supposed to, it stopped again on the way back and picked them up.

When Jeremy came home, we just looked at each other and I said, "Well...that was fun." Now I have a lot of laundry to do and more diarrhea bums to change.

Later that day, Isaac came to snuggle with me in bed while I worked on my computer. He wore his typical at-home attire: an adult size diaper. I thought it was sweet he wanted to be by me, but Jeremy and I were both skeptical, wondering if he would make a mess of our brand new down duvet and white cover. Don't ask me why I bought white—I should know better.

"But he's so cute when he's snuggly," I said to Jeremy, pleadingly. He just rolled his eyes and I could read what he was thinking: *This isn't going to turn out well, but I'll let you have your moment.* As I laid there, typing, Isaac suddenly hopped off the bed and I noticed a wet spot where he was. At least he realized his mistake and got up before any more leaked out of his diaper.

"Aw, man. Isaac, really? I trusted you," I sighed in frustration.

Sadly, I looked at the pee spot and took off the cover and sheets to put in the laundry and clean up the mess. At this point, the newer mattress was completely exposed and Isaac was still in the room. He was sitting cross-legged by the bed. I was still getting things.

Barf!

My eyes shot to Isaac as he finished his first throw up on my floor and bed skirt.

Barf!

"Dude! Stop!"

Barf!

"Millie, hurry get me some cleaner!" I hollered over my shoulder. Soon the little girls and dog came in to see what the commotion was all about and I tried to keep them out of the mess. Millie came in with a cleaner and a rag.

"Here, Mom," she said breathlessly.

"Thank you. Can you take the dog and the girls outside to play or something?"

"Yeah. Come on guys, let's go jump on the tramp!" Millie said, leading the little clan out the door.

I moved my mattress to get the soiled bed skirt out from underneath, but it was so heavy and awkward to lift I ended up getting chunks on my box spring. With my head and neck holding up the mattress, I scrubbed at the spot and move the mattress to the side so the wet spot could dry.

Then I smelled something. It's not throw up. It's not pee.

"Isaac, did you poop?"

He looked up at me, in the pooping crouch position, with a small pile of poop behind his leg. There's still throw up in front of him on the floor. Thankfully, Jeremy came to my rescue.

"Come on, bud. We gotta go take a shower. Come on, stand up," Jeremy coaxed. He took Isaac downstairs with poop dripping from his diaper and poop heel prints following behind. I finished cleaning up. I'm not even sure this was from him being sick, because he throws up all the time if there is a certain smell, a food he doesn't want to eat, or the look of his food is off. Later, Jeremy speculated he smelled the foulness of his own poop and that's why he threw up. Whatever it was, it was gross. This type of thing happens whether he is sick or not.

Jeremy and I tag-teamed cleaning the floors with me getting the chunks and him doing the sanitation spray while Isaac washed off in the shower. I finished cleaning him up, helped him get dressed, and we went back to our day like normal. Our normal.

If it isn't messes, it's meltdowns. Other days, we deal with aggression, yelling, screaming, public displays, and the dangers of getting hurt. I will never forget one day when we decided to make a ten-mile trek on our surrey bike (with no assist) to the local grocery store for donuts and snow cones at a nearby shack. After waiving at passersby, seeing smiling faces in tinted car windows, and almost causing a wreck after one truck stared at our family circus too long, we made it to the store. Jeremy and I decided I would take his place driving the bike around to keep the littles happy and grab the snow cones while he and Millie ran in to get the donuts. We stopped in front of the automatic sliding glass doors and the two ran in while I peddled away.

"Daddy!" Evelyn shouted.

"I wanna go!" Eliza screamed.

"It's okay. We are going to get a snow cone right over there and ride the bike. They will be back soon," I said, trying to reassure them everything would be okay. Then I realized I didn't have my card to pay for snow cones, so we would have to wait for Jeremy. I started to sing a song and just tootle around the parking lot when I looked behind me. Isaac always sat in the backseat with a belt strap to help hold him in. He wasn't there.

I panicked.

I couldn't let the girls know that. I kept peddling and singing while praying over and over to find my little boy. He could've ran anywhere at this point.

I did a quick glance around to see if there was any commotion. No honking horns or screeching tires. Traffic was normal, so I sighed in relief, thinking it was unlikely he went out on the road. I searched the parking lot as I rode back and forth, but found nothing. I didn't have my phone to call Jeremy or anyone. I craned my neck to hear any of Isaac's whines, crying, singing, or other loud noises he makes, but I heard nothing. It was business as usual all around me and I could not think for the life of me where he could be. Now I know I should have immediately started yelling his name, shouting out to everyone around that a special needs boy was lost, but at that moment, I sat in front of the store, not knowing what to do next, when I saw Jeremy coming out.

Isaac jumped forward on his bare feet, following behind his dad, and loudly "singing" with a bag of chips in his hands. I immediately knew what happened.

"Oh my gosh!" I said as Jeremy came out with a smile.

"Yeah, he followed us in, I guess," Jeremy said. "I knew you would be worried, so we hurried and came out."

"I found him!" Millie said proudly. "I heard something and I knew it was Isaac's noises, so I told Daddy."

"Yeah, and sure enough, we followed the sound and there he was, looking at the bags of chips," Jeremy laughed.

"He must've known there were chips in there," I said in disbelief. "I can't believe he got out of his seat and just ran in there!"

"I can," said Jeremy with a smile.

"Yeah, he does love his chips," I said and laughed. "But I was so worried! I really thought he was lost! I worried he'd been run over by a car!" I started to put Isaac back in his seat.

"I'm sorry, hon. That would be scary. I'm glad he just wanted chips and he is so loud he provided his own homing beacon," Jeremy said and laughed.

We got settled, bought the snow cones, and went on our way. Of course, the kids had meltdowns, because some had a donut and some had a snow cone—we will always get them all the same thing from now on. Besides, I felt stupid in a surrey bike with fringe on top going down the road with everyone staring and my kids are bawling their eyes out. I jokingly told them, "You can't cry when you're on this bike. It doesn't look right. We draw enough attention with this as it is!"

Honestly, I can't count how many times my days likely looked like a nightmare to others. Just recently, I prepared a dessert. I didn't feel like it, but I made myself, because I knew it would make Millie and Jeremy smile. I like doing things like that for them. Unfortunately, I chose the wrong time. I was just about finished with the batter when Eliza came up. I reminded her it was time to go potty, to which she plainly replied, "I pooped."

"Oh...okay." I've stopped having much of a reaction, because she poops in her underwear at least once a day. We are still working on that second part. "Well, let me get this in the oven and then we will change you." I quickly finished the batter, poured it in the pan, and set the timer for thirteen minutes.

"K, let's go clean you up in the bathroom," I said. We trudged downstairs and I began to undress her.

"Whoa. Did you get Evelyn's diarrhea? This is looser than usual," I said as I tried peeling off the brown, gooey mess of underwear.

Eliza giggled, then said, "Sorry, Mommy."

"It's okay," I said, trying to slide the underwear down her legs without getting it everywhere. It wasn't working. "You know what? This isn't going to work this time. Hop in the shower. I'm going to hose you down."

She obeyed and I grabbed my handy dandy detachable shower head. I turned it to the most direct flow and hosed down her underwear and backside. The whole time I'm thinking, *Okay, thirteen minutes. This is taking longer, but still, I have thirteen minutes.*

"Okay, stay in here and rinse off. I'll be back." I wanted to give it some time to soak and wash off before I took to her body with a loofah. Poop chunks in a loofah aren't fun. Believe me, I know.

I quickly ran up the first part of the stairs to the landing to see if my brownies were done when I saw Millie coming up to the door. Our door has large glass windows with opaque designs, so you can always see who's there. I opened the door, surprised.

"Hey!" I said as I opened the door. I looked past her to see Isaac's bus already there with Isaac almost unloaded from the wheelchair ramp.

"Oh, crap!" I said and shut the door—in Millie's face—and ran up the rest of the steps so I could go through the back door and get Isaac through the garage. We keep his stroller there so I know he won't run off down the street when I let him out. Routines, right? As I ran up the stairs, I heard the timer. I grabbed my hot pads, turned off the oven and timer, and removed the pan from the oven so the treat didn't burn. Then I rushed out to get Isaac.

"Hey! Sorry!" I said, running out to the bus.

"Oh, it's fine. He's just jabbering away and so happy today!" the bus driver said.

"Oh good," I replied. Then I looked at Isaac with a smile. "Hey bud. Come on, let's get inside!"

I hurried to get him in the house, because Eliza was still playing in the shower. We walked in and Millie greeted me.

"Hey, sorry about that," and we both laugh.

"It's okay," she smiles.

"I didn't realize it was that time already!"

Millie hung up her backpack. She then looked past me and said, "Isaac!" I followed her stare to the floor and Isaac somehow peed a puddle and took off his pants and diaper.

"Aw, man! Isaac! Seriously?" I ran to get cleaner and a rag. I had so many pee rags upstairs and downstairs ready to go for this sort of thing.

"Millie, Eliza is downstairs in the shower. Can you get her out, dried and dressed, please?" I said quickly.

"Oh! Uh, yeah, sure," she said. Love that girl!

After I cleaned up Isaac's mess and got him back in a diaper, I hurried downstairs to help Millie. That's when I heard Evelyn was awake from her nap.

"Oh good, we can get Eliza's clothes out of there now," I told Millie, who was toweling off a wet Eliza. I stepped in and immediately smelled something strong: lacquer. I opened the door all the way and saw Evelyn in the reclining rocking chair with an open bottle of purple nail polish.

"Oh my gosh!" I said with wide eyes. "Are you kidding me?" My eyes scanned the room and I saw she had painted on her sheets, the walls, the closet doors, the recliner, and herself. She was purple from toes to knees and fingers to elbows—but hey, at least it wasn't in her hair.

"Nevermind, go grab some clothes from the laundry and get dressed out in the TV room, K? Evelyn, let's go hop in the bath!"

I stripped Evelyn down, threw away the nail polish, and started a bath for her. While the water filled up, I grabbed my nail polish remover and cotton balls. I tried to get most of it off of her body, but she just turned a light purple and I didn't want to put acetone all over her. I decided to let her soak.

"Can I take a bath, too?" Eliza asked from behind as I scrubbed Evelyn.

"No, sweetie, there's purple nail polish flecks all in the water and I need to get this off your sister."

Eliza screamed. And wouldn't stop screaming.

"Sorry, but you just got clean and I don't want you in here right now," I said, ignoring her screams. She continued to scream as I scrubbed the walls and chair with acetone that took off more than just nail polish and left a purple hue everywhere it touched. She finally decided no one was going to let her in the tub, so she stopped crying. I'm surprised she didn't just jump in.

I tried my best, but things were still purple. Evelyn had flecks on her legs like purple freckles for days afterward. For the longest time, she sported two purple painted toenails. Unfortunately, that wasn't the last fingernail polish incident. We have so many messes constantly in my home. For a time, the most dreaded sound was the drip, drip, dripping of water *somewhere*.

We had moved from an old home to a newer-ish home in the same neighborhood. Jeremy had fixed water leak after water leak and pipe after pipe in that old home. We were ready to be done with water damage and issues, but Isaac had another plan for us.

A nice, sunny Saturday came along and I decided it was a good time to "nap while the baby is napping." Apparently, at the same time, my husband decided it was a good time to go work outside in the garage. I remember waking up to Millie yelling something. Soon I heard Jeremy yelling something at Isaac. I let my sleeping baby lie and softly crept out of my room and to the kitchen where I saw a disaster. Isaac was crying on the floor with a squirt toy and bucket.

"What in the world?" I asked, inspecting my flooded kitchen floor.

"I don't know. Where were you?" Jeremy asked, frustrated.

"I was sleeping with the baby, where were you?" I retorted.

"I was working outside. I thought you were in here," he said.

"Well, I thought you were keeping an eye on the other kids," I said. We both sighed, frustrated, and yelled at each other, "Get a towel!"

"Hurry! Millie, go downstairs and bring up all the towels, quick!" I said, getting on my hands and knees and grabbing kitchen rags as substitutes to soak up the water.

"It's under the fridge and through the vents," Jeremy said, angry. "It's probably downstairs." With that, he took off to see what the damage was. I heard some muffled anger through the floor before stomping sounded up the stairs.

"It leaked into the basement. I'm going to have to redo the whole ceiling in that part of the house!" Jeremy yelled. He had seen enough leaks, dry wall, and paint since fixing our last house and it was not something he wanted to do again.

Apparently, Isaac simply wanted to play with the water bucket and squirters outside, but no one was around to play, so he took matters into his own hands and brought the bucket inside. We have a sink with a faucet that comes out of the base and he decided to let it run directly onto the floor for who knows how long. It was such a disaster.

"I'm turning off the water under the kitchen sink for a while," Jeremy informed us all after we'd cleaned the immediate mess. "Isaac won't leave the faucet alone and we can't sit and stare at him all day to make sure he doesn't touch it."

Isaac was obsessed. We had to hide all the squirters and buckets, turn off the water, and watch him closely. Thankfully, that has since passed and he has (hopefully) learned, but every single day he wets our floor using the water feature on the fridge. We have a permanent rag that gets rotated under the fridge to prevent our wood floor from getting any more warped. Still, it's better than filling up a sippy cup every five seconds for him and having him pee more.

On many days, Jeremy and I decide to laugh rather than cry, but sometimes the crying comes before the laughter. Some days are just so hard we wonder if we can go another day or even another minute. Jeremy and I have both come to our breaking points time and time again. The more Jeremy is involved in family life, the more understanding he is toward how I have felt over the years. Jeremy happened to write his feelings down one day as a coping mechanism to vent. We want things we can't have. Even with more financial security now than as college students years ago, there's things we just can't buy or change. This is hard to read, but it is also how I've felt many a day and I know others have felt this many days, too. This is what he wrote:

Was there ever a time in your life when you just wanted to give up and stop, where you were so tired you didn't want to carry the load anymore, when what little good does keep you going is overshadowed by yet another sour experience, or when because of all these things together you wallow in the aftermath of getting angry and yelling because that seems to be the only thing that brings order in your life full of disorder?

I know venting seems to have merit, though it might do some harm, too.

I'm tired of cleaning up pee on the floor everyday. I'm tired of walking past laundry that smells like urine because there's already a mountain of laundry that needs to be folded and both the dryer and washer are full. I'm tired of yelling. I'm tired of wearing out my life to only have my kids bicker and fight. I'm tired of the tablet and its noises and obnoxious sounds, but that seems to be our lifeline keeping sanity between us and Isaac. I'm tired of cleaning poopy underwear because we've been trying to potty train Eliza since August. I'm tired of pulling clothes out of the trash can because Isaac doesn't comprehend the difference between throwing his diaper away and his own clothes.

I'm tired of the feeling of being trapped. I'm tired of not seeing any ray of sunshine at the end of the tunnel of Isaac improving in his behavior. I'm tired of going to extraordinary measures to make our life normal in a world that seems to fight us at every turn. I'm tired of "normal" people treating my wife and kids as problems when they have no idea the load and energy expended just to get us where we are. I'm tired of chasing goals in life that are only goals because it's the only way we can put out the fire. I'm tired of wasted food. I'm tired of buying things for my kids, because they don't care. I'm tired of the bus drivers from three different buses who get mad at us because we were a few minutes late. I'm tired of packing snacks, multiple changes of clothes, drinking utensils, and entertainment for our kids whenever we want to go someplace. I'm tired of having to leave someplace early because my kids are having a meltdown and I'm embarrassed and can't get them to calm down. I'm tired of Isaac stripping down in places outside the home. I'm tired of performing all this service and receiving only ungrateful whining and crying as thanks. I'm tired of trying to pursue my faith in Christ only to be met with the demons of Christ's time and hearing others say they are angels. I'm tired of picking up the tablet that Isaac throws out in the road because we went out of WiFi range. I'm tired of administering multiple medications day and night just to make it through the day. I'm tired of knowing I need to figure out how to take care of my kids after I die because they won't be able to work. I'm tired of seeing things not change. I'm tired of cleaning the couches again because of Isaac's diaper leaks. I'm tired and I don't want to do this anymore.

We have had so many days like this. I could go on and on with such day-to-day stories, but I will say this: even through all the craziness we face every day, it makes it all worth it on the days I see my kids giggling and playing with one another; the day Evelyn said, "I love you, Mommy" for the first time; the night Isaac showed affection by saying, "Happy Halloween," and later telling me "Iwuhoo" (I love you). I take all I can get. I'm grateful my kids can speak. I'm grateful Eliza says, "I'm so happy you're home, Mom! I missed you!" And even Evelyn has grown in her language and comes to give me a hug when I've been gone even an hour. But even before they could say any words, their laughter and giggles, smiles and sparkling eyes made my day and still do. It makes everything feel worth it. Those times keep me going. I recall a time when Isaac was much younger and didn't use many words at all. We had a tender moment I won't forget:

Isaac grabbed my hand and led me out the side door with no words. He is autistic, nonverbal, and has Fragile X Syndrome. But that is not all Isaac is to me. He is sweet, smiley, funny, and loving. As I turned my attention to him, he just smiled and looked up at me. At the time, I was in the middle of eating dinner. My husband made his homemade tortillas that we all love. Of course, Isaac had been in the living room watching his tablet at the time. I, however, wasn't in a hurry to leave the table as I enjoyed the delicious food.

Sometimes Isaac ate at the table if I gave him rice, but usually it was a pricey PediaSure and goldfish on the go. He's always on the go. I savored the times we all sat together at the table. It was few and far between and usually did not last more than five minutes. Isaac even had a special chair at the head of the table to keep him secure so he didn't fall off the bench...again. He didn't know where he was in space like I do.

Normally, I would have told Isaac I couldn't come out with him because I was still eating. Normally, I would've been too tired, too busy, and too overwhelmed—but something in those dark brown eyes and pure smile had me going out the door without a second thought. He used the best form of communication he had: pulling me where he wanted to go. As usual, I knew what he wanted before he brought me to his destination: the swing. There are very few things he ever wants and the swing is one of his favorite sensory activities. Something about swinging through space with the wind in his face brought a joy only he truly knew.

Unfortunately, he was getting too big for the baby swing. He can't swing in a regular "big kid" swing because he doesn't have the balance required, nor the knowledge of how to pump his legs. Maybe one day. As I secured him in his swing, just me and him in the shade of a lazy summer day, I enjoyed every moment. For once I didn't worry about my other children, because they were eating with their daddy. I knew it could be just me and him. There would be no jealousy, competing for attention, aggression, or guilt.

As we enjoyed this time, our "conversation" was limited, but I did my best. Through years of speech therapy and parenting classes, I learned that the more you talk, even if it seems to be only to yourself, it can pay off in the long run for a child's vocabulary. But that's not the only reason I kept the conversation going. This was OUR time. Special time. Natural. Our conversation went something like this:

"Swing! Swing. Do you like the swing?" I asked. He just smiled with his fingers in his mouth, drool threading through the air.

"Let's count! One...one...what comes next? One, two...three!" I said. He looked up and sang his usual tune of "eeee" and "uuhhhh."

"You know more than you let on," I said as I smiled at him knowingly. "You're smart." He smiled back at me. "When are you going to talk to us, bud?" I asked.

For a moment, that familiar sadness began to creep in my heart and mind, but I decided, at least for now, not to let it stay and said, "That's okay, bud. I'll talk to you." So I talked about his clothes, the color and type, and I talked about his age. I casually chatted to him about the day like I usually did with no response from him. I was happy. He was happy.

He looked in my eyes, and I could see his joy and contentment. I could see that he knew I genuinely loved him. In moments like that, I feel that no matter if he ever learns his numbers, ABCs, or how to speak in sentences, if he knows I love him, that's all that really matters in the end. I went on with that day, hoping for a bright future for my little buddy.

Sometimes we feel like these special, peaceful moments are few and far between. Sometimes we feel other families must have it more often, but that just makes those times even more special for us. A day in my life may be a nightmare to many out there, but I know I have moments of joy and appreciation most individuals can't comprehend. I can't count how many times I have thought how lucky and blessed I am.

24

Final Thoughts

Millie, Eliza, Isaac, and Evelyn

Life is not so much about beginnings and endings as it is about going on and on and on. It is about muddling through the middle.
—Anna Quindlen

I t's hard to know when to end a book when you feel things are only beginning. My life is full of untold stories, even after this book, but at some point I have to bring it to a close. Things change every day. I have already edited a lot in this book, because changes have occurred to make my past writing obsolete. Even now, I don't know where life will lead. I don't know what tomorrow will bring, but if there is one thing I have learned, it's that everything is going to be okay. When I get overwhelmed, anxious, and worried, I stop myself and think, *This will one day pass. God is in control. In the eternal perspective of things, one day everything will be made right. I've made it this far—I can make it another day.*

I have to tell myself to keep pushing forward day to day and minute to minute. That includes taking breaks when I need them *without* feeling guilty. Sometimes that means turning on the TV for the kids so I can lay on my bed and recoup. I know the only way I get through day-to-day is because people around me are constantly praying for me and my family. I pray daily for the Lord to give me strength and patience to handle my children, to show them love, and to find joy. God gave me these children for a reason. I believe He will help me through. Even in times I felt alone and wondered if He cared, I know He was there, loving me all along the way.

It's not easy. Life isn't easy for anyone, really. It's a matter of choices. I choose to continue to care for my kids. My husband and I choose to stay together. I choose to keep waking up in the morning. Not everything is in our control to choose. Awful things happen every day to amazing people. Loved ones die. Life turns things upside down. But we *can* choose the way we react to what happens to us, and I choose to trust in God, I choose to love my children, and I choose to keep trying, because in the end it's always going to be okay.

There is a poem by Sara Teasdale that sums up how I feel about my children and myself as a Carrier. Jeremy actually gave me this poem one day after I was feeling down about all my imperfections and wondering why he still sticks around. It goes like this:

They came to tell your faults to me,
They named them over one by one;
I laughed aloud when they were done,

I knew them all so well before;—

Oh, they were blind, too blind to see

Your faults had made me love you more.

We all are children of God; human beings that need and deserve to be loved. Life is hard for us all, so why not help each other out along the way? We got this!

If you'd like to hear more stories, ideas, or just relate to someone who has "been there," feel free to visit kirstenfowler.com. There you can subscribe to my email list for further stories and helpful tidbits. You can email me directly at contact@kirstenfowler.com.

Acknowledgements:

Writing a book isn't easy, especially when you are wrestling four kids—three with disabilities. I want to take this page to thank the many people who helped me make it here:

My coach, Kerk Murray, who helped me go even when I just wanted to stop!

Isaac's caregiver, Diana, who took the time to love and help my whole family, especially in giving me time to write this book.

My editors, Katherine Birch and Jess Nielsen Beach, who turned this mess of a book into a masterpiece.

My sister, Rachael Gibson, who designed the cover of this book and also watched Isaac on many occasions so I could take a break to write.

My parents, Judy and James Reimschiissel, for helping me along this tough journey, being my best friends, and loving my children.

My husband, Jeremy, for his constant encouragement, despite times when I didn't believe in myself or didn't think I could finish this book.

My oldest daughter, Millie, for helping watch the kids when I needed a break or had to write another chapter to meet my deadline.

My son, Isaac, who changed my life forever and taught me there are better ways to live and love. You can either laugh or cry and we try to laugh as much as possible.

Author Bio:

Kirsten Fowler has had a love for writing since she was a young girl and always kept a journal for expression, therapeutic value, and family history. Throughout high school and college, she wrote and designed for several newspapers. She currently lives in a small town in Utah with her husband, Jeremy, and their four children, Millie, Isaac, Eliza, and Evelyn, as well as their dog, Luna and their cat, Ebony. She is a jack of all trades, master of none. Kirsten dabbles in music, including singing, guitar, ukulele, fiddle, and, of course, the recorder. She also likes to draw and paint, whether on canvas or furniture. Dancing is a love of hers, but she now simply enjoys waltzing around the kitchen with her husband or jamming out to tunes with her kids. When she really takes the time, she will even do needlework, and when she is feeling adventurous, she loves indoor rock climbing. Otherwise, she is cleaning, cooking homemade meals, chasing her kids, serving in the community, and keeping in touch with family and friends as best she can.

Thank you for reading this book. Please don't forget to leave a review!
Every review matters, and it matters a *lot!*
Head over to Amazon or wherever you purchased this book to leave an honest review for me.
I thank you endlessly.

www.ingramcontent.com/pod-product-compliance
Lightning Source LLC
Chambersburg PA
CBHW071144130626
46553CB00004B/1508